Bankers Systems, Inc.
Human Resources Dept.
6815 Saukview Dr.
P.O. Box 1457
St. Cloud, MN 56302-1457

OFFENSIVE STRATEGY

OFFENSIVE STRATEGY

Forging A New Competitiveness in the Fires of
Head-to-Head Competition

Lee Tom Perry

HarperBusiness
A Division of HarperCollins*Publishers*

International Standard Book Number: 0-88730-435-4

Library of Congress Catalog Card Number: 90-4381

Printed in the United States of America

Library of Congress Cataloging-in-Publication Data

Perry, Lee Tom.
    Offensive strategy : forging a new competitiveness in the fires of head-to-head competition / Lee Tom Perry.
        p. cm.
    Includes bibliographical references.
    ISBN 0-88730-435-4
    1. Competition. 2. Competition, International. 3. Efficiency, Industrial—United States. 4. Industrial management—United States. 5. Strategic planning—United States. I. Title.
HD41.P45 1990
338.6'048'0973—dc20   90-4381
                                                                         CIP

90 91 92 93 PS/HC 9 8 7 6 5 4 3 2 1

For my wife, Carolyn, and my children—
Audrey, Thomas, Justin, Diana, and Christina

Contents

Preface

Late in 1986 I read David Halberstam's *The Reckoning* and began to see global competition in a different light. Halberstam's book raised a question I found especially thought-provoking: Why were the Japanese so successful economically, especially when the keystones of Japan's economic miracle were cut from a quarry of ideas originally excavated by American management theorists? After exploring a variety of possible explanations, I settled on the only answer that made any sense to me. The U.S. and Japanese economies were at two very different places in the early 1950s, when Edward Deming, Joseph Juran, and William Gorham originally introduced their new management ideas in the United States. U.S. companies, enjoying unprecedented success, were mostly unchallenged by domestic and foreign competition. Their recurring successes created hubris and complacency. They assumed they were already the best in the world and were therefore not looking for new ways to manage. Moreover, when a few progressive American companies adopted new approaches to management, they tended to evolve in irrelevant ways, without the discipline of competition.

The Japanese economy was devastated following the Second World War. When Deming, Juran, and Gorham could not find honor at home, they quite naturally gravitated to Japan, where their ideas were readily accepted. Japan was the ideal seedbed for developing new management ideas because the Japanese economy was intensely competitive, as hundreds of new ventures struggled to survive in the 1950s. Head-to-head competition subjected management ideas to intense scrutiny. With little margin for error, it was clear when something improved performance and when it did not. Moreover, abstract ideas were refined quickly and appropriately because they had to be. Many of the principles of Japanese management may have originally been American management ideas, but they were recast and strengthened in the refiner's fire of domestic competition before they were sharpened by foreign competition.

I owe a deep intellectual debt to David Halberstam, because his history of Nissan and Ford Motor Company helped me realize how competition improves organizational performance. Because companies are only as good as they have to be, they need competition to make them better. This became the foundation of my argument for offensive strategy.

I came to the study of competitive strategy as an outsider—my training is in the field of organizational behavior. I consider this a great advantage because I have never felt constrained by the dominant ideas in the strategy field. Organizational research shows that companies operating outside established industry structures develop most radical innovations. This is because once companies within an established industry settle on a dominant design they foster only incremental innovations. An outsider's perspective becomes necessary for innovation to move beyond existing design parameters. A similar dynamic affects the study of organizations. I was able to develop my ideas about offensive strategy and move radically beyond traditional competitive strategy because I had the benefit of an outsider's perspective.

I have explored offensive strategy from many perspectives and through innumerable sources. I consider myself to be a collector and synthesizer of ideas. Accordingly, countless people have contributed something to *Offensive Strategy*—both people I know and people, like David Halberstam, I don't know but admire a great deal. I am deeply grateful for the insights, criticism, and encouragement I have received from so many people.

I feel especially indebted to several of my colleagues at Brigham Young University. My longtime friend and mentor, Gene Dalton, holds a special place in my heart. He has been willing to share his wisdom and insight with me. On numerous occasions his encouragement has lifted my spirits and rescued me from a web of despair. I will always be in his debt.

Wonderful colleagues like Howard Barnes, Gary Cornia, Gibb Dyer, Reba Keele, Heikki Rinne, Bonner Ritchie, Alan Wilkins, and Warner Woodworth have also unselfishly shared their ideas, research, criticism, and support with me. Moreover, the two deans I worked under while writing this book, Paul Thompson and Fred Skousen, have been immensely helpful in providing me with encouragement, resources, and support. I would also like to thank Jill Jacoby, Marilee Matheson, Catherine Shumway, and Cathleen Cornaby for their friendship and secretarial and word processing help.

I have learned a great deal from several of my students. I am indebted to Kurt Sandholtz for first introducing me to the metaphor of jazz and its liberating form. Mark Nyman and Greg Pesci have helped me find relevant books, cases, and articles to read. Moreover, discussions with Paul Carlile, Mark Kizilos, Rob Page, and Eric Rebentisch have helped fine-tune my thinking.

I have had the privilege to learn from some thoughtful executives and managers. I am especially grateful to David Evans at Evans and Sutherland; Bill Belgard and Kim Fisher formerly at Tektronix; Kyle Powell and Ray Noorda at Novell; Steve Domenick at Identronix Corporation; and John Newkirk at Silicon Solutions for the time they spent teaching me about their organizations.

I also have benefited greatly from interviews and articles found in *Inc.* and *Fortune* magazines. What wonderful resources these business publications provide to the study of organizations. While I have extensive hands-on experience inside organizations, I relied heavily on these two publications for supplemental case material. The descriptions of companies and insights provided by their writers have greatly enriched *Offensive Strategy*.

I have been fortunate to have had a wonderful professional support system to inspire and sustain me. I am grateful to my literary agent, Michael Snell, for helping me connect with the people at Harper Business. Virginia Smith, my editor, has been extremely patient and understanding with me. Much credit is owed her for shaping and honing the final manuscript. The editorial eye of Mark Greenberg has been immensely helpful and greatly appreciated, as has the administrative support provided by Lee Watson.

Most of all, I am grateful to my family. My mother, Virginia, died 15 years ago, but I still feel her presence. She nurtured the writer in me from an early age and insisted that I write well. My father, L. Tom, has been an anchor and source of strength throughout my life. I appreciate his ceaseless enthusiasm and competitive spirit. Moreover, much of what I know about business I learned first at my father's knee. I also want to acknowledge my sister, Linda Gay, for her friendship, love, and loyalty. Finally, I am dedicating this book to my wife, Carolyn, and my five children—Audrey, Thomas, Justin, Diana, and Christina. They are my principal source of inspiration, and I feel richly blessed by their unconditional love.

OFFENSIVE STRATEGY

1 Introduction

"The business of America is business," said Calvin Coolidge, and until recently most Americans assumed that business was *America's* business. Then, the American business machine jammed, and none of the vaunted tools of American management could get it rolling again. According to Felix Rohatyn, the investment banker and social critic: "In just twenty-five years we have gone from the American century to the American crisis. That is an astonishing turnaround—perhaps the shortest parabola in history."[1]

Now at the beginning of a new decade, there is new hope for America's resurgence on the international business scene. American managers are talking about turning their companies back around. But if American companies are to show the world that business is still *America's* business, they must divest themselves of their outmoded competitive strategies. Traditional competitive strategy, an American invention adopted by most of America's corporate elite, is uncompetitive. Companies that adopt it attempt to find positions where they can best defend themselves against competitive forces and gain sustainable competitive advantages.[2] But competition is like exercise: The harder companies compete, the stronger they become. Those with sustainable competitive advantages forfeit the benefits of direct competition and lose their ability to compete in open markets. Global competition can be the salvation of American companies, but only if they go on the attack to recapture worldwide competitive leadership.

The purpose of this book is to help American companies become competitive leaders. Companies that are competitive leaders both compete head-to-head against world-class competitors and lead their industries. They prove they are the world's best by meeting the

1

test of competition every day. They are also the companies that other companies most respect, watch, and follow because their decisions, methods of operating, and successes set the standards for their industries.

If American companies are to recapture worldwide competitive leadership, they must make two changes in the way they conduct business. First, they must change their attitude toward competition. They need to rekindle their competitive spirit. Lester Thurow, the dean of the Massachusetts Institute of Technology's Sloan School of Management and a noted macroeconomist, suggests that when businesspeople celebrate free enterprise, the freedom they are talking about is the freedom to make money. They are not talking about the freedom to compete.[3] Companies, however, do not become competitive leaders unless they are willing to enter the forge of head-to-head competition, the refiner's fire that recasts, strengthens, then sharpens organizational capability. Companies with a strong competitive spirit seek opportunities to compete head-to-head because they realize that to become the best in the world they must compete against the world's best.

Competitive spirit also provides the motivational force to drive the second change—from defensive to offensive strategy. While traditional competitive strategy includes both offensive and defensive components, it clearly emphasizes the defensive. An offensive strategy is launched from a position of strength and is sustained by developing new organizational strengths. The success of this strategy depends more on lessons learned from head-to-head competition than on finding a defendable position in the business environment. The intent of this strategy is to gain worldwide competitive leadership.

REDISCOVERING COMPETITIVE SPIRIT

During the 1980s many U.S. companies looked to Japan for new, more effective management ideas when what they needed to do was rediscover what once made U.S. companies the best in the world. What made them great was their competitive spirit. It was a "can do" attitude, bolstered by the will to do whatever it took—as long as it was ethical and legal—to lead competitors. Both large and small companies were more offense-minded, more entrepreneurial. They avoided complacency and fostered the drive and determination necessary for constant improvement.

A company that has never lost its competitive spirit is the Marriott Corporation. A page from the company's history illustrates why. On the night of 20 January 1964, J. Willard "Bill" Marriott could not sleep. The next day the board of the Marriott Corporation was to meet to appoint Marriott's son, Bill Jr., to succeed him as head of the company. At four o'clock in the morning Bill left his bed and went downstairs to his study. He found a pen and a pad of paper and wrote a letter to his 32-year-old son. Then on a separate sheet of paper he wrote a few guideposts, all born out of his experience as the founder of Marriott Corporation.[4]

Today, these guideposts serve as the seven core values of the Marriott Corporation. The first five core values tell managers "what" to do. They emphasize "productivity through people," "staying close to customers," and "hands-on management"—three of the characteristics Tom Peters and Robert Waterman found in most of the excellent companies they studied in their book *In Search of Excellence: Lessons from America's Best-Run Companies.*[5] But the last two values are different. They are prescribed attitudes that, when followed, provide the determination, will, and energy that drive Marriott's competitive strategy.

The sixth of Marriott's core values is "Strive for success and never be satisfied." How does Marriott define success? Marriott employees are quick to recite lists of their company's most recent recognitions, such as being rated first overall by *Business Travel News* and being given "most preferred" ratings by travel organizations like Business Transients, the Association of Meeting Planners, and Corporate Meeting Planners. The fact that Marriott hotels and motels report the highest profits in the industry from food and beverage sales is another source of pride for employees. To Marriott Corporation's people, success depends on how the company stacks up against its competitors. Because Marriott's employees want their company to lead its competitors in all businesses it operates in, they are extremely competitive.

Marriott Corporation's seventh core value is "Work hard and be determined in everything you do." Rather than telling managers "what" to do, this core value suggests "how" things should be done. Managers are instructed to take the initiative and to persevere. If at first they don't succeed, they are encouraged to try harder until they do.

Marriott's sixth and seventh core values are the foundation of the company's indomitable competitive spirit. Many of the company's successes over its 63-year history can be attributed more to the competitive spirit that Bill Marriott and Bill Jr. were able to instill in their managers and employees than to a clever and distinctive competitive strategy.

Traditional thinking about competitive strategy focuses on mechanics, not on the forces that drive strategy. This is a significant oversight. The example of Marriott Corporation shows how competitive spirit both creates and harnesses new energy. Competitive strategies are neither aggressive nor competitive unless they are propelled by competitive spirit. This spirit provides the fuel to launch offensive competitive strategies.

A recent change in strategic direction at Marriott Corporation shows how a strong competitive spirit provides competitive strategy with an offensive thrust. J. Willard Marriott, Jr., announced on 19 December 1989 that Marriott was negotiating to sell its 600 Roy Rogers fast-food restaurants and that the company's other 430 family restaurants—including those in their Bob's Big Boy, Wag's, Bickford's and Howard Johnson's chains—were also on the sales block. While some analysts will question "what" Marriott Corporation is doing, others will interpret the announcement as Marriott's surrender to McDonald's and Burger King in the so-called burger wars. But knowledge of Marriott's competitive spirit leads to another conclusion: The company is simply regrouping to launch an even more ambitious offensive strategy.

According to Bill Marriott, Jr., Marriott Corporation is positioning itself for earnings per share growth of 15 to 20 percent a year. After jettisoning its two oldest businesses, the company will continue to build its international hotel business. Marriott's strategy is to double the number of hotels and motels it operates by the mid-1990s, with most of its growth to come from new Marriott Courtyards and Residence Inns. The company also expects to build and manage 150 senior residence homes in the 1990s to capitalize on the opportunities created by an aging U.S. population. Finally, Marriott plans to enter the day-care business, providing high-quality day-care services to corporate clients.

Made in America, the report of the Massachusetts Institute of Technology's Commission on Industrial Productivity, decries America's loss of competitive leadership and blames American industries for it. According to the report, "American industry is not producing as well as it ought to produce, or as well as it used to produce, or as well as the industries of some other nations have learned to produce." The report tells the sad tale of the sorry state of most American industries. It details the lopsided, negative balances of trade in the automobile, consumer electronics, machine tools, microelectronics, steel, and textile industries. It concludes that even though Americans are trying harder in most industries, they are slipping further behind global competitors.[6]

Amid all the pessimism about American industry, there is still reason for hope. One of the more compelling rays of hope may at first seem otherwise. Lester Thurow observed that American industry has "consistently tended to underestimate the competition." And it has. In 1970, for example, few Japanese companies possessed the resources, manufacturing volume, or technical prowess to be taken seriously by their American competitors. But, as Gary Hamel and C. K. Prahalad note, American companies misread the situation because their competitor analysis focused only on the existing resources of existing competitors. In a recent article in the *Harvard Business Review,* they say that "the lesson is clear: assessing the current tactical advantages of known competitors will not help you understand the resolution, stamina, and inventiveness of potential competitors."[7] Here is the twist that offers a ray of hope. The Massachusetts Institute of Technology report, like American competitor analysis of the early 1970s, is at best only a partial view. It tells us where American industry is, but provides little information about the speed and direction it is moving in. It misses the inventiveness, stamina, resolution, and—most importantly—the newfound competitive spirit of many American companies.

OFFENSIVE STRATEGY

According to Bill Emmott, the author of *The Sun Also Sets: The Limits of Japan's Economic Power,* "American solutions have to use American methods: free enterprise, open markets, individual initiative. That is how Americans work best."[8] Emmott also believes that, unlike his native Great Britain, the United States has no shortage of entrepreneurs. This is good news and the key to America's resurgence. There is still no more potent force in the global economy than the competitive spirit of American entrepreneurism. Even the Japanese, who operate from a completely different economic model, show deep respect for American entrepreneurship. *Fortune* magazine, for example, reported that in four surveys of Japanese executives in the past five years, and most recently in one published in 1989, Kyocera Corporation earned the distinction of being Japan's most admired company. Why was Kyocera Corporation chosen over highly regarded companies like Sony, Toyota, and Honda? It was Kyocera's distinctly American entrepreneurial nature that Japanese executives admired most.[9]

Kyocera's charismatic chairman, Kazuo Inamori, stated the creed of American entrepreneurship when he said, "When a company is no longer on the offensive, that company is already beginning to go downhill."[10] The principles of American entrepreneurship provide the foundations for offensive strategy. Companies that implement offensive strategies behave like entrepreneurs by promoting aggressive expansion. Offensive strategies aim to take business away from competitors and to create new business.

Offensive strategies are the key to American companies' recapturing worldwide competitive leadership. While Kodak never lost its competitive leadership, it was severely tested by Japan's Fuji Photo Film. In a celebrated marketing coup, Fuji outbid Kodak to become the official film of the 1984 Summer Olympics in Los Angeles. The move gained Fuji immediate recognition which it backed with a full advertising, promotion, and retail campaign.[11]

How did Kodak respond? It went on the offensive. The company unleashed a series of product improvements. Two years after introducing Kodacolor Gold film, the world's best, Kodak introduced the Ektar series films, a new industry standard. Moreover, the company vows to continue introducing new and improved films so Fuji never catches up. To keep these improvements coming, Kodak restructured itself in 1985, shifting from functional management to business units. It divided its photographic products division into six units that address separate industry sectors, such as professional photographers and the motion picture industry. By segmenting its organization into business units, Kodak provided focus. Its people were encouraged to think about prevailing over specific competitors for leadership in specific markets.[12]

Kodak's experience tells us that companies do not need to engage in battles of size and brute strength to go head-to-head against competitors. In many cases, such an approach is self-defeating. Rather, they do best to approach head-to-head competition as a battle of wits and finesse, in which they gain leverage from their unique strengths. Notice that Kodak did not challenge Fuji on its strength in marketing. It challenged Fuji with innovation—that is, from a position of strength that Kodak has always held. In addition, Kodak restructured itself to focus more attention, effort, and strength on head-to-head competition in specific markets.

Five years ago Tektronix's plant in Forest Grove, Oregon, decided to go head-to-head against global competitors. Until then the plant had supplied circuit boards only to Tektronix customers. The critical turning point came when people at the Forest Grove plant decided to sell to outside customers. They launched their offensive strategy with the goal of making their plant a world leader, offering unmatched value to all market segments it competed in. Over the last five years, most U.S. production of circuit boards has moved offshore, but the Forest Grove plant has continued to take away market share from foreign producers. It now produces 50 percent of its boards for external customers.

Why has Tektronix's Forest Grove plant succeeded in the highly competitive circuit board assembly business when most other U.S. producers have failed? The transformation of the plant into a worldwide competitive leader began with a simple strategy of going head-to-head against world-class competitors. As employees learned about it and understood it, the strategy became increasingly sophisticated. By gradually raising their expectations and continually setting new challenges for themselves, then meeting the test of competition every day, Forest Grove's employees developed distinctive competitive strengths that drove the plant's phenomenal success.

Xerox invented the modern copier but lost its competitive leadership in 1979, when its manufacturing costs were twice those in Japan, its product development time was twice as long, and its product development teams required twice as many people. But Xerox came back with an aggressive offensive strategy. First, the company tried to learn everything it could from its own Japanese subsidiary, Fuji Xerox. Then, it required every department to conduct a global survey to identify the company or business unit that was best at performing the same function the Xerox department did. To promote competitive leadership, the performance level of the world's best company became the target for each Xerox unit.[13]

The goal of an offensive strategy is to gain worldwide competitive leadership. It is to be the best by competing and winning against the world's best, as the case of Xerox illustrates. All companies, however, do not gain competitive leadership in the same way. Competitive leaders can implement any of three distinct offensive strategies, which define them as Opportunists, Visionaries, or Capitalists.

Opportunists are competitive leaders in the development of new business opportunities. Their offensive strategies are guided by opportunities that generate a continuous flow of entrepreneurial activity. To gain competitive leadership, they rely on surprise and the ability to respond quickly to changes in the business environment. Because they do not develop radically innovative products or services, the windows of opportunity for their new products or services are narrow. Only by continuing to generate new business opportunities do Opportunists remain competitive leaders.

Superior technology is the key element in the offensive strategies of Visionaries. Visionaries operate on the cutting edge of new technology and product development and are competitive leaders in innovation. They pursue visionary offensive strategies that promote fundamental change: They either create new industries or redefine existing ones. In many respects, they are idealists following technological visions of what should be.

Finally, Capitalists provide competitive leadership by serving as models of the world's most effectively run organizations and most successful developers of topflight management talent. Capitalists' offensive strategies are guided by both opportunities and visions, and the key determinant of success is a superior work force. They envision themselves as being distinctive, excellent companies run by satisfied and motivated work forces. They both create and find new business opportunities by involving *all* their people in developing unrelated, interrelated, and even competing ideas, and they evaluate opportunities based on expected positive contributions to their performance.

GOOD AND BAD COMPETITORS

Traditional competitive strategy strives to achieve a stable and profitable industry equilibrium. Accordingly, a company's competitors are good when they have clear and recognizable weaknesses; understand the industry's rules and do not attempt strategies that involve technological or competitive discontinuities to gain position; and employ strategies that preserve the structure of the industry. Competitors are bad when they have the opposite characteristics.[14]

When, however, the goal of competitive strategy changes from achieving a stable and profitable industry equilibrium to gaining competitive leadership, the characteristics of good and bad competitors change—good becomes bad and bad becomes good. First, competitive leaders want their competitors to be strong. They learn more by competing against strong competitors and feel more pressure to improve internal efficiency and effectiveness when strength is pitted against strength. Challenges launched by strong external competitors also increase internal cooperation. Internal cooperation never just happens. It occurs when companies compete aggressively against

strong competitors and their people realize they need to band together to prevail against them.

Second, while competitive leaders want their competitors to
behave morally and ethically, they expect neither their competitors
nor themselves to abide by gentlemen's agreements that discourage
competition. In other words, they want their competitors to play fair,
but they also expect them to act aggressively. When the noted management and systems theorist Kenneth Boulding suggested in the
Harvard Business Review that free market competition be a symbol for
peace, he captured this essential idea. According to Boulding, the
trader and merchant historically have been peaceful, abiding by implicit rules and conventions to foster noncoercive cooperation. Moreover, free markets have been important mechanisms for resolution
because they offer myriad alternatives.[15] But traders and merchants
were never passive, and neither are competitive leaders. They are
confident in their ability to compete. They believe the only true test
of their competitive leadership is head-to-head competition, which
demands that both they and their competitors compete as hard as
they can until the best company wins.

Third, competitive leaders want competitors who shake up industries. They believe that volatility, not stability, is critical for a
healthy industry because it provides a way for draining out failure.
Of course, competitive leaders are companies that promote industry
change. But according to Kenneth Olsen, Digital Equipment Corporation's president and CEO, change is "something you have to keep
after all the time, because people fall into tradition. It gets too easy
to do things the way we've been doing them."[16] Good competitors,
therefore, send a clear message to competitive leaders: "If you want
to stay on top, you can't be complacent. You need to be changing and
improving faster than we do."

Recently it has become popular to attribute the failure of American industries to new, more aggressive forms of foreign capitalism,
but it is more likely that American companies have been vulnerable
to foreign competition because for decades they avoided aggressive
domestic competition. Good competitors make it hard, not easy, to
succeed. They are strong and are determined to become stronger.
While they play fair, they show no mercy; they are relentless in their
pursuit of industry leaders. Good competitors do not create comfortable industries, but they perform an indispensable role in the creation
of world-class industries and worldwide competitive leaders.

2 The Power of Competing Head-to-Head

U.S. companies in the automobile, consumer electronics, machine tools, microelectronics, steel, and textile industries were caught off-balance when global competitors challenged them for shares of their domestic markets. They had avoided competition for decades and had forgotten how to compete. When newly faced with competition, the managers of companies in these fields responded in an interesting way. Even though economic conditions threatened the survival of their companies, they were unwilling to accept the new competitive realities and go head-to-head against competitors. They tried everything else first.

It was widely assumed before global competitors mounted their initial attacks that U.S. companies operating in these six key industries were the world's leaders in innovation and new product development. Therefore, one of the first responses to global competition several companies made was to increase spending on research and development. American managers generally believed that if their companies could develop next-generation products they could halt the advance of foreign competitors. But American companies discovered that even though new technology and products gave them a temporary advantage, foreign competitors kept catching up. Because competitors caught up so fast and could produce higher-quality, less-expensive versions of new products, U.S. firms lost most of the benefits of new product development.

In the microelectronics industry, for example, new high-tech companies exploded into prominence with brilliant initial products

11

but could not repeat their initial successes. When early products became obsolete and the funds needed to finance internal growth became scarce, employees defected to newer firms, and proprietary knowledge was sold, often to foreign firms. Then foreign competitors used the knowledge they purchased to push prices down, and the U.S. firms that created the new markets were unable to compete.[1] The case of Honeywell and NEC offers the ultimate ironic twist to this often repeated sequence of events. Honeywell transferred computer technology to NEC in the 1960s. Now, NEC owns part of Honeywell's computer business, and Honeywell is the U.S. marketing agent for NEC supercomputers.[2]

Other U.S. companies operating in these six key industries adopted an if-you-can't-beat-them-join-them attitude. Managers examined closely how their competitors managed, then tried to imitate them. Quality circles, just-in-time inventory systems, bottoms-up management, and lifetime employment guarantees became part of the lexicon of American managers. But Americans have never been good at borrowing ideas from other cultures. They do not possess the borrower's inclination or facility. Moreover, most Americans believe that both they and their institutions are unique, and American pride has always discouraged learning from foreigners.

U.S. companies that adopted quality circles provide perhaps the best examples of America's failed effort to imitate the Japanese. In 1985, over 90 percent of Fortune 500 companies reportedly had quality circle programs. But well-designed empirical studies suggest that quality circles have been successful less than half of the time.[3] Their high failure rate has been attributed to many causes, but the most commonly cited problem is transplanting such programs from Japan to the United States without altering their nature and their organizational and cultural surroundings. American managers create widespread disaffection among employees when they introduce programs that promise to alter work relationships dramatically and increase their employees' sense of participation in decision making without relinquishing control. According to Gregory Shea, a professor at the University of Pennsylvania's Wharton Business School, "an approach to group problem solving [quality circles] developed in Japan and bottled in America is misused because of insufficient knowledge of the product and its side effects."[4]

The managers of several U.S. companies also responded to global competition with corporate downsizing strategies. They reduced investments and head count to improve short-term financial ratios. It seemed obvious to American managers that if they trimmed off the fat, their companies would become lean and mean. But corporate downsizing was really just another way to avoid competition. It was a quick fix that sent organizations farther down the path of long-term decline. Lee Iacocca, for example, believed that he turned Chrysler around by lowering its break-even point. But a lower break-even point did not come without costs. Chrysler lost significant production capacity. Because managers did not carefully address the question of why they were cutting back, they seldom knew how much or where to cut. Moreover, their downsizing strategy was inherently unfair. Laid-off employees were expected to bear most of the consequences of mismanagement.

American managers tried to infuse their organizations with new life through mergers and acquisitions, joint ventures, and other strategic alliances. In the cases of several megamergers, giant corporations assumed they could gain new advantages over their competitors with increased size. Nobody, of course, knows whether a $20 billion company enjoys improved economies of scale over a $10 billion company, or if the question is even relevant. Increased size, however, does create added buffers between organizations and their environments. For example, large organizations can use mergers and acquisitions to become more vertically integrated. In effect, they become their own suppliers and customers, reducing the uncertainty associated with market upturns and downturns. Vertical integration, however, also seals off companies from competitive forces in the business environment, which, unfortunately, can dull incentives and blunt initiative.[5]

Other large U.S. companies acquired high-tech firms, assuming they could buy the innovative capacity they had lost. In many cases, however, this strategy met with disastrous results for both the acquiring and acquired firms. Acquirers gained new technologies but destroyed innovative capacity because they did not know how to manage it. Acquired firms lost their creative vitality once they were engulfed by huge corporate bureaucracies and disconnected from life-giving competitive forces.

General Electric, for example, acquired Intersil in 1981 to jazz up its product line. GE went out of its way to leave Intersil's culture whole, except for one thing. When Intersil's original stock option plan expired, GE replaced it with an incentive system that was more consistent with those found in other parts of the company. But top Intersil managers and engineers were unimpressed by the opportunity to earn cash bonuses of up to 30 percent of their salaries. They saw GE reneging on its original agreement. The most confident and capable employees, including at least one-third of Intersil's engineers, went elsewhere, and new product development slowed down significantly.[6]

Finally, U.S. companies sought protection from foreign competition, claiming they needed some breathing space from direct competition to become competitive. And what happened? In the auto industry, Ford and General Motors made significant improvements in product quality, but unfortunately Toyota made dramatic improvements. The quality gap between American and Japanese automobiles actually grew wider while the Voluntary Restraint Agreements were in force. The most obvious consequence of protection was not increased competitiveness. Rather, each of the Big Three U.S. automakers used the significant sums of money generated by the Voluntary Restraint Agreements to move out of the auto industry: General Motors spent over $5 billion on Hughes Aircraft; Chrysler bought Gulfstream Aerospace; and Ford invested billions in insurance companies and other businesses.

Innovation, imitation, downsizing, forming strategic alliances, and seeking protection were not necessarily the wrong strategies for gaining competitive leadership, but they were taking companies in the wrong direction—away from competition. The power of competing head-to-head becomes most evident when we see how simple redirection toward competition begins a remarkable process that transforms these failed strategies into the strategies of competitive leaders.

INNOVATION STRATEGIES

Innovative American companies maintain their competitive leadership by never giving competitors a chance to catch up. Companies must remain on the cutting edge of new technology development to provide worldwide technical leadership. This requires unusual amounts of self-criticism and analysis. It also requires being constantly on the move. The engines of innovation stall quickly unless they propel companies toward competition.

Present thinking about organizational innovation has been influenced by Stephan Jay Gould's "punctuated equilibria" theory of evolution. According to Gould's theory, periods of relative stability are punctuated by periods of rapid change, during which new species arise and old species either change in dramatic ways or die. The punctuated equilibrium model of organizational innovation argues that organizations evolve from entrepreneurial strategies, informal structures, and radical innovation toward increasingly competitive strategies which emphasize formalized structures, tight managerial control systems, incremental innovation, and a focus on efficiency. The process, drawn from observing the innovation patterns of many U.S. corporations, consists of periods of stability and convergence around a dominant technological design that are interrupted or "punctuated" by chaotic periods of rapid change caused by emergent, innovative technologies.

Two problems with the punctuated equilibrium model of organizational innovation deserve attention. First, what was initially a model for describing the evolution of innovation in firms has become a prescriptive model. Laced through most discussions of innovation strategy is the assumption that companies ensure their success by converging around existing technologies and settling on a dominant design. The crux of the argument is that organizations are highly vulnerable to other competitors until both a technology and its manufacturing processes become well established and innovation becomes little more than incremental process and product enhancements. The problem with a prescriptive punctuated equilibrium model of organizational innovation is its conservative nature. It argues that once companies have carved out product market niches they should direct all their resources toward defending them.

Second, the punctuated equilibrium model does not explain how companies adapt to inevitable environmental change. The model, returning to its descriptive roots, predicts that organizations will either go into decline or adapt by pursuing new technologies through radical innovation. The model also posits that effective organizations align their cultures, strategies, structures, and controls to changing environmental demands. But the model never discusses how they do this. The convergence prescribed by the punctuated equilibrium model results in organizational inertia and a progressively stronger resistance to fundamental change. In other words, the more prolonged the period of stability, the less likely it becomes that organizations can or will respond effectively to environmental change.

Most observers of the global economy argue that it is becoming increasingly turbulent. Periods of stability are becoming shorter and are punctuated by longer periods of dramatic change. These new descriptions of accelerating economic change suggest that the punctuated equilibrium model may not apply to business and economic trends.

In his book *Innovation and Entrepreneurship: Practice and Principles,* Peter Drucker writes, "The best way to predict the future is to invent it."[7] His statement suggests a more appropriate response to new competitive realities. In turbulent business environments, competitive leaders destabilize or puncture equilibria rather than wait for them to be punctuated by change. The best way for companies to avoid the turbulence associated with the many waves of change is by riding on the crest of a wave of their own creation.

How do companies continue to puncture equilibria? They keep innovating. New products must always be moving through the R and D pipeline. Chuck House, of Hewlett-Packard, recommends that by the time a first-generation product is introduced in the marketplace, a third-generation product should already be in the works. His reasoning is simple: New product development takes a long time, and unless companies like Hewlett-Packard keep developing next-generation products one after another, they will miss what have come to be extremely narrow market windows.

Too many companies that rely on innovation strategies to gain competitive leadership think only in terms of a single product at a time. Adam Osborne invented the portable computer and then went bankrupt. SmithKline Beckman's ulcer drug sold under the brand name Tagamet became the biggest-selling drug in the world and the first to top $1 billion in annual revenues. But competitive drugs from Glaxo, Merck, and Eli Lilly challenged Tagamet's dominant position, and SmithKline Beckman was slow to respond. It spent hundreds of millions of dollars on research to find a superdrug like Tagamet only to come up empty-handed.[8]

It is not easy for companies like Osborne Computer and Smith-Kline Beckman to repeat their phenomenal successes. Perhaps, in a nutshell, that is the problem. SmithKline Beckman may have struck out because it was swinging for the fences. Even in the pharmaceutical industry, where R and D budgets are among the highest, the second hit does not have to be for extra bases. Many rallies are started with bloop singles and helped by bunts that move runners into scoring position. Moreover, companies are usually better off scoring on a series of small hits than on one big hit.

Even in the case of heavy hitters, technical leadership is never based on one-time successes. It is based on the capacity of individuals or companies to innovate time after time. This is why at Novell, the maker of NetWare, the leading computer networking software, Ray Noorda, the CEO, focuses his technical people's attention on creating an industry, not just a successful product and company. It is why the founders of other technology-based companies innovate by looking out as far as they can to products with ultimate capabilities. Then, by thinking backwards, they identify the steps necessary to create the products they imagine.

Finally, innovation strategies do not always need to be guided by ultimate product visions. They can be opportunistic. Kent Archibald confided in his wife, who was a nurse, that he wanted to leave 3M to start a medical products company. Then, in an attempt to stay close to an exceptionally well-placed potential customer, Archibald asked his wife to be on the lookout for new product ideas while she cared for patients at the hospital.

One day Archibald's wife came home with a promising idea. She explained that it was difficult for nurses to regulate the intravenous delivery of medications to patients because they could not monitor flows precisely. Why don't you invent a precision monitoring device for IVs? she suggested. Fascinated by the idea, Archibald soon resigned from 3M to form AVI. He spent the next two years working in the basement of his house designing a prototype. Because his precision monitoring device responded to a bona fide need, it met with success as soon as it was introduced into the marketplace.

When annual sales climbed to $10 million, Archibald sold AVI to 3M. Archibald immediately turned over day-to-day management of the company to a team from 3M but agreed to remain with AVI for three more years as the director of research and development. In that role, he led the development of second- and third-generation precision monitoring devices. But two years into his contract, Archibald started getting restless. He began to think more and more about what he would do once his contract with 3M expired. When it did, he moved to Colorado and launched Lorax Medical to go head-to-head against a new set of competitors.

IMITATION STRATEGIES

Imitation strategies vary depending on (1) the *target* of imitation, (2) the target's *complexity,* and (3) the *availability of information* about the target. Generally, technologies are easier to imitate than are management systems that involve a good deal of tacit knowledge, which by its very nature is idiosyncratic. Obviously, it is easier to imitate something simple or novel combinations of simple things than it is to imitate something complex. Moreover, imitation becomes more and more of a guessing game in cases where information about the target is unavailable.[9] At one extreme, where the target is a technology made up of highly standardized components and a great deal of information is available about it, many Japanese companies have often proven that an imitator can approach replication through backward engineering. Rather than do their own research and development, they simply develop engineering drawings from existing components. But when the target of imitation is Japanese management—a highly complex system that is mostly tacit and, therefore, not easily observed—American managers, their resolve bolstered by the knowledge that problems do have solutions, are better advised to create their own management systems than to try to imitate what they can't see and can barely begin to understand.

When Caterpillar was on the ropes in 1985, an executive vice president in charge of revitalizing the company's manufacturing capability, Pierre Guerindon, traveled the world studying other companies' modernization efforts. Did Guerindon believe he could imitate the competitive leadership of other companies? Not exactly. He quickly realized that imitating another company's advanced technology would never transform Caterpillar into a competitive leader. Moreover, the whole of a competitive leader's strategy was more than the sum of parts borrowed from other competitive leaders. Guerindon learned that even though the strategies of competitive leaders could vary dramatically, they all had a basic integrity. Although parts of a strategy could be acquired elsewhere, the overall strategy needed to be homegrown, evolving from head-to-head competition against world-class competitors.[10]

The argument against imitating competitive leadership goes deeper still. Even if U.S. companies could imitate elements of the Japanese success, they may not want to. Companies are like racers who conserve needed energy and gain an added boost by drafting onto competitors and being pulled along in the vacuum they create. But if, like Caterpillar, they seek to gain or regain competitive leadership, they can only draft on to their competitors so long. Eventually, they must challenge their competitors for the lead, then shoot past them. According to Hayes, Wheelwright, and Clark, authors of *Dynamic Manufacturing: Creating the Learning Organization,* companies "have to learn how to grow their own technology and their own skilled people, not simply scavenge the leavings of others."[11] In other words, companies cannot imitate competitive leadership: They must create it out of their own competitive struggles.

Because U.S. companies cannot imitate competitive leadership, however, does not mean that they should not learn from foreign competitors. Hayes, Wheelwright, and Clark discuss how dangerous it is when managers believe—often without apparent justification—that their plants are better at certain activities than any others in the world. These managers spend very little time observing how their plants compare with competing ones. Convinced that they are doing the best they can and that no one else could possibly do better, they assume that they can learn nothing from anyone else. But many industries are undergoing profound changes, and the best way those in such industries can keep abreast of these changes is to visit sister plants, corporate advanced-process development labs, equipment suppliers, customers, and world-class competitors.[12]

A learning-from-others strategy is different in purpose from traditional competitor analysis. The objectives of competitor analysis are (1) to develop a profile of the nature and success of the likely strategy changes each competitor might make; (2) to determine each competitor's probable response to the range of feasible strategic moves other firms could initiate; and (3) to predict each competitor's probable reaction to the array of industry changes and broader environmental shifts that might occur.[13] While companies that use competitor analysis learn about competitors' strategies, the underlying purpose of the strategy is to avoid direct confrontation, especially with world-class competitors. When companies adopt a learning-from-others strategy, however, they learn what they can from world-class competitors in order to compete more aggressively against them. They understand that to be the best in the world they need to compete head-to-head against the best.

Early in 1981, Vaughn Beals persuaded twelve other Harley-Davidson executives to join him in taking over the company in an $81.5 million leveraged buy-out. Harley's sales were holding steady at the time of the buy-out, but the Japanese were mounting a serious challenge to the company and siphoning off market share in the heavyweight motorcycle market. Manufacturing was Harley's Achilles's heel in head-to-head competition against the Japanese. Harley's management had tried to improve manufacturing, but the Japanese continued to produce better bikes at lower costs. When Beals and other managers visited Honda's assembly plant in Marysville, Ohio, they finally understood why. According to Beals, "We were being wiped out by the Japanese because they were better *managers*. It wasn't robotics, or culture, or morning calisthenics and company songs—it was professional managers who understood the business and paid attention to detail."[14]

Only a few months after Harley's management visited the

Marysville Honda plant, the company began to use a just-in-time inventory program. When the plan was proposed to Harley's York, Pennsylvania, assembly plant, however, most workers were skeptical. The York plant already had a state-of-the-art, computer-based control system with overhead conveyors and high-rise parts storage. Parts were made in large batches for long production runs, stored until needed, then loaded onto the 3.5-mile conveyor. The proposed system was going to replace all this with *push carts.* [15]

In designing the new system, however, Harley's management began with the principle that employees needed to be involved in planning and working out details. Managers met for months with groups from all departments, from engineering to maintenance. No changes were made until people first understood them, then had a chance to experiment with them, and, finally, accepted them. Commenting on how Harley's employees responded, Beals said, "That reaction demonstrated the true value of employee involvement. Normally, the engineers would figure out how to make changes. They would have made them with the usual number of errors, and the reaction [from the employees] would have been, 'Those dummies screwed up again.' And worse yet, the employees wouldn't have lifted a finger to help solve the problems."[16]

What do we learn from Harley-Davidson's learning-from-others strategy? First, Harley's managers believed in what Hayes, Wheelwright, and Clark call the open-door policy: They opened their doors and went out, visiting Honda's Marysville plant. Second, Harley's managers learned something. Initially, they learned about just-in-time inventory systems; later, they learned about statistical tools for monitoring and controlling the quality of work, training plant managers to become team leaders instead of bosses, and helping suppliers to adopt similar methods. The entire strategy for transforming Harley's factories was formed and executed around these core ideas. But Harley did more than learn from competitors. Because the company competed head-to-head against the Japanese, its strategy was as much a product of management and worker improvisation as these core ideas. Over and over again, Harley's people took what they learned elsewhere another step. The company was able to shoot past its Japanese competitors only because it was also able to transcend their ideas. The process not only enabled Harley to develop an array of new and distinctive competencies, but it also cemented employee commitment to the new strategy. So even the fact that the strategy's core ideas came from a Japanese auto assembly plant could not diminish employees' sense of ownership. It was their strategy because they had invented it in response to head-to-head competition.

DOWNSIZING STRATEGIES

I was interviewed recently in Washington, D.C., by a woman who wanted to learn more about my views on organizational downsizing. She was interested in an article I had written about alternatives to layoffs for companies operating in declining industries, and wanted to discuss it further. In the article I had built a typology of organizational responses to industry decline based on two dimensions: (1) the extensiveness of declining market demand (widespread decline versus isolated decline) and (2) the expected duration of industry decline (short-term versus long-term). I discussed *survival* (widespread, but short-term industry decline), *maintenance* (isolated and short-term industry decline), *divestiture/disinvestment* (widespread and long-term industry decline), and *realignment* (long-term, but isolated industry decline) strategic responses to industry decline. My basic argument was that in most cases layoffs do not make sense because they are inefficient. When compared to other options available to managers of firms operating in declining industries, layoffs are high-cost rather than least-cost strategies. Moreover, a wide assortment of alternatives to layoffs are available to companies committed to avoiding them whenever possible.[17]

Many interesting ideas surfaced during the interview, but the interviewer's final question really started me thinking. Referring to organizations' recent efforts to trim fat, she asked me if there was an ideal organizational size. I thought for a moment, then responded that although many growing organizations are not competitive leaders, I don't know of any competitive leaders that are not growing. There is no ideal organizational size, because organizations will grow if they continue to compete head-to-head and learn from competitors.

When organizational scientists began to write about industry and organizational decline, they challenged the assumptions of growth in organization theory. They noted that many organizations were retrenching and that they needed to understand the processes by which organizations become smaller. But organizational scientists never suggested that organizations should become smaller. The reason, of course, is that when managers see themselves managing organizations in decline their management becomes a self-fulfilling prophecy: They believe a business unit is a dog, so they treat it like a dog, and if it is not already a dog it soon becomes one. General Electric, for example, believed it was selling off a dog when it unloaded its consumer products division on Black & Decker. But with a little imaginative marketing, new product development, and by going head-to-head against global competitors, Black & Decker has transformed the business into a star.

The initial impetus for downsizing strategies came from managers who were interested in exorcising the inefficiencies that had stacked up inside their firms after years of operating in noncompetitive environments. When a firm's very survival hinges on immediate and drastic reductions in costs, downsizing may be a company's only alternative for putting its house in order. But if companies had not avoided competition, the need for layoffs would never have arisen because inefficiencies would never have stacked up. Moreover, downsizing will continue to be a necessary quick-fix solution if companies do not adopt long-term, offensive strategies.

A related argument against the indiscriminate use of downsizing strategies, based on maintaining an appropriate tension between freedom and discipline, is also an argument against lifetime employment guarantees. On the one hand, it is too easy for companies to lay off workers. Managers too often depend on layoffs to hide their mistakes. Boeing, for example, laid off 20,000 workers—one-fifth of its employees—when high oil prices, a recession, and uncertainty about airline deregulation stalled market demand for new commercial aircraft in the early 1980s. Today Boeing has an unprecedented demand for its jets, but the company does not have the kind of experienced, well-trained work force it needs to take full advantage of the situation. The principal problem is Boeing's tremendous backlog of orders. Some commercial airlines have already given up waiting for Boeing and have taken their business elsewhere. To reduce the extensive backlog, Boeing recently contracted with Lockheed's Georgia operation to "borrow"—at premium pay and generous housing allowances—670 skilled workers with an average of ten years of experience who had been laid off at Lockheed when production of the Air Force's C-5B heavy cargo plane ended. Another problem is that many of Boeing's customers who have received aircraft have not been satisfied with the company's quality control. The Federal Aviation Administration found 95 cases of misconnected wiring and plumbing in systems used to detect and put out fires in all versions of Boeing jets. Japan Air Lines and British Airways were so furious with flaws in their Boeing aircraft that they wrote blistering letters to Frank Shrontz, Boeing's CEO.[18]

Lifetime employment guarantees, on the other hand, suffer from inflexibility. Managers' freedom is severely limited when they cannot use layoffs under any circumstances. Companies like Ford Motor Company that have experimented with lifetime employment guarantees agonize over decisions to expand plants because of the lifetime commitments they are forced to make to unionized workers. Even Japan's system of lifetime employment is being severely tested as that nation moves into a period of slower economic expansion. Guarantees made to older workers have limited the numbers of younger workers being hired by elite Japanese companies. Moreover, the system has always been buffered by a massive part-time work force, composed mostly of women and the employees of satellite companies. Accordingly, serious concerns are being raised about both the viability and fairness of Japan's system of lifetime employment.

What alternatives, then, to downsizing strategies or to lifetime employment guarantees represent the appropriate balance between freedom and discipline? Recent moves at IBM suggest one alternative. IBM has always tried to avoid layoffs but found itself over-staffed. Therefore, the company moved 20,000 people from staff and laboratory jobs to the sales force, where they could boost revenues and increase contacts with customers. Bolstered by these redeployed technical and staff people, IBM's sales force now has more time for the smaller accounts it used to neglect. Moreover, salespeople are instructed to "Just say yes" to customers' requests. Salespeople, for example, will service other brands, tie them to IBM computers, design computer centers and install equipment, or recover lost data after a disaster. Although some analysts estimate that keeping the redeployed people on the payroll has pulled IBM's profits down 35 percent, it has also created a new profit center. IBM, for example, presently captures only 9 percent of the $100-billion-a-year computer maintenance and service business. But with a new, 20,000-strong army of aggressive salespeople going to great lengths to serve their customers, IBM is likely to grab an increasingly larger share of the market as it goes head-to-head against competitors.[19]

Another alternative to downsizing strategies and lifetime employment guarantees is structuring organizations as small profit centers, then making people's employment contingent on whether their profit centers meet minimum performance standards. In this kind of organizational structure, entrepreneurial rewards can be tied directly to entrepreneurial gains. In other words, profit centers function much like small, independent businesses, with all the attendant benefits and risks.

The owner of a building maintenance company was shocked to

learn one day that the client that accounted for almost 70 percent of his company's business did not intend to renew its contract. He gathered his six key managers together to share the bad news and to offer them an alternative to shutting the company's doors the day the major client's contract expired. The owner told his managers that he would fund each of them for one year as they tried to generate new business for the company. After the year, he would retain those managers who generated at least $50,000 in new business; the others he would let go. Moreover, the owner offered to pay each manager 50 percent of the profits from the business he or she generated. All six managers eagerly accepted the offer.

A year later, the owner reviewed the amount of business each of his six managers had generated. Five of the managers did not reach the $50,000 minimum and were let go. The sixth manager, however, generated over $500,000 in new business. The owner was so impressed with what this manager had accomplished that in addition to giving him 50 percent of the profits he made him a full partner.

Many companies are using internal markets as an alternative to downsizing strategies to cut the costs of services provided by their headquarters staffs. Such staffs, instead of forcing their services onto line operators, must sell to audiences that are no longer captive. This involves a three-step process. The first step is identifying where costs are incurred. Then, the prices of corporate services must be set accurately so that they are not overused or underused because of underpricing or overpricing. Finally, operating managers must be allowed to shop around for services both inside and outside the company. According to *Fortune,* forcing the corporate staff to compete with outside suppliers keeps the pressure on them to charge no more than the market rate. If they can't bring their costs in line with the market and have no advantage over competitive services, they lose their customers.[20]

Bell Atlantic CEO Raymond W. Smith estimates that the use of internal markets can reduce the costs of a headquarters staff by about 25 percent, while unleashing "an absolute flood of creativity and responsiveness." Weyerhauser, which began creating internal markets in 1985, has reduced costs significantly and has given birth to a new entrepreneurial spirit. Weyerhauser's Information Services Department, for example, felt threatened when line managers balked at the prices it charged for computer work. To compete against outside providers of services, the department was forced to drop prices, lay off staff, and invest in newer, more cost-efficient equipment. Then, to cover costs and more fully leverage its capital and human resources, the Information Services Department began competing on the open market by selling laser printing services. It gained several new outside customers from ads run in local papers touting its ability to generate hard copy from IBM, HP, DEC, and Honeywell computer tapes. More importantly, a remarkable psychological transformation has occurred in the Information Services Department. Its people no longer see themselves as consumers of wealth generated by Weyerhauser's operating units. Instead they see themselves as entrepreneurs providing services to customers.[21]

The real power of internal markets is that they encourage natural selection. Because they remove decisions about the allocation of resources from the political arena, they tend to be fairer and less biased. Ideally, only reduced demand for services determines if, when, and where downsizing occurs. Moreover, internal markets create new entrepreneurial energy that drives new growth in companies that use them. Because many of a company's employees actually compete head-to-head against external providers of services, the entire company becomes more competitive.

FORMING STRATEGIC ALLIANCES

Many companies form strategic alliances to avoid competition. Vermont Castings was rebounding quite nicely following the return of its visionary founder, Duncan Syme. The company all but owned the high end of the market for wood-burning stoves. But a new competitor, Consolidated Dutchwest Incorporated (CDW), a marketer based in Plymouth, Massachusetts, that manufactured stoves in Taiwan, made Vermont Castings's management nervous. CDW started out making a basic stove, stressing value for the dollar, then gradually worked its way up in the market with new, higher-priced models. Nobody at Vermont Castings believed that CDW would ever make the best stove in the world, but because of CDW's $18.5 million in sales in 1987 and a 1,637 percent five-year growth curve, they did fear that CDW might soon be making the best-selling one. So in April 1988, Vermont Castings acquired CDW.[22]

In many ways the acquisition made a great deal of sense. Vermont Castings could finally solve the problem of absorbing unused foundry capacity by moving production of CDW's stoves to Vermont. It made marketing sense, too. CDW sold many of its stoves through a carefully positioned catalog that also could provide new customers for Vermont Castings's stoves. The acquisition also gave the company a mid-range line of wood-burning stoves, which it advertised as providing basic heat at half the price. Moreover, Vermont Castings produced 15 percent of the stoves sold worldwide and 20 percent of the industry's revenues following the acquisition.[23]

But the acquisition brought Vermont Castings new problems as well. Vermont Castings and CDW were successful using two very different strategies. Under Duncan Syme's leadership, the people at Vermont Castings were obsessed about product quality. The company had a long tradition emphasizing the sacredness of the product. CDW's managers, on the other hand, were concerned about producing stoves of acceptable quality. The company grew by finding needs, then filling them.[24]

In theory it may be possible to build a stronger company by combining two companies as different as Vermont Castings and CDW, but the actual acquisition has done more harm than good. Why? Because by acquiring its chief competitor, Vermont Castings destroyed the competitive pressures that would have promoted organizational improvement. CDW stoves remain quarantined on a separate production line, built on the second shift by a dedicated work crew. Even though Vermont Castings continues to build the stoves that set the industry standard for quality, it drags its feet in introducing new models and tapping new markets.

Another example of a strategic alliance to avoid competition is the attempt by Visa and Master Card to form a joint venture called Entrée that would offer subscribing banks a nationwide debit card system. Before forming the joint venture, Visa bought Plus and Interlink, two of the nation's largest automated teller and debit card networks, while Master Card acquired Cirrus, another large national teller network. Recently, however, thirteen states joined together in filing a complaint in a New York district court, asking the court to stop Visa and Master Card from introducing Entrée and to reestablish the Cirrus, Plus, and Interlink systems. According to the attorney representing one of the states, "When Entrée negotiations stalled and Visa saw that it might be forced to compete with Master Card, it was able to formulate detailed plans to introduce its own product at prices and fees from 20 to 30 percent less than those contemplated in the Entrée joint venture. Had Visa and Master Card not joined to eliminate competition, consumers would in all likelihood already have available to them a national point-of-sale debit card system at a price much less than is contemplated by the Entrée venture."[25]

Competitive leaders do not form strategic alliances to join with competitors so they can avoid competing against them or to grow larger so they can dominate an industry. They form strategic alliances to go head-to-head against competition. This perspective is evident in the strategies of many of the U.S. companies that are forming joint ventures with foreign competitors to attack global markets. Black & Decker, for example, negotiated a partnership with Shin Daiwa Kogyo, an outdoor products and tool company, to distribute Black & Decker products in the Japanese domestic market dominated by Hitachi and Makita.[26] Ford Motor Company's joint venture with Mazda has been instrumental in developing several new components and car designs. The partnership has also aided Ford's entry into fast-growing Asian markets. It was Mazda that initially brought Ford into South Korea, and Ford's link with Mazda has led to another joint venture with South Korea's Kia Motors.[27]

AT&T is one company that has had a difficult time managing several joint ventures with foreign competitors. For example, a fifty-fifty joint venture with Philips, the Dutch electronics giant, resulted in four straight money-losing years because adapting AT&T's electronic telephone switches to Europe turned out to be a longer and more expensive effort than expected. AT&T and Philips also disagreed on how much should be invested in product modernization. Eventually Philips decided to end the battle by cutting its equity to 40 percent and turning over operating control to its U.S. partner. AT&T's joint venture with Olivetti has also had its moments of uneasiness as the American company has struggled to create a European identity. Nevertheless, it has drawn AT&T into competing in new markets and has provided valuable contacts and coaching. For example, AT&T, with Olivetti's help, recently prevailed over three European competitors to become the leading candidate to join with Italtel, Italy's state-owned telecommunications equipment company, in a venture that promises access to a market worth an estimated $7 billion annually.[28]

At Corning, the diversified glass products company, Roger Ackerman, the group vice president of specialty materials, said, "You need allies to invade a market." Corning, a veteran alliance builder, looks on joint ventures as a form of leverage that enables the company to extend its reach throughout the world. Corning has formed partnerships with other multinational corporations like Switzerland's Ciba-Geigy, Japan's Asahi Glass, and South Korea's Samsung. It usually prefers fifty-fifty ownership in its joint ventures but often will let its partners run the show. The company wants strong teams to manage its joint ventures, ones that can operate without constant intervention from the parent corporations. Joint ventures not only assist Corning in establishing new foreign markets but also help it regain domestic market share. Corning Asahi Video Products, for example, sells glass bulbs for TV picture tubes to the numerous Japanese tube makers that have moved their manufacturing facilities to the United States.[29]

STRATEGIES FOR GAINING GOVERNMENT PROTECTION FROM COMPETITION

Common sense tells us that companies that lobby for trade protection from global competitors from the government are not driven by head-to-head competition. Head-to-head competitors are companies that are concerned about what they can do for themselves, rather than what the government can do for them. Of course, such competitors voice their opinions to government leaders, and they certainly oppose government intervention that puts them at competitive disadvantages. But they do not try to manipulate government policy to create artificial competitive advantages for themselves.

Tom Peters urges that "the answer [to American companies' becoming more competitive] is to turn *up* the heat, not turn it down [through protectionist legislation]."[30] Recently, high-definition TV (HDTV) has generated a lot of heat in Washington. Lobbyists for U.S. electronics companies are flooding Washington, asking Congress and the Bush administration to help them catch up in the race to develop HDTV. Proposals range from protectionist measures to a $1.3 billion federal cash infusion.

The case of Zenith, the only American-owned company that still manufactures TVs, helps us understand why companies that focus too much attention on gaining government protection from competition do not become competitive leaders. Jerry Pearlman, Zenith's CEO, spent a lot of time trying to push the government into identifying exporters that were violating U.S. dumping laws. He complained that South Korea, Taiwan, Malaysia, and Singapore were artificially holding down currency values. But Pearlman's critics complain that he should have spent less time looking for help from the government and more time running his company. For example, Pearlman failed to develop markets for several new products developed in Zenith's labs because he ignored distribution. More importantly, he did not build a strategy around HDTV technology. As one analyst remarked, "I wish Zenith would learn that it can take charge of its own destiny."[31] Companies like Zenith fall behind global competitors because they keep looking to the government for solutions and forget that they can solve most of their problems by themselves.

Is protectionism ever a good idea? Many companies argue for government protection as a reprieve. If you'll just let us get back on our feet, they plead, we'll fight back. A few companies mean it. Harley-Davidson's management concluded that the company was trying to compete too broadly against Japanese motorcycle manufacturers. They decided to concentrate on what had always been Harley's principal strength—the big-bike market. At the same time, management lobbied for and won protection against Japanese big-bike producers. Extra tariffs were slapped on heavyweight bikes from Japan, adding 45 percent to the existing 4.4 percent tariff and declining in stages before expiring in five years. Of course, the Japanese were eventually able to avoid much of the new tariff's impact by assembling more heavyweight bikes in their U.S. plants, but the tariffs did buy Harley some needed time. In 1988, when the tariffs were scheduled to be phased out, Harley did not approach government leaders and ask for an extension. The company had already gone back to the government in 1987—to ask that the tariffs be removed a year ahead of schedule.[32]

Other companies argue that foreign competitors do not play fair. But instead of seeking protection—that is, trading one artificial competitive advantage for another—why don't they sue their unfair competitors, like Joseph Parkinson, the CEO of Micron Technology, did? In the fall of 1984, Micron was selling a memory chip for $3; six months later the price was under $1, with some spot business going at 50 cents. Micron went from revenues of $12 million a month to less than $2 million a month. What had gone wrong? Japanese chip manufacturers were dumping their products on the U.S. market, pricing them well below what it cost to make them. So with encouragement from the International Trade Commission, Parkinson went to the government, told them that what the Japanese chip makers were doing was illegal, and brought suit against the Japanese. The Japanese were later found guilty of unfair dumping practices, and the resulting penalties against them tightened up supply and drove the prices of memory chips back up to previous levels.[33]

Micron's legal campaign against Japanese chip makers served two purposes that government protection would not have served. First, the case offered convincing evidence that Micron's claims about Japan's unfair business practices were true. Once Micron proved its point in court it was much more difficult for the Japanese or others to argue that they were on top *only* because they were better. This helped restore Micron employees' pride in their company. They had a right to make the argument: The Japanese had to cheat to beat us. Second, the legal campaign was a way of fighting back. The company was able to retain its combative spirit because it was battling the Japanese in court, not seeking the government's protection in the marketplace. This helped Micron's people adopt an aggressive posture toward their Japanese competitors outside the courtroom as well.

A FINAL TESTIMONIAL

Under government ownership, British Airways reached nearly $1 billion in losses in 1981. Service was so poor that the airline became the target of many British comedians. "What does BA really stand for?" a popular joke opened. Then came the punch line: "Bloody Awful." At Prime Minister Margaret Thatcher's insistence, British Airways was privatized in February 1987, and almost immediately it began to transform itself. Today it is the farthest thing from a laughingstock. Its profits over the fiscal year that ended in March 1988 were the highest in the industry, at $284 million on revenues of $7 billion. Its average revenue per passenger was $266, also the industry's highest. British Airways was also the world's largest international airline in 1987 both in terms of passengers carried (23 million) . . . and passenger miles flown (31 billion). According to one respected analyst, British Airways is the model global airline of the future.[34]

The story of British Airways is just one more testimonial of the power of competing head-to-head. Under government ownership and subsidy, it amassed a huge, unproductive work force and a lax management. Uncompetitive organizational practices flourished because the company was never challenged to be competitive. But with privatization, the chemistry of the airline could finally change. Of course, the airline needed to add many ingredients to transform itself into the competitive leader it is today. It listened to its customers and began to pay more attention to detail. It trimmed down from 59,000 to 36,000 employees to get into better shape and changed its advertising and flight schedules to appeal more to business-class customers. It also formed important strategic alliances—first by acquiring British Caledonian Airways and then through a so-called marketing merger with United Air Lines. But all the ingredients that reinvigorated the company's strategic mix followed an ingredient of singular importance in the making of competitive leaders. Although there is no secret formula for gaining competitive leadership, head-to-head competition is a key ingredient in the formula of every competitive leader.

3 An Uncompetitive Competitive Strategy

Travis Services Corporation[1] was founded in 1980 and reached $40 million in sales in 1985. "I didn't expect the company to get as big as it did," admitted René Travis, the company's founder.

Before starting her company, Travis worked teaching tennis for the Parks and Recreation Department of Big Bear, California. She wanted to build her own tennis court but considered the idea frivolous because she could only play outdoor tennis three months out of the year in Big Bear. She concluded that she needed to find a way to earn the money herself.

Travis's neighbor earned extra money assembling circuit boards at home. Travis contracted to assemble boards for Allison Electronics. She recalled how pleased Allison was with her work: "They made a big deal out of me doing my job the way it was supposed to be done. I thought that was what I was paid to do."

Travis had involved a dozen other women in her business by 1981. Allison agreed to supply more boards if Travis committed to on-time delivery. The women worked in Travis's home and assembled 60,000 boards a month.

Travis realized that many of the women who worked for her depended on the money they earned to pay their bills. She decided that their jobs would be more secure if they supplied more than one company, so she contracted to assemble circuit boards for three additional electronics firms.

Travis Services moved to a 600-square-foot shop in Apple Valley, California, in 1982. The company's trademark was simple, if not old-fashioned: Attention to detail, coupled with the determination to make the best product, delivered on-time. The company struggled through 1982, however, with only $76,000 in sales; Travis had to borrow money from her husband, Carl, to break even that year.

Following 1982's dismal performance, Travis decided that offering the best quality was not enough in the highly competitive circuit board assembly business. She needed to offer the best prices, too. Other circuit board assembly companies were charging between 7 and 8 cents a board. Travis Services, while promising to maintain its high quality standards, began charging 4 to 4.5 cents a board. It also offered packaging services.

Fueled by the demand for its low-priced circuit boards, Travis Services's business took off. In May 1983 the company received an order the supplies for which required two semitrucks to deliver. Sales in 1983 reached $321,000. Then, in 1984, sales shot up to $21 million. By 1985 the company had relocated several times, finally settling in an 85,000-square-foot facility.

Through this period of rapid growth, the Travises retained sole ownership of Travis Services. An enormous amount of effort, emotion, and sacrifice went into building the company. The Travises were justifiably proud of what they had accomplished, but they also felt that the time had come to consider selling out.

Carl Travis, who had joined the company in 1984, felt they had taken the company as far as they could. People he trusted repeatedly told him that he and René could not run a $100 million company, and he also believed that they did not have the financial resources necessary to sustain projected growth. But most of all, Carl was anxious. He wanted to cash in their chips before competitors started to move in and take some of their business away. He also convinced René that they should enjoy some of the wealth they had earned and do some of the things they'd always wanted to do.

Selling Travis Services was one of the most difficult decisions René Travis had ever made. She and Carl found three potential buyers, then decided to sell to a man who offered them $10 million for the company, to be paid out over several years, and who also possessed the financial resources necessary to sustain company growth. The acquirer still wanted the Travises to manage the company for at least five years. In addition to their salaries, the acquirer promised to pay them a bonus of 1 percent of gross revenues over ten years. The Travises were delighted with the offer, and the deal was finalized in June 1986.

The acquisition of Travis Services, however, soon turned into a nightmare for the Travises. The company's new board of directors appointed additional managers when they concluded that the company had outgrown the Travises' ability to manage it. Inadequate controls led to climbing overhead costs, and, in such a low-margin business, profits immediately plummeted. New policies and procedures slowed production, making most deliveries late. The goodwill that Travis Services had built over several years by providing on-time, quality service to customers was rapidly disappearing.

The Travises also discovered that the new owner was using the profits from Travis Services to support other ventures, instead of vice versa. This discovery was even more troubling to the couple because a substantial payment from the new owner was already several months overdue. They were sitting in front-row seats watching the company they had built come apart at the seams. What they had originally seen as a way to secure their future was destroying it.

The irony of Travis Services Corporation is repeated over and over again in small and large businesses. Companies do something to decrease risk and secure their future, but they instead discover that their risks have increased and their future is no longer secure. Kierkegaard told the story of a knight who saw a rare bird and chased after it because it always seemed to be near. But whenever the knight reached out to grab the bird, it flew away. Perhaps security in business is like Kierkegaard's rare bird: It is only an illusion that we can have it. If we continue to pursue security, our experience will be the same as Kierkegaard's knight: Our companies will become inescapably lost and uncompetitive.[2]

There is another irony in American business. The traditional approach to competitive strategy most American companies accept, the very thing they rely on to make their companies more competitive, is one of the fundamental reasons why they have lost their competitive leadership. As Gary Hamel and C. K. Prahalad have observed, "As 'strategy' has blossomed, the competitiveness of Western companies has withered."[3]

INITIAL WRONG TURNS

Traditional competitive strategy is a way to think about managing organizations. It is a management perspective built on a set of assumptions about the determinants of organizational success. Like all management perspectives, however, traditional competitive strategy has its strengths and weaknesses. In providing a unique frame for business decisions, it enhances perception but also deceives. Even though I believe that traditional competitive strategy provides an immensely helpful management perspective, it has also contributed to the loss of America's competitive leadership. Why? Because some of the assumptions underlying traditional competitive strategy have not been explored or challenged.

Specifically, I want to explore and challenge three sets of assumptions that form the foundation of traditional competitive strategy. First, microeconomic assumptions encourage companies to avoid competition, not go toward it. They promote strategies in which a little offensive thinking is mixed with a lot of defensive thinking. Second, traditional assumptions about who should formulate competitive strategy make it complex and, therefore, less accessible to all organizational levels. Third, assumptions about strategic positioning being the key to organizational success mean that the effects of traditional competitive strategy on the internal workings of organizations are ignored.

Chaos theorists discuss how in modeling systems tiny differences in input can quickly result in overwhelming differences in output. They have named this phenomenon the *sensitive dependence on initial conditions.* [4] The analog in traditional competitive strategy is a sensitive dependence on initial *assumptions.* These three assumptions are *initial* wrong turns that invoke a series of consequences that make companies increasingly less competitive.

A Defensive Competitive Strategy

Even though Michael Porter, a Harvard Business School professor and the author of *Competitive Strategy* and *Competitive Advantage,* suggests that most successful companies combine offensive and defensive components, he emphasizes defensive strategy, and his approach to offensive strategy is surprisingly cautious. According to Porter, "Defensive strategy aims to lower the probability of attack, divert attacks to less threatening avenues, or lessen their intensity. Instead of increasing competitive advantage per se, defensive strategy makes a firm's competitive advantage more sustainable." [5]

Gaining competitive advantage is an appropriate and realizable strategic goal. Good baseball hitters work hard at disciplining themselves not to swing at pitches outside the strike zone so they can work the count to their advantage. Having a competitive advantage is like "sitting on the catbird seat," a phrase famed Brooklyn Dodgers announcer Red Barber used to use for a batter whenever the count was three balls and no strikes. Companies with defensive strategies that seek sustainable competitive advantages, however, *always* want to be sitting on the catbird seat. The problem, of course, is that companies, like batters, assume defensive postures when they occupy advantageous positions for too long. They think more about defending what they already have than about going on the offensive to increase their competitive advantage.

Hamel and Prahalad discuss the problem with companies wanting—even expecting—competitive advantages to be sustainable. They suggest that "competitiveness ultimately depends on the pace at which a company embeds new advantages deep within its organization, not on its stock of advantages at any given time." The point is that few competitive advantages are long lasting. A strategy's success depends on whether a company can create new competitive advantages faster than competitors mimic present advantages.[6] Accordingly, the hope of gaining a sustainable competitive advantage is a dangerous one for companies to have. It is the same mental snare that led to the hare's demise in Aesop's fable of the tortoise and the hare. The speedier hare figured that because he was way ahead he could stop and rest. But he rested too long, lost the advantage he assumed he could not lose, and the tortoise won the race.

There is a reason that traditional competitive strategy emphasizes defense more than offense. Traditional competitive strategy is based on microeconomic theory, according to which competition should be avoided because it continually drives down the rate of return on invested capital toward the competitive floor rate, "or the return that would be earned by the economist's 'perfectly competitive' industry." The argument goes that investors will not be attracted to companies that approach free market returns because they can invest in other industries. Conversely, rates of return that are significantly higher than free market returns stimulate the inflow of capital through additional investments in existing companies or through the formation of new companies. Therefore, the ultimate goal for a firm adopting traditional competitive strategy is to find a position where it can best *defend* itself against competitive forces, because there is a high negative correlation between the strength of competitive forces in an industry and the ability of firms to sustain above-average returns.[7]

Although microeconomics is extremely useful for modeling behavior between firms, it is difficult to understand why it has become the foundation for traditional competitive strategy. Clearly, not all companies are created, develop, or operate equally. It would be as unlikely for every team in the National Basketball Association to finish with the same .500 record season after season as it would for all firms in a competitive industry to earn free market returns. Over the course of many years and while competing at the highest level, teams in every sport and companies in most industries outperform their competitors. Moreover, much of the capability of these overachieving teams and companies is developed in response to competition and would not exist without competition.

Microeconomists distinguish between "existing" and "potential" competition. They argue that even when companies are successful at avoiding competition (there is no existing competition), the threat of potential competitors pressures them to continue to improve. But potential competition does not impose the same sense of urgency as existing competition does. Also, implicit in the idea of potential competition is the adoption of a defensive posture. Companies wait for potential competitors to come to them rather than take the offensive and go toward competition. Defensive strategy also dictates that when companies do act, the first thing they try to do is place entry barriers in the way of potential competitors to prevent head-to-head competition.

Boeing's decision to delay development of a hypersonic transport illustrates why potential competition seldom increases organizational capability. Boeing engineers completed initial designs for a hypersonic transport, a plane estimated to fly six times as fast as the Concorde. The expected $12 billion in project development costs, however, frightened management. The company decided to wait until Airbus or one of its other potential competitors had plans for its own hypersonic transport before developing the technology further.

The wait-and-see attitude Boeing's management adopted is a clear-cut departure from the company's early history. In 1952, Boeing was the potential competitor. It bet the company by boldly gambling $16 million—most of its net worth—on a prototype passenger jet when the market was dominated by Douglas Aircraft's propeller-driven DC series. The resulting Boeing 707 made propeller planes obsolete.[8]

Boeing's present CEO, Frank Shrontz, has said, "We don't want to get into the position they [Douglas Aircraft] were in at the beginning of the jet age, when they were complacent about their product line and didn't innovate. They were unwilling to take the risk that somebody else did." But Shrontz was talking about the $2.5 billion investment associated with developing the 767-X, a 350-seat plane with only a slightly longer range than Boeing's 767, not the five-times more risky hypersonic transport. With $4 billion in cash, little debt, and an $80 billion backlog in orders from commercial airlines, Boeing, by waiting for a potential competitor to make the first move, may be letting a golden opportunity to reshape its industry simply slip away. Certainly, it would be hard to imagine a better time to take the offensive by shouldering the risk associated with developing the hypersonic transport.[9]

Obviously, Boeing's capital budgeting procedures have also discouraged management from making a $12 billion investment in a hypersonic transport. But, again, because Boeing's management believes it has the option of sitting on its lead and waiting for potential competitors to step forward, it is reluctant to say "to hell with the numbers" and send the offensive team onto the field.

Because on the surface its logic is compelling, employing defensive strategies to make competitive advantages more sustainable continues to influence strategic business decisions. Many companies that employ defensive strategies lead their industries. But they are not competitive leaders because they do not compete head-to-head. Moreover, when companies rely on defensive strategies to avoid competition they are extremely vulnerable. Potential competitors eventually break through entry barriers and overcome competitive advantages, and companies that have only played defense discover that they do not know how to play offense.

George Stalk, Jr., in his analysis of SKF, a Swedish producer of bearings, points out how the shortcomings of defensive strategies show up when competition becomes unavoidable. Stalk described how in the late 1960s the Japanese became formidable competitors in the bearing industry by fielding product lines that had one-half to one-quarter the variety of those of Western competitors. By targeting high-volume industry segments, the Japanese used the low costs of highly productive, focused factories to undercut the prices of companies like SKF.[10]

SKF reacted to the Japanese intrusion in a predictable way: It tried to avoid head-to-head competition. The company added, then emphasized higher-margin products and served specialized customer applications. But in Stalk's opinion, SKF did not go far enough because by not simultaneously dropping low margin products, it complicated its plant operations and added to production costs. Stalk's argument has merit, of course, because, in effect, SKF provided a cost umbrella for the Japanese. As long as the Japanese operated beneath it, they could expand their product line and move into more varied applications.

According to Stalk, SKF was able to beat back the Japanese advance by adopting the Japanese strategy. After a review of its factories, the company focused each factory on the products it was best suited to manufacture. If a product did not fit a particular factory, it was either placed in another, more suitable plant or dropped altogether.[11]

But is Stalk correct? Did SKF really adopt the Japanese strategy? Although both the Japanese and SKF implemented focus strategies, the Japanese never intended to remain focused. Their strategy from the beginning was to establish a presence at the low end of the bearing market, then gradually move up until they owned the entire market. It was an offensive strategy. Even though SKF's strategy was in many ways similar to the Japanese strategy, it was a defensive strategy. SKF's focus strategy ran only in reverse gear. The Japanese continued to attack, and SKF retreated.

SKF had two strategic options that it never considered. It could have held its ground, met the Japanese head-on, and improved its internal organization enough to repel the Japanese challenge. Or it could have initially retreated to establish a position of strength but then attacked the Japanese to regain its lost market share. George Stalk is right: At one level SKF won because it found a way to stay in business. But at another level SKF lost out because it gave up competitive leadership to the Japanese. The Japanese were able to lead because they were willing to go head-to-head against SKF, while SKF pursued neither of the options that would have taken it toward competition.

A Complex Competitive Strategy

In Herman Wouk's *The Caine Mutiny*, Tom Keefer describes the U.S. Navy as "a master plan designed by geniuses for execution by idiots." Keefer saw the Navy as an organization in which the work had been fragmentized by a few excellent brains at the top. For these organizational designers, the Navy offered a challenging, long-term career; they would become the nation's admirals. But for the rest, the Navy was a third-rate career, making its employees third-rate. This was largely the result of the organizational designers' assumptions about people. They assumed that near-morons would be responsible for each fragment of their designs. According to Keefer, "If you're not an idiot, but find yourself in the Navy, you can only operate well by pretending to be one."[12]

Keefer's description of the Navy also applies to traditional competitive strategy: It can also be "a master plan designed by geniuses for execution by idiots." This happens when well-trained, elite staffs formulate traditional competitive strategy. Accordingly, the people who formulate competitive strategy are never the same ones who are responsible for implementing it. This creates problems for both the strategic planners and the line managers who implement strategy.

Strategic planners have difficulty learning from the rest of the organization. Not enough people in strategic planning departments challenge conventional wisdom. The starting point for next year's strategy is usually last year's strategy, so any change in strategic direction is incremental.[13] Moreover, strategic planners formulate elaborate but impractical strategies because they are separated from the realities of organizational performance. Because the consequences of their strategies do not affect them, they do not learn when and how to make appropriate strategic adjustments.

Line managers, on the other hand, have a commitment problem. According to Hamel and Prahalad, "Japanese companies win, not because they have smarter managers, but because they have developed ways to harness the 'wisdom of the anthill.' "[14] Japanese companies also harness the energy of the anthill. Many U.S. companies, however, lose the wisdom and energy of their line managers because they do not involve them in strategic decisions. Line managers are left in the dark about the reasoning behind strategic decisions. They are less committed to decisions they have no role in making. It is easy for them to distance themselves from the decisions of an aloof strategic planning staff. Managers ask, "If the strategic planners wanted me to be involved, then why didn't they ask what I thought?"

Recent experiences at General Motors highlight another problem with complex strategies: They are difficult to communicate to employees. Roger Smith, writing in *Fortune,* claimed that his plan to reindustrialize GM was working. He was certain that if he had the opportunity to do everything over again he would make exactly the same decisions he made when he became CEO in 1981. Then he said:

> But I sure wish I'd done a better job of communicating with GM people. . . . Then they would know why I was tearing the place up, taking out whole divisions, changing our whole production structure. If people understand the *why,* they'll work at it. . . . There we were, charging up the hill right on schedule, and I looked behind me and saw

that many people were still at the bottom, trying to decide whether to come along. I'm talking about hourly workers, middle management, even some top managers. It seems like a lot of them had gotten off the train.[15]

Roger Smith and GM's corporate planning staff developed strategic responses to the new realities of global competitiveness. The challenges Smith faced in sharing his strategy with GM employees, however, were compounded by the strategy's complexity. Clearly, that strategy's complexity, more than its appropriateness, has hampered GM's turnaround.

The grand strategies strategic planning staffs positioned at the tops of organizations develop are difficult to communicate throughout organizations. When strategies are not communicated throughout organizations, they do not guide people's behavior. Employees do not adjust their activities to merge them with an uncommunicated strategic thrust. Moreover, employees become alienated by the changes they do see going on around them because they cannot tie separate events to broad strategic intentions.

Another problem with a complex competitive strategy is that only large organizations can use it. Small organizations do not possess sufficient resources to support separate strategic planning staffs. Of course, this could also be seen as an advantage to small companies. Even though the strategies of small organizations are not always better than those of large ones, they are usually simpler.

When so many problems are associated with complexity, why do we have complex competitive strategies? A subtle but significant contributing factor to complex competitive strategies is the practice of *competitor analysis.* Companies that rely on such analysis are always trying to second-guess their competitors. Traditional competitive strategy loses its simplicity and focus because it is continually being developed in response to the actions or expected actions of existing and potential competitors.

Another problem with competitor analysis is that even though it helps companies avoid competition, it can lead them away from the simple things they do best. In their efforts to predict, then respond to, what competitors do, companies forget their own competitive strengths. This is the essence of the argument John Wooden, the legendary coach of the UCLA basketball team, makes when he questions the amount of effort other coaches put into scouting other teams:

Like most coaches my program revolved around fundamentals, conditioning, and teamwork. But I differ radically in some respects. . . . I never worried about how our opponent would play us. . . . I probably scouted opponents less than any other coach in the country, less than most high school coaches. I didn't need to know that his forward likes to drive outside. You're not supposed to give the outside to any forward when he tries you. Sound offensive and defensive principles apply to any style of play.

Rather than having my team prepare to play a certain team each week, I prepared to play anyone. I didn't want my players worrying about the other fellows. I wanted them to execute sound offensive and defensive principles we taught in practice.[16]

Although it is helpful to know something about a competitor's strengths, companies that rely too much on competitor analysis establish a pattern of reacting to their competitors. They forget the simple principles of business success and their own competitive strengths because they come to view strategy formulation as a series of countermoves. In their efforts to avoid competition, to be one up on their competitors, they develop enormously complex strategies and become less competitive.

The Effects of Strategic Positioning on Internal Organization

Traditional competitive strategy does not consider the effects of strategic positioning on the internal workings of organizations. It does not account for internal improvements that occur when organizations go head-to-head against competitors and does not address what happens internally to companies when they too successfully avoid competition.

One way to view organizations is as receivers of messages from the external business environment. These messages act as stimuli, prompting employees to call on routines in their repertoires. Their performance of routines generates a stream of messages to others. These messages are interpreted, generate performances of other routines, messages, interpretations, and so on.[17]

Given this view of organizations, if companies operate in noncompetitive business environments before behavior becomes routine, only uncompetitive routines will likely develop. Why? Because companies are only as good as they have to be. In a noncompetitive business environment no natural selection process favors the development of competitive routines because almost anything companies do results in good enough performance.

Allan Kennedy, the coauthor of *Corporate Cultures* and a thirteen-year veteran of McKinsey & Co., the management consulting firm, decided to start his own business. After an extensive search of business opportunities, he decided to develop microcomputer software for sales and marketing management. In February 1983, Kennedy resigned from McKinsey and formally launched Selkirk Associates Incorporated with five of his friends.[18]

Kennedy saw Selkirk as a kind of laboratory for his theories about corporate culture. He wanted the company to function as a society of professional colleagues committed to building a culture, to be a company that would stress all the values he had written about, such as collaboration, openness, decentralization, democratic decisions, respect, and trust. In the beginning, Selkirk was everything Kennedy had hoped for. It was a familial enterprise, infused with the qualities Kennedy had laid out in his core beliefs. Most mornings the staff feasted on doughnuts, which they called "corporate carbos" (playing on the phrase "corporate cultures"). They began a scrapbook to serve as an impromptu cultural archive. To strengthen relational bonds even further, they began to experiment with so-called rites, rituals, and ceremonies. There were barbeques on the beach and Friday afternoon luncheons of pizza or Chinese food, at which everyone in the company shared their experiences and feelings.[19]

But even though Selkirk's cultural goals were noble, its organizational routines were uncompetitive. The company grew from twelve people in June 1983 to twenty-five in January 1984, without any product or sales to show for it. When Selkirk introduced its initial product, Correspondent, few customers were willing to pay its $12,000 price. Even more astounding, three of Selkirk's four salespeople took vacations during the same month. The result was that sales for the month all but vanished. At one point, Selkirk was losing over $100,000 a month.[20]

What was the source of Selkirk's uncompetitiveness? By continuing to pour money into the company, Kennedy in effect created a noncompetitive business environment. Therefore, organizational routines developed without the discipline of competition. How did Kennedy get Selkirk back on track? He gave notice that he was unwilling to sink any more of his money into the company. Selkirk had to compete on its own. Either the company paid for itself or Kennedy would let it go under. Almost immediately Selkirk began to rebound. By 1986 the company had a durable product and an installed base of about 1,000 units. Moreover, uncompetitive routines had been replaced by competitive ones. Because it was forced to operate in a competitive business environment, Selkirk has a reliable order-filling process, a sales force that is paid on straight commissions, and specific sales targets.[21]

Uncompetitive routines would be less problematic if it were easy for organizations to change them. At Selkirk Associates, Kennedy responded early enough to turn around his small company. But the bigger companies are and the longer they avoid competition, the more entrenched their uncompetitive organizational routines become.

At Esso Chemicals, for example, entrenched organizational routines prevented the company from implementing a new competitive strategy. In the early 1980s, executives and managers at Esso concluded that the company faced new competitive realities and needed to change. They agreed that in addition to becoming the low-cost supplier of basic products, they should also develop new products through joint ventures and joint-development agreements with customers. The new strategy required faster, more flexible production and new relationships with customers. Both strategic thrusts were significant departures for the company but were critical to regaining competitive leadership.[22]

After several months very little had changed at Esso. Why? Because many entrenched organizational routines ran directly counter to the new strategic thrusts. For example, people believed it was an ironclad rule that managers should not give more than a gallon of product to customers. Customers, of course, needed much more than a gallon of crude oil in jointly developing new products. Where did this uncompetitive routine come from? In 1975 an internal audit team concluded that the company was giving away too much product to customers. Employees were personally criticized, and so they adopted a rule that they would not give more than a gallon of product to a customer.[23]

Why do uncompetitive organizational routines become entrenched? Because they (1) become an organization's memory, (2) serve as targets for organizational behavior, and (3) provide bases for comprehensive truces formed across coalitions of organizational members.[24]

Organizational routines constitute an organization's *memory* because individuals remember only the routines they perform.[25] If they only perform routines stimulated by messages from a noncompetitive business environment, they are likely to forget competitive routines. The longer organizations continue to operate in noncompetitive environments, the more likely it becomes that the only routines individuals remember will be uncompetitive ones.

Paradoxically, another reason organizational routines become entrenched is because of the difficulty of keeping existing routines running smoothly. In a complex organization with many interrelated routines, one routine cannot usually be changed without affecting others. Thus, any change in an organizational routine is likely to create a ripple effect of change. For this reason the policies and practices of most organizations are biased against change, and managers invest significant time and energy developing mechanisms to buffer routines from unexpected disruptions. Therefore, another reason organizational routines become entrenched is that they become norms or *targets*. [26]

Established routines also involve a comprehensive *truce* to minimize intraorganizational conflict.[27] This truce further entrenches established routines. Organizational change that may appear sensible to an outside observer is resisted internally because it may be interpreted as "provocative" and destroy the delicate balance of interests existing truces are built on. As established routines become further entrenched, the likelihood decreases that anyone will want to upset the fragile political equilibrium by proposing change. When change does occur, it requires incredible amounts of energy from organizational members and is confined to increasingly narrow corridors of indifference. Ultimately, a state of political inertia overwhelms any felt need for change.

George Romney, a former president of American Motors, said, "There is nothing more vulnerable than entrenched success."[28] After organizations operate for a long time in noncompetitive business environments, their routines become so entrenched that they become closed systems. Or, as Karl Weick suggests in *The Social Psychology of Organizing*, organizations become "autistic" as they detach themselves from the business environment in which they operate and automatically recycle organizational routines entrenched in memory.[29] Autistic organizations falsely assume that their business environments will never change. But because of shifting business cycles and because other firms invent new ways of competing, change is inevitable, even in noncompetitive business environments. When environments do shift, autistic organizations are late to recognize that they are no longer as good as they have to be.

Fortune recently published a scathing attack on Sears, the

Figure 3–1.   The Effects of Strategic Positioning on Internal Organization.

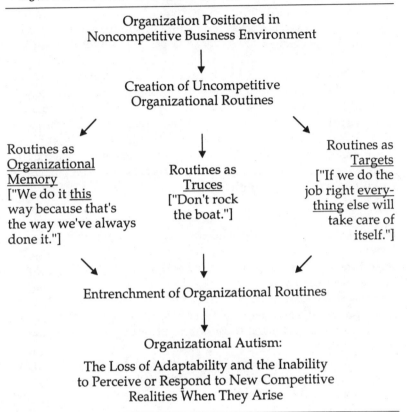

Organization Positioned in
Noncompetitive Business Environment

↓

Creation of Uncompetitive
Organizational Routines

Routines as
Organizational
Memory
["We do it this
way because that's
the way we've always
done it."]

Routines as
Truces
["Don't rock
the boat."]

Routines as
Targets
["If we do the
job right every-
thing else will
take care of
itself."]

Entrenchment of Organizational Routines

↓

Organizational Autism:

The Loss of Adaptability and the Inability
to Perceive or Respond to New Competitive
Realities When They Arise

world's largest retailer. The article described Sears as a "2,000-pound centipede":

> The antennae work poorly, so the creature is directionless. When some of the 101 legs try to move ahead, others interfere and even move backward. . . . [Sears] is a century-old, muscle-bound behemouth crushed by its lumbering corporate culture, needing new strategy and probably new management. Sears's half-hearted, clumsy efforts to adapt to a competitive retailing environment reveal an American institution in decline, a textbook example of what happens to any company that settles too comfortably into its market.[30]

Sears is a company losing the competitive lead it held for many years because it is being smothered by uncompetitive organizational routines. Its sales and administrative expenses are 13 percent higher than those of Wal-Mart and 6 percent higher than those of J.C. Penney and K Mart. Sears has the highest distribution costs in retailing, about 8 percent of sales, versus 3 percent at Wal-Mart and K Mart.

A recent experiment to cut costs showed how entrenched uncompetitive routines have become at Sears. Five Sears stores agreed to reduce inventories in a line of men's apparel from the usual 22-week supply to an 8-week supply. Employees in the five stores packed up the leftover 14 weeks of goods to ship back to the supplier. But the merchandise was never sent. It sat in boxes for five months until it was unpacked, ironed, and placed back on store shelves. A consultant who worked with Sears on the test blamed the failure on turf battles.[31]

The way Sears displays its apparel is also troubling. *Fortune* reporters visited the large Sears store at the Paramus Park Mall in New Jersey and noted that every female mannequin they saw in the store had torn stockings. In the maternity department the pillows beneath several of the mannequins' clothes had slipped out of place. The jewelry department, which six months earlier had moved to space previously occupied by the cosmetics department, still had empty cosmetic racks and huge photos of heavily made-up models on the walls.[32]

Sears also has problems with its vendors. Name brand manufacturers don't like the company's sloppy displays and claim the stores don't treat their goods with respect. The company also communicates poorly with its vendors. Nike, for example, pulled out its $40 million worth of business after Sears, without telling Nike, decided to run a coupon for Nike sneakers on the back of Kelloggs cereal boxes.[33]

Fortune's most damning words were reserved for Sears Chairman Edward A. Brennan. According to the article, Brennan was completely out-of-touch, oblivious to the company's enormous problems, and reluctant to change anything at the retailing giant. He believed Sears was responding well to its new competitive realities and felt good about how the company was positioned strategically.[34] In the midst of so many uncompetitive routines, Brennan failed to see that fleet-footed competitors were shooting past Sears. He could not admit that the only remnant of competitive leadership at Sears was its Teflon reputation or that the company was dangerously close to not being good enough even to be competitive.

THE RECKONING

The title of David Halberstam's book about the U.S. and Japanese auto industries fascinates me. Why did he call his book *The Reckoning*? A *reckoning* is a time to settle accounts or to account for past mistakes. Halberstam believed that the U.S. auto industry's day of reckoning had not come in 1980 when the floor fell out of the U.S. auto market and that the industry turnaround beginning in 1983 was only temporary. The true day of reckoning, a day when U.S. automakers would be completely overpowered by their Japanese rivals, was yet to come.

Although I prefer to interpret Halberstam's vision of a day of reckoning as a warning rather than a prediction, I still believe it is important to understand why he saw so many ominous signs in the U.S. auto industry's future. At Ford, the U.S. company that Halberstam studied in depth, we can examine his reasoning. According to Halberstam, in 1979, the last good year at Ford before the crunch, the company made a profit of $1.2 billion on sales of 4.7 million cars and employed a work force of 500,000 people worldwide. In 1983, the year Ford returned to the black, the company made $1.1 billion on sales of 3.6 million cars and had a work force of 380,000. Even then there were questions about whether Ford's turnaround was based more on skilled financial rearrangements than on industrial resurgence.[35]

Halberstam saw Ford as a company desperately trying to improve itself, even though it still had many fundamental problems. He argued that it would be extremely difficult to restructure a company that had grown careless and sloppy over more than twenty-five years of virtual domestic monopoly.[36]

But the challenges facing Ford were not only internal. The Japanese were under voluntary trade restrictions until 1985, but they were not standing still. Halberstam saw the Japanese auto industry as being pushed by an obsession with excellence and by its own fierce domestic competition. It was also pushed by the vision of an ascending Korea and by the fear of a resurgent United States. Above all, the Japanese were pushed by a cultural spirit that made them more comfortable in adversity than in success. As Keith Crain of *Automotive News* said, "The Japanese remind me of a race car driver who's five laps ahead but doesn't know it and keeps driving as if he's five laps behind."[37]

Why is there such a significant difference between U.S. and

Japanese automakers? In his book, Halberstam described two very different automobile industries. In the Japanese auto industry, only Toyota made a consistent profit in a crowded field of domestic competitors. Other Japanese automakers were forced to develop foreign markets to make profits. In the U.S. auto industry, before the Japanese invasion, a country club atmosphere prevailed. Both Ford and Chrysler followed GM's lead in pricing in what Halberstam called a "parody of competition."[38] Where did these two dramatically different competitive environments lead? U.S. automakers stood still in product innovation and actually lost ground in the area of product quality. Japanese automakers, even after rocketing past their American rivals, continued to improve on all fronts.

The central message of Halberstam's book is that companies need competition because they are only as good as they have to be. The Big Three U.S. automakers lost their competitive lead because they operated in a noncompetitive environment for over twenty-five years. Japanese automakers are such a strong force because over the same twenty-five year period they went forward, survived, and improved under the intense pressures of their domestic competition.

The reason I see Halberstam's day of reckoning as a warning, not a prediction, is that the monopoly shared by the Big Three has been shattered. GM, Ford, and Chrysler are competing for their very survival. Japanese automakers clearly hold the upper hand, and they will not give up their competitive leadership as easily as the Big Three did in 1980. Nevertheless, the Big Three have already learned a great deal from a decade of real competition, and they will continue to learn. Of course, the Big Three are still far behind. There is also the possibility that the Big Three will deny their own culpability and by blaming others ignore the immense work that they need to do internally. But if the Big Three will play offense, simplify their competitive strategies, and challenge themselves to improve at an accelerating rate, they can undo the effects of twenty-five years of not competing. They can still catch up to the Japanese, if they continue to compete head-to-head.

4 Offensive Strategy

The founder of a small but successful software company decided to relocate his corporate headquarters. His love for mountains and outdoor recreation led him to search the Rocky Mountain area for a site. After doing some research, he decided to visit a community near Brigham Young University in Utah.

The founder arrived at the Salt Lake City airport and was greeted by a group of state and local government leaders, who offered to drive him to the community he was considering, explaining that it was located about an hour away from the airport. After driving for forty minutes, the car carrying the founder and government leaders climbed to the top of a steep hill overlooking their destination. The founder, looking out over the community for the first time, saw something in the distance that surprised him. "What's that?" he asked, pointing to a huge complex of black and gray buildings. One of the government leaders explained to the founder that what he saw was the Geneva Steel Plant, the major employer in the community for nearly forty years until it was recently shut down by USX Corporation. Hearing this, the founder said, "Turn around. We can't locate here."

Why did the vacant Geneva Steel Plant change the founder's mind about this community as a potential site for his corporate headquarters? He explained later that it portrayed the wrong image. He did not want to relocate near a steel mill, even an abandoned one, because it was a symbol of the old order. "How could I stand in the shadow of an empty steel mill and tell my people that we can compete and win against worldwide competition?" he asked.

The founder realized that there are two approaches to corporate

51

strategy: Companies either defend themselves against competition and seek sustainable competitive advantages or they go on the offensive to gain competitive leadership. USX, formerly U.S. Steel Corporation, had defended itself against competition for decades, successfully sustaining a competitive advantage. Still, the company was only as good as it had to be while operating in a noncompetitive business environment. When foreign competitors converged on attractive U.S. markets, USX lost its competitive advantage and much of its steel business because it had forgotten how to compete. The founder of the software company, however, wanted his company to become a competitive leader. The basic principles of his company's strategy, therefore, were very different from USX's.

Even though I agree with those who promote traditional competitive strategy—that successful corporate strategies combine both offensive and defensive components—I disagree on the desired balance between offense and defense. Traditional competitive strategy is uncompetitive because it gives too much attention to defensive components. Competitive leaders show that a good offensive strategy is also the best defense. Their strategies consistently stress offense over defense. Given this, I have chosen to focus my attention on laying a foundation for offensive strategy.

THE FOUNDATIONS OF OFFENSIVE STRATEGY

What are the foundations of the offensive strategies of companies that become competitive leaders? First and foremost, their strategies take them head-to-head against competitors. Companies do not become competitive leaders by accident. Daily, they meet competitors head-on and outperform them. Second, companies that become competitive leaders have simple offensive strategies. The attention of all their people is riveted on a few key strategic goals. When offensive strategies are simple they become the driving forces behind all organizational activity, blending effort at all levels and across all functional areas of an organization. Finally, the offensive strategies of competitive leaders consider effects on the internal workings of organizations. Competitive leaders develop liberating, not routinized, organizational forms, which enable them to lead out. They are progressive organizations—always the first to do something. And even though other companies try to imitate them, competitive leaders remain a step out in front.

Increasing Organizational Capacity by Going Head-to-Head Against Competitors

How do companies go head-to-head against competitors? They challenge potential competitors, pitting strength against strength. Going head-to-head begins with a belief that resistance builds strength. Companies that go head-to-head choose to attack competitors when they occupy positions of strength, not weakness. They want their competitors to be strong because the stronger they are the better they themselves become.

Competition forces organizations to improve. It destroys complacency and increases organizational capacity. A case can be made that no company can ever rest on its laurels and that companies become competitive leaders only by meeting the test against worthy competitors every day.

Evans & Sutherland, a maker of state-of-the-art flight simulators, assumed it had the high end of the market cornered because it had never lost a competitive contract. Then General Electric, a company that most E&S engineers assumed wasn't even in their league, beat them out on a major contract bid. Initially, E&S engineers were devastated, but before long they resolved never to be embarrassed like that again. The loss to GE marked the beginning of a period of intense work and innovation during which E&S engineers reestablished themselves as the unquestioned technical leaders in their industry.

Another illustration of the importance of competition comes from the experience of the so-called excellent companies identified by Thomas Peters and Robert Waterman in their national best-seller *In Search of Excellence.* In the fall of 1984, *Business Week* conducted a survey of the 43 excellent companies listed in the book and discovered that at least 14 of them had lost some of their luster. Although several of these companies have since rebounded, the *Business Week* findings still beg the question what happened? Why was excellence lost, even temporarily? *Business Week* offered two explanations. First, some of the companies failed because they walked away from the principles that had been key to their earlier successes. Atari, for example, had clearly broken all the commandments of excellence except one—"sticking to the knitting." Second, some companies were simply inept at adapting to fundamental changes in their markets.[1]

Related to *Business Week*'s second explanation is another possibility. Perhaps the designation of excellence led to the downfall of
at least some of the companies. Why? Because being called excellent
created a corporate hubris. Assuming they had arrived and no longer
needed to try as hard, some so-called excellent companies failed to
go head-to-head against competitors.

Whether or not hubris was the cause of the downfall of these
companies, one of the risks of working for a highly successful company is falsely assuming you are no longer at risk. Excellent companies are no different than other companies. They must prove how
good they really are by pitting their strengths against those of competitors. They have no guarantees that they will be successful tomorrow doing the same things they are doing today. The only way for
them to avoid complacency and increase competitiveness is to continue to play offense against strong competitors.

Competitive leaders generate a different kind of internal energy
because they are running toward, not away from, competition. Competition vitalizes human resources. It increases people's interest in
their work and captures more of their attention. People know that the
company's survival depends on their ability to rise to the occasion.
They do things they would never do without competition because of
the compelling sense of the here-and-now that competition brings.
When people feel more challenged, their desire to meet further challenges more often increases than decreases.

H. Ross Perot, the founder of Electronic Data Systems and Perot
Systems, has always believed that eagles will separate themselves
from the flock. "You put them in the field," he says, "right in the
thick of competition, and the eagles emerge." Perot's eagles go head-
to-head against competition. They enjoy the challenges that competition brings. They excel because they have learned how to win in a
variety of competitive situations.[2]

A useful way to view employee motivation is as an exchange
between people and organizations (see Figure 4-1). Both people and
organizations have resources to exchange and outcomes they desire
to receive from exchange. Organizations want people to perform so
they accomplish organizational goals, and individuals' desired outcomes are based on their needs. Organizations, then, offer people
resources to satisfy their needs, as long as they work to accomplish
organizational goals.

At first glance, this exchange model appears to argue for the use
of organizational routines. Because routine behavior requires less of
people, organizations would need to give up fewer resources to sat-

Figure 4-1. An Exchange Model of Employee Motivation.

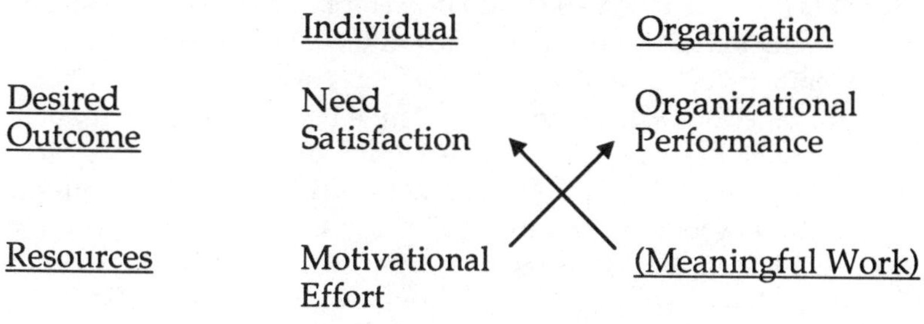

	Individual	Organization
Desired Outcome	Need Satisfaction	Organizational Performance
Resources	Motivational Effort	(Meaningful Work)

isfy their people's needs. Based on return on investments, organizations would be way ahead using organizational routines.

But consider this: When people have higher order needs, they desire significant and meaningful work assignments. They want to work with more than their hands. They want to use their minds, too, and think about what they do rather than perform mindless routines. The only resources organizations expend to satisfy higher order needs are job assignments that require increased thought and involvement. By going head-to-head against competition and moving away from routines, organizations create new resources to motivate employees with higher order needs. Moreover, organizations replenish these resources and, in turn, increase their capacity when they provide new challenges for their people.

Dana Corporation provides a powerful example of how competition increases organizational capacity through people. Dana operates mostly in the highly competitive automobile and trucking parts industries. The company offers an interesting kind of employment security to its workers: As long as their plants remain profitable they will remain open. Each plant is a profit center, and its people know that they hold the fate of the plant in their hands.[3]

Dana's corporate philosophy is built around the importance of people. People are a company's most important asset, and people determine if a company remains competitive. The expert on any job is the person performing it. All of Dana's people are expected to find ways to increase their productivity. Moreover, information is freely shared so people know how their performance affects plant performance.[4]

Of course routines exist at Dana Corporation. But because all employees are finding new ways to increase their performance, routines are constantly evolving. Where does the constant pressure to improve performance come from? Clearly a lot of peer pressure operates at Dana's plants. Workers are intolerant of coworkers' mistakes, because the industries Dana operates in have little margin for error. Every employee knows that Dana competes against firms that badly want to take their customers away. There is nothing abstract about the challenge that each person in each of Dana's plants faces every day. Dana's people are willing to do whatever it takes to beat out the competition because they know that they determine whether or not they will have a job tomorrow.

Experiences at Dana Corporation illustrate another point. Only when people are aware of competition does it affect their work and benefit their organizations. In many companies management is unwilling to share information about the challenges of competition. They leave workers in the dark, then expect them to feel the same imperative to compete as they feel. When workers resist demands on them, managers assume they are either lazy or uncommitted. In reality they are only uninformed. A colleague of mine, Gene Dalton, observes that in competitive organizations employees have their "noses up against the glass." They know about the challenges that competitors are forging against their companies, and they rise to the occasion because they understand what's at stake.

Simple Offensive Strategies

In laying the foundation for an offensive strategy I have been influenced by the metaphor of jazz. Jazz differs from other musical forms in important ways. Figure 4-2 is an example of a simple piece—the *Sesame Street* theme song—represented in traditional musical format. This particular example is written in the key of F, for alto saxophone and string bass. The music leaves little to the imagination. All notes are specified; the musicians know exactly what, when, and when not to play.[5]

In contrast, Figure 4-3 is the same *Sesame Street* theme song, represented in a jazz format. It could be played by any collection of instruments, in any key. Chords and their duration, rather than notes and rhythms, are specified. The pattern is stable—twelve measures, always played in the same sequence, at an agreed-upon tempo—but open.[6]

This openness gives jazz musicians license to invent a melodic line (or accompaniment) that fits the song's basic harmonic sequence.

Figure 4–2.   Traditional Musical Format.

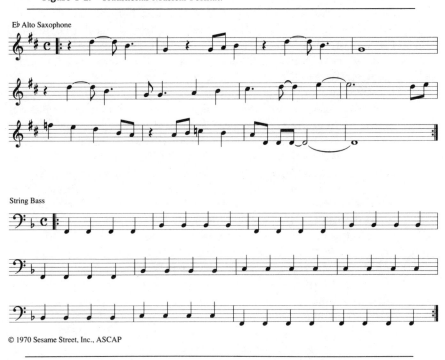

Figure 4–3.   Jazz Format.

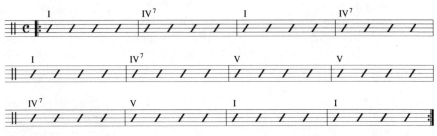

Figure 4-4, a transcription of a sax solo, is an example of what a soloist can do with such deceptively simple harmonic sequences.[7]

Traditional competitive strategy is like a traditional musical format. Strategic planners who formulate strategy specify all the options, leaving little to the imagination of the managers who implement strategy. Offensive strategies to gain competitive leadership, however, are more like jazz. They are open, providing for improvisation. Managers formulate and implement offensive strategies together in real time. The ideal is realized when managers create offensive strategies from a deceptively simple strategic logic.

What are simple offensive strategies like? Below, I will propose a process for formulating offensive strategy that is simple, general, and takes companies head-to-head against competition. But there are many examples of simple, specific offensive strategies from both the present and the past. Ray Noorda had a simple offensive strategy for Novell, the maker of NetWare, when he became CEO. He told Novell's people, "We're going to concentrate on four-letter words, like *cash,* being the *best* at what we do, or working as a *team.*" Everyone understood Novell's four-letter words, and the basic principles conveyed by them provided a simple offensive strategy that everyone could implement.

Many years ago, J. C. Penney proposed a simple offensive strategy for retail establishments. According to Penney, a Main Street Merchant started with an *idea.* Penney's idea was "to give the most— for the least!" What came next? A *store,* then *goods.* Experienced *people* provided another critical ingredient in the simple strategy of the Main Street Merchant. Then, the final ingredient brought everything together. The *leadership* of the Main Street Merchant combined the idea, store, goods, and people into a competitive retail operation.

The movie *Big* illustrates how simple offensive strategies become when viewed through the eyes of a child. The MacMillan toy company had a typical MBA-formulated, uncompetitive strategy based on double-blind studies of children fitting eight demographic categories. But Josh Bascum, a child in the body of a man, questioned the relevance of the company's scientific findings. To Josh the toy business was simple: If you make fun toys, kids will buy them.

Jan Carlzon, the CEO of Scandinavian Airlines Systems and author of *Moments of Truth,* has formulated a simple offensive strategy for his company's becoming the preferred airline for frequent business travelers. It is based on three priorities—safety, punctuality, and other services. So, according to Carlzon, "if you risk flight safety by leaving on time, you have acted outside the framework. . . . The same

Figure 4–4.   Invented Melodic Line Based on Jazz Format.

is true if you don't leave on time because you are missing two catering boxes of meat."[8]

Simple offensive strategies are the secrets of charismatic founders like Wal-Mart's CEO, Sam Walton. *Fortune* describes one of Sam's self-improvement videos as something that Dale Carnegie would have envied. From *Fortune* we read:

> Sam rambles on about the hunting he's been doing and demonstrates his bird dog whistle, then gets down to his idea. "I don't think any other retail company in the world could do what I'm going to propose to you," he says. "It's simple. It won't cost us anything. And I believe it would just work magic, absolute magic on our customers, and our sales would escalate, and I think we'd just shoot past our K Mart friends in a year or two and probably Sears as well." He proposes that whenever customers approach, the associates should look them in the eye, greet them, and ask to help. Sam understands that some associates are shy, but if they do what he suggests, "it would, I'm sure, help your personality develop, you would become more outgoing, and in time you might become manager of that store, you might become a department manager, you might become a district manager, or whatever you choose to be in the company. . . . It will do wonders for you." He guarantees it.[9]

Simple offensive strategies have clear advantages over traditional competitive strategies because everyone in both large and small companies can understand, remember, and use them. This enables every line manager to think strategically. Simple offensive strategies provide what L. J. Henderson, a former professor at the Harvard Business School, called "walking sticks" to assist all managers as they go head-to-head against competition.

A Liberating Organizational Form

What needs to happen to companies internally for them to become competitive leaders? What role does offensive strategy play in the process? Companies are held back from becoming competitive leaders by entrenched, uncompetitive organizational routines. Offensive strategy, therefore, liberates them from such behavior. This does not mean that they abandon routine and form, which clearly offer some advantages, just as freedom and adaptability do. What competitive leadership requires is a liberating organizational form.

Marden Clark, in a penetrating essay on life and art, explores the paradox of freedom and form in literature. Some of the loveliest, most energetic poems in the English language are written in one of its most restrictive forms—the sonnet. Clark suggests that a poet often finds that conventional poetic forms can anchor, channel, refine, and control creative energy. Of course, the poet supplies the energy, and mere knowledge of the form never guarantees significant creative achievement. Still, most of the time poets have more difficulty creating meaningful forms than creating within available and proven forms.[10]

Borrowing from the world of aeronautics, Clark offers another analogy:

> A glider soars, a jet plane flies not just because the wind blows or because the motor develops a half million pounds of thrust. The energy of wind or motor must be exerted on or within significant and controlled form. Imagine all that power being released by a jet engine unattached to anything, like the balloon you blew up as a child and let go—how it hissed and darted and sputtered aimlessly.[11]

Offensive strategies foster organizational forms that enable people to glide and soar. But only through directed, not aimless, flight do organizations and people continue to ascend to the loftier altitudes of competitive leadership.

As we see in the case of entrenched organizational routines, too much form can be stifling. For example, what if the sonnet form were even more rigid and restrictive? What would be the effect on creative effort? I know a short story writer who grew up in a small, remote town. He started dreaming about becoming a writer at an early age. But he knew very little about what writers did, and there were no writers in his community to consult. His only source of information about writing was a small town library with fewer than a hundred books, all old and worn. So he read every book in the library, decided he understood what writing was all about, and began writing his first book. After writing only a few pages, however, he became discouraged and temporarily gave up his dream. Why did he give up? Because writing was too hard. Why was it so hard? Because he assumed every line of his manuscript had to be of equal length. Every time he wrote a line that did not have the same number of letters as the previous line he thought he had to start over. And why did he conclude that every line needed to be the same length? Because every line in every book he read was.

Obviously, this writer's performance was stifled because he

mistook the process by which books are printed for the process by which they are written. His understanding of the form writers were required to follow made writing hopelessly cumbersome. Not until someone told him that he was mistaken and all the lines of a manuscript did not need to be of equal length did he begin to write again.

When forms are too loose, performance also suffers. For example, WICAT Incorporated was going to change the world of education using computer-assisted teaching. The company was launched with much fanfare and received almost $90 million in capital when it went public in 1981. The founders of WICAT believed that technical people should be given a free rein to create, and they encouraged them to pursue interesting ideas for their own sake. As long as WICAT's "burn rate" was held within reasonable limits there was no pressure to translate ideas into saleable products. After all, the founders assumed, the company could continue to operate indefinitely given its vast capital reserves.

WICAT continues to operate, even though its capital reserves have been seriously depleted. But the company has never realized its creative potential. Why? For many reasons, of course, but clearly WICAT's founders were ineffective at interpreting the business environment in a way that provided the needed form for creative endeavor. Technical people never felt compelled to develop practical products because the founders continued to emphasize the company's extensive capital reserves. Time after time, the founders hired bright technical people with promising ideas, then several years later felt forced to fire them because no progress had been made. It is obvious why technical people were not making progress: They did not see the company as a competing business because management never raised their consciousness about competitive challenges. Even though technical people loved working for WICAT because the company offered them unlimited freedom, much of their creative energy was wasted because it was never anchored, channeled, refined, or controlled.

We usually think of uncompetitive organizational routines as being too restrictive. But WICAT's experience suggests that too much freedom without the form that competition imposes can also create uncompetitive routines. A liberating organizational form evolves out of the discipline competition imposes and the freedom granted to organizational members to meet the test of competition.

Ideas about worker participation developed in the 1950s and 1960s gradually lost credibility for reasons similar to those behind WICAT's disappointing performance. Worker participation was assumed to be good simply because it made people feel better about themselves and their work. In other words, worker satisfaction, not performance, was the desired outcome of early efforts to increase employee participation.

It took the new realities of global competitiveness to resurrect ideas about worker participation. When U.S. companies became concerned about meeting the relentless test of competition, the logic of employee participation expanded beyond making people feel better about themselves. It incorporated better solutions and much faster rates of improvement through the mobilization of untapped human resources. In several U.S. companies, the freedom of employee participation mixed with the form imposed by competition to create a liberating organizational form and promote competitive leadership.

A liberating organizational form, however, results only when the tension between freedom and form is managed effectively. An experience at Evans & Sutherland illustrates this point. E&S had promised a flight simulator with specific performance capabilities to the U.S. Marine Corps by a specific date. The project team struggled with the design for several months but made little progress. Time was running out, and everyone on the project team was feeling immense pressure and frustration.

The project leader, reluctantly assuming that the deadline for completing the flight simulator could not be met, decided to attend an out-of-town technical conference. On his way to the conference, a path-breaking insight came to him, and he spent the next three days holed up in a hotel room writing the complex specifications for the system architecture on hotel stationery and envelopes. When the project leader returned, everyone on his team worked around-the-clock to build the state-of-the-art flight simulator. The simulator was delivered to the Marine Corps on the date promised because when it was finished the team plugged it in and it worked the first time!

The flight simulator contract with the Marine Corps was like other E&S contracts in that it promised more than the company knew how to deliver. This is how E&S's management created challenge and form for technical people. Contracts were used to provide a sense of urgency and channels for creative effort. But E&S also gave immense freedom and responsibility to its project leaders and project teams. This is why what did not happen in the Marine flight simulator story is as interesting as what did happen. While E&S's management was certainly aware of the lack of progress being made on the project, it did not panic or intervene. It trusted that the contract provided the necessary form for channeling creative effort. Accordingly, management did not feel the need to restrict the project team's freedom. Even when the project leader decided to attend a technical conference at a critical time, management did not question his judgment.

Basic to E&S's offensive strategy was the assumption that if the deadline could be met the team would meet it and that if it could not be met then unrealistic expectations had been created. This assumption offered immense freedom to the project team, but also discipline in the form of an extremely challenging project with a tight deadline. It created a liberating organizational form for E&S's continued technical leadership.

Competitive leaders dominate their industries because of the liberating forms that direct the collective creative energies of their people. Liberating forms involve everyone in formulating and implementing offensive strategies. They don't divide people up into those who think and those who act. Everyone thinks and acts. People at every organizational level have important information and insights that help competitive leaders learn how to do things right as well as how to do the right things.

In today's competitive global economy most discussions of what companies need to learn focus on how they should do things better and faster, while lowering costs. Certainly these are important lessons, but they do not apply to all competitive leaders. The lessons of competition are unique. They begin with companies defining what they are and what they want to become. The lessons continue through liberating organizational forms that energize collective efforts and channel organizational learning.

FORMULATING OFFENSIVE STRATEGIES

Figure 4-5 represents a simple process for formulating offensive strategies, one that promotes head-to-head competition in different ways depending on the interactions of opportunity, vision, and persistence.

Two strategic thinking processes are represented in Figure 4-5, which suggests that offensive strategy can be viewed as a way of thinking or a mental discipline. First, opportunities are identified and selected in a process similar to what Edward deBono calls lateral thinking, which helps identify different areas to focus effort and expend energy on. DeBono uses the example of digging a hole. Lateral thinking is used to decide on different places to dig a

Figure 4–5.   A Process for Formulating Offensive Strategies.

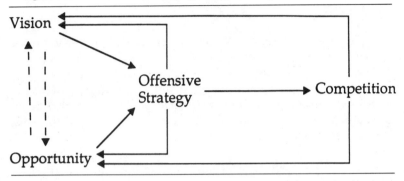

hole.[12] The purpose of an opportunity-guided approach to strategy is to explore all the opportunities that exist and then pursue those that appear to be the most promising. Opportunity-guided offensive strategies are clearly opportunistic. They require a broad network of contacts to assist in identifying and selecting significant business opportunities.

The second strategic thinking process represented in Figure 4-5 involves forming and developing a vision—a way of thinking similar to what deBono calls vertical thinking. While lateral thinking is used to generate new opportunities, verticle thinking is used to make the most of existing opportunities. Returning to deBono's example of digging a hole, vertical thinking is used to dig the same hole deeper. Accordingly, vision-guided offensive strategies involve moving forward in sequential steps toward an envisioned end.[13]

The two strategic thinking processes depicted in Figure 4-5 are complementary. Although one process is often emphasized over the other, both are required. Opportunities enhance vision, and vision develops opportunities.

The process represented in Figure 4-5, like jazz, provides a basis for improvisation. Why is it important that companies improvise their own offensive strategies? Because as Peter Vaill suggests in his discussion of high-performing systems, how something is done is less important than a belief that what is being done is right.[14] When companies improvise their offensive strategies they are more committed to them. They are more likely to believe they are right. This belief gives companies the confidence they need to continue to go head-to-head against competitors.

Opportunity

The Chinese word for crisis consists of two characters meaning "danger" and "opportunity." Competition, like crisis, creates both danger and opportunity. Although every company wants the opportunities that competition brings, many are unwilling to face the necessary dangers. In the long run, however, companies that avoid competition create another danger for themselves. Once they exhaust present opportunities, they are incapable of finding new ones.

The process depicted in Figure 4-5 suggests that opportunities are both found and created. The more offensive strategies are guided by opportunities, however, the more Figure 4-5 becomes an opportunity-finding process.

How do companies find new opportunities? Finding opportunities requires information, and relationships are sources of information. But what kinds of relationships provide information for finding the most new opportunities? Reba Keele discusses the information-gathering potential of different kinds of relationships. Strong ties include kinship, friendship, and love relationships; relationships based on their usefulness at particular times are weak ties. Strong ties connect people of similar backgrounds who move in the same circles; they provide little new information because everyone shares the same sources of information. Keele observes that the only way to connect with new sources of information is through weak ties. The most valuable weak ties are those that connect clusters of strong ties. Therefore, weak ties are often more useful than strong ties in providing information about opportunities.[15]

In many ways, finding opportunities is limited only by human imagination. But opportunities are also fleeting. Why? One reason is that when a company does not exploit an available business opportunity, a competitor will. Of course, the resulting competition may be good for a company if it goes toward it and the playing field remains level. But because most companies want to avoid competition, they will pass up these kinds of opportunities.

Another reason opportunities are fleeting is that companies and people lose energy for them when they stop to analyze them. Therefore, when opportunities guide offensive strategy, it is usually best to strike when the iron is hot. There are clear advantages associated with jumping into the middle of an opportunity and making something happen before analysis paralysis sets in.

I serve on the board of directors of Isis Medical Technologies Development Corporation, a small company that invests in and provides management assistance to new medical start-ups. The president of Isis was approached by a man wanting to sell a small company with a promising product. When Isis' board met, every member was excited about the acquisition. Board members decided that the man was asking a fair price for his company and that Isis should proceed immediately to acquire it. When an offer was extended to the owner of the company, however, he got cold feet. Over a three-month period the owner vacillated back and forth on whether to accept Isis' offer. Finally, he decided to sell his company.

Isis' president reconvened the board to decide if they should proceed and discovered that all enthusiasm for the acquisition was gone. He reported back to the company owner the decision of the board not to acquire his company, and the owner offered to cut his asking price in half. The president took this counteroffer back to the board, but board members still had no interest in proceeding with the acquisition.

Why did the board members change their minds? As one of the board members, I know that in the beginning I was captivated by the company's product. I devised different ways to improve it and market it. I was anxious to get started, then frustrated when the owner dragged his feet. I maintained my excitement for a few weeks, assuming the owner would soon change his mind. But the longer nothing happened, the more doubts I began to have about the acquisition. Like Aesop's fox, who concluded the grapes were sour after failing to reach them, I reduced my frustration by seeing the acquisition in a less attractive light. Then I gradually lost interest in the acquisition. I focused on other opportunities, and my excitement about the acquisition never returned.

As depicted in Figure 4-5, competition both generates new opportunities and creates a sense of urgency around finding new opportunities. New opportunities promote changes inside organizations because companies must adopt different operating procedures as they enter new businesses. The challenge of adjusting to different operating procedures then increases the pressure to identify new opportunities. This creates higher levels of volatility in the business environment as competition between companies intensifies around identifying and pursuing new opportunities.

Vision

Visions are different from plans. In the process depicted in Figure 4-5,
a vision begins as an undeveloped image of future accomplishments.
It can be a feeling about what is to be attained as much as a visual
preview. Visions become increasingly well defined through action,
not passive thought. They also provide checkpoints. A way to keep
offensive strategies on track is to look back at the original vision and
compare it to the evolving one. Such reflective glances, according to
Karl Weick, keep organizations from wandering too far afield.

Weick, a critic of traditional views of planning, suggests that it
is wasteful spending time trying to anticipate future contingencies
because one can never know how things will turn out. He recommends that instead of planning people should take action, then reflect
on what has occurred. Random trial and error, which is typically
viewed as a highly inefficient way to approach a problem, often
produces the best results because it generates data sense can be made
from.[16]

The process depicted in Figure 4-5 mixes together Weick's
views and more traditional views. In it visions are reviewed both
prospectively and retrospectively. They guide but do not shape the
process. Depending on how they interact with opportunities, visions
can be either moving or stationary targets.

There are many examples of human visions in both fictional
and nonfictional accounts of great men and women. Clearly vision
often precedes great accomplishments. Perhaps this is why King
Solomon wrote, "Where there is no vision, the people perish" (Prov-
erbs 29:18).

John Steinbeck's novel *East of Eden* provides an example of a
great man's vision. The novel tells the story of Adam Trask and his
progeny. Adam grew up in Connecticut, then moved to the Salinas
Valley in California to make a new life for himself. As Adam looks
over the farm he has recently purchased, he envisions what he wants
to accomplish. In his mind he can see the wheat growing tall and
squares of green alfalfa near the river. He hears the hammering of the
carpenters behind him and knows in his heart that he has found the
place to plant his dynasty.[17]

Adam Trask "foretasted comfort for himself and his descend-
ents," but his vision was not realized without hard work. There was
manure to scrape out, old floors to tear up, and neck-rubbed window

casings to rip away. Steinbeck described the men who, like Adam Trask, came to the Salinas Valley during this era as "notched and comfortable in the present, hard and unfruitful as it was, but only as a doorstep to a fantastic future."[18]

An executive's vision tells people where to go and what to do to realize a "fantastic future" and provides direction to all organization members so their efforts converge around common purposes. Visions define the values and skills that are critical to meet competitive challenges. Moreover, an executive vision falls short if it does not also capture the imagination of organization members, inspire and motivate them to do whatever it takes to make the vision a reality.

Ray Kroc founded McDonald's with a vision like Adam Trask's. He pictured his empire long before it existed, and he saw how to get there. He invented the company motto—"Quality, service, cleanliness, and value"—and kept repeating it to employees for the rest of his life.[19] His people internalized the values he articulated and contributed to McDonald's fantastic success.

How does the process depicted in Figure 4-5 affect an executive's vision? The process either brings the vision closer to reality or reality closer to the vision. In many respects, this is a process of natural selection. In order for their visions to survive, executives must prove to themselves and enough of their people that at some point their visions will connect with reality. When they cannot offer such proof they must change their visions or they will die from lack of support.

Persistence

Ross Perot said, "If I had to write a handbook for the American entrepreneur and put everything in one sentence I'd say, 'Persevere, no matter what the pain, persevere.'" Perot's actions speak even louder than his words. One Electronic Data Systems veteran observed about the company when it was still guided by Perot: "EDS was like a tank. Put it in low gear, and it could run over anything." Another EDS employee said, "Our gunner's command was simple: Ready, aim, fire, fire, fire, fire, fire."[20]

Before strategic decisions are made or deals are consummated, one often changes one's mind, just as my experience on the board of Isis Medical Technologies Development Corporation showed. Backing out at this stage may be the right or wrong thing to do, but either way nothing is ventured so nothing is gained or lost. But once commitments are made, the rules of the game change. The time for having second thoughts is over.

Persistence is what makes offensive strategies work. It drives the process described in Figure 4-5 in two ways. When offensive strategies are guided by opportunities, persistence continues to identify opportunities, to select and exploit them. When offensive strategies are guided by vision, persistence keeps attention riveted on doing whatever is necessary to realize the vision. It is also the force that preserves the vision until it is realized.

Reggie Jackson, the baseball star, once said, "I never believed that giving 110 percent meant anything. Give me whatever it takes to win." Jackson was describing situations in which important games hung in the balance. According to him, these were the times when great players raised their performance another notch. By reaching deep inside themselves, more often than not they found a way to overcome the odds and win the game.

Competition demands the kind of persistence Reggie Jackson describes. Persistent people and companies keep going head-to-head against competitors until they win. Their persistent desire to win eventually wears down the competition.

The story of Identronics [IDX] demonstrates how persistence can turn disappointments and failures into successes. The founders of IDX believed they could eliminate the massive waste associated with branding cattle by developing a passive transponder that could function as a license plate beneath the skin of a cow. They also concluded that through a combination of analog, digital, microwave, and radio wave technology, they could monitor the temperature of cattle to assist ranchers in the early detection of sick animals.

IDX's founders worked on the development of the technology for nearly three years before a working prototype was finally developed. Then they conducted the "critical experiment." They sprayed water on dairy cows and monitored their temperatures using the passive transponder. The founders were shocked to discover that their device mistakenly reported that the cows were clinically dead.

At about the same time, one of the founders asked the "critical question": Was there a market for devices that could passively identify and monitor the temperature of cattle? The founders knew how many dairy cows there were, but they did not know how many dairy farmers would buy their device or at what price they would buy it. The founders believed that eventually they could sell their devices for $1, and then by pointing a gunlike device toward a cow they could read its identification number and determine its temperature. But none of the dairy farmers they surveyed wanted to buy the devices for $1. So the founders asked the dairy farmers if they would use the devices if they gave them away. Again, the dairy farmers said no. Finally, IDX's founders asked the dairy farmers how much they would have to pay them to use the devices. The dairy farmers told the founders they would need to be paid a lot of money because the devices would be such a nuisance to use.

After discovering the results of the "critical experiment" and the "critical question," IDX's founders met together in one of their homes. They knew they either needed to find an alternative application for their technology or throw in the towel. They reasoned that if a device could passively transmit through an inch of cowhide, fat, and skin, then it could operate in a fairly hostile environment. But where? And for what use? After several hours of persistent deliberation an idea surfaced. One of the founders recalled reading an article in the *Wall Street Journal* about a legal suit brought against a bar code manufacturer by the Southern Pacific Railroad. The railroad claimed that the bar code devices sold to them by this company to identify railroad cars were useless when covered by dirt and mud.

Why couldn't their devices be used to identify railroad cars? IDX's founders asked. One IDX founder taped a prototype device to his car and drove it to the Santa Cruz airport after it closed. He ran his car at 120 miles an hour past an antenna and was able to get a reading from the device. Then he covered the device with dirt and mud and repeated the experiment. He still got a reading.

The next day the founders called General Railway Signal and Westinghouse Air Brakes, two railway supply companies. They described the technology over the telephone and both companies sent representatives to evaluate the technology that same week. Within a month, IDX negotiated a contract with General Railway Signal to buy exclusive rights for applications of the technology to wheeled vehicles.

This improbable story demonstrates the power persistence adds to offensive strategy. IDX could have done a better job at anticipating technical problems and the market potential of its devices. But no offensive strategy is foolproof. Success is often blocked by circumstances that companies cannot anticipate; only through persistence are companies able to succeed.

THREE OFFENSIVE STRATEGIES

The process depicted in Figure 4-5 is adapted from Herbert Simon's description of how levels of aspiration change in response to changing circumstances.[21] Simon's work and my own empirical observations suggest that organizations improvise unique offensive strategies around three core themes. I call organizations: (1) Opportunists (opportunity-guided offensive strategies), (2) Visionaries (vision-guided offensive strategies), or (3) Capitalists (both opportunity- and vision-guided offensive strategies), based on their different approaches to head-to-head competition.

The Japanese word *nemawashi* means "preparing the ground for planting." One of the reasons for the success of many Japanese companies is the *nemawashi* they do before entering new markets. In the next three chapters I will discuss the offensive strategies of Opportunists, Visionaries, and Capitalists. This chapter has provided the *nemawashi* in the form of a conceptual foundation for this discussion.

5 Opportunists: An Opportunity-Guided Offensive Strategy

If venture capitalists were deciding whether to invest in an Opportunist, what would they consider first? Many firms that provide venture capital emphasize the management team heading new ventures or the founding idea, but such firms specifically interested in Opportunists make decisions based on the size and readiness of potential markets. Why? Because those firms that serve Opportunists are equally opportunistic. They are interested in short-term investments and want to build a company quickly so that it either attracts acquirers or they can take it public.

Ideally, firms that deal in venture capital reinforce the natural growth strategies of Opportunists. Opportunists look for opportunities to enter existing markets with products or services offering enough unique features to attract market share away from competitors. They live with the thought of "What else?" or "What next?" as they move from one success to another. Accordingly, Opportunists avoid long-term attachments to specific opportunities, telling themselves that "You never fall in love with a deal" or "You can't be married to a deal forever." They build an exit mentality into every enterprise.[1]

When venture capitalists reinforce the strategies of Opportunists they encourage them to persist in finding new opportunities. Accordingly, the relationship between venture capitalists and Opportunists promotes new economic activity in the form of new products and services that respond to newly identified needs in the marketplace.

The case of Data-Disk Corporation,[2] however, shows that venture capitalists can also distort the natural opportunity-finding strategies of Opportunists. While working for a Fortune 500 company, Data-Disk's founders developed a new data storage technology. The data storage project was scrapped because the larger project it was a part of was cancelled. One of Data-Disk's founders suggested starting a company to develop the technology into a marketable product, and others signed on. As one of the founders recalled, "I was ready for the challenge and jumped at the opportunity."

Although there was a definite demand for Data-Disk's technology, the company was entering a crowded market with a product offering only marginal advantages over alternative ones. Moreover, the scientific literature was reporting advances in laser disk data storage technology that, in time, would render Data-Disk's technology obsolete. What this meant was Data-Disk's window of opportunity was relatively narrow, requiring an immediate response to current market conditions. To take on the competition, Data-Disk needed a quick infusion of venture capital.

Data-Disk was financed with venture capital from Beta Partners,[3] which made an initial investment of $750,000 in the company to develop its first product. Beta's managing partner became Data-Disk's chairman of the board but did not assume an active role in the company's management. On average, he spent a day and a half a month working with Data-Disk.

One of Data-Disk's founders served as the company's president. Data-Disk's initial strategy was to market exclusively to original equipment manufacturers, but none was interested in its products because they were unproven in the marketplace and the company's manufacturing capabilities were suspect. Several technical problems further hampered Data-Disk over a period of two and a half years, and Beta was forced to make significant additional investments in Data-Disk to keep it afloat.

Once Data-Disk's technical problems were solved, Beta replaced the company's president with one of its board members, who joined Data-Disk on an interim basis until a permanent replacement could be found. Under his direction Data-Disk formulated a new and highly successful strategy, developing an IBM-compatible version of its product and marketing it to end users. By the time Data-Disk's third president was hired, sales had already started to take off.

Beta Partners offered Data-Disk's third president, a former

marketing director for a Fortune 500 company, an attractive compensation package that included an annual bonus equal to 1 percent of the company's gross revenues. In each of the next three years, Data-Disk's sales more than doubled, and the president received a commensurate annual bonus.

During the president's fourth year at Data-Disk, sales leveled off. But Beta Partners refused to allow the president to lower projections and pressured him to revitalize sales. The president responded by offering attractive incentives to Data-Disk's network of dealers. The strategy worked, but only temporarily. Dealers became overstocked, and sales again plummeted. Undaunted, the president continued to pressure manufacturing to produce more product. When all of Data-Disk's storage facilities were filled with unshipped product, the president leased additional storage space.

Beta Partners eventually realized the severity of Data-Disk's problems. It fired the president and replaced him with the man who had served as Data-Disk's second president. He immediately furloughed 400 hourly workers and nearly 250 salaried employees.

Data-Disk continues to limp along as the market continues to shrink for its data storage technology. During the tenure of Data-Disk's third president, the company was taken public. A total of 2.3 million shares were sold through an initial public offering at $10 a share. At that time Beta sold all but 17 percent of its holdings in Data-Disk, realizing a significant return on its original investment. The fact that Beta retained a 17 percent stake in Data-Disk indicated that it still considered the company a solid, short-term investment. Data-Disk's stock did, in fact, peak at nearly $25 a share. Then, coincident with eroding company performance, the price of Data-Disk stock dropped until it finally leveled off around $2 a share.

What lessons do we learn from the story of Data-Disk and Beta Partners? The first lesson is that Opportunists remain strong and vital organizations only as long as they are fed by a continuous stream of opportunities. They do not develop radically new products or services. The windows of opportunity for their products or services are narrow. Therefore, a key element to their offensive strategies is continuing to generate new opportunities. Data-Disk should have continued to look outward to identify new technologies to develop within its existing market or to identify new markets to enter. Instead, it milked dry the demand for its only technology.

Another important lesson learned from Data-Disk and the experiences of thousands of other new ventures is that some liabilities are clearly associated with newness. New ventures are clumsy, undisciplined, and, therefore, unready to enter the forge of head-to-head competition. This is why new ventures usually require some initial protection from competition. Venture capital is one of the means of providing this initial protection while new ventures work out some of their bugs. Thus, new ventures do not start out by going head-to-head against competition, just as sports teams do not begin their official seasons directly but rather practice and play preseason games first. But this initial protection is best when it is temporary. New ventures should always be pointed toward competition. Too much protection is as destructive as too little protection. Gradually, this early protection should be lifted, exposing new ventures to significant competitive challenges.

Finally, timing is a key variable in the Opportunist's offensive strategy. Opportunists retain their independence from venture capitalists by staying on schedule. The sooner they get their new products to market, the more benefits they reap from narrow windows of opportunity. But Opportunists can also move too fast. One of the most disastrous mistakes they can make is introducing products before the market is ready for them. Moreover, Data-Disk's story warns about the disruptive effects of forcing market penetration too fast. Critical to an Opportunist's offensive strategy is quickly identifying new market opportunities, but the success of the strategy depends on its timely execution.

IMPROVISING AN OPPORTUNIST'S STRATEGY

An Opportunist's offensive strategy is an opportunity-finding strategy. Opportunists become competitive leaders when they identify and pursue new opportunities faster than their competitors do. They literally redefine industries by pioneering new markets or new concepts, with their major focus on customer needs. They find new areas of opportunity by asking questions about what potential customers want but don't have.

Opportunists improvise, more than plan, their offensive strategies. Planning, of course, is one of the staples of corporate life. Organizations that underplan are unprepared for even the most predictable events. But organizations that overplan are equally at risk, because planning always delays doing. In fact, it is sometimes used to avoid doing or becomes an excuse for not doing. Planning, especially detailed planning, can also create a false sense of security. Because many events are unpredictable, even the best plans are only rough approximations, which should never preclude improvisation. The greatest danger of overplanning is its restrictiveness. When Opportunists adhere too closely to plans they close themselves off to the opportunities they cannot plan for.

The ideal Opportunist's strategy is guided by opportunities that generate a consistent flow of entrepreneurial activity. Opportunists are hungry for action and experience. They are forward-moving, intensely inquisitive organizations.

How do Opportunists improvise offensive strategies? First, Opportunists are outward-looking organizations, led by outward-looking managers. Second, they are problem-solving organizations, solving problems in two ways—either by developing solutions then seeking problems or by seeking problems then developing solutions. Third, they form, then use networks of relationships to help identify and evaluate new opportunities. Finally, Opportunists view competition as an opportunity.

Outward-Looking Organizations

The founders of organizations we call Opportunists are outward-looking managers who are constantly looking for emerging areas of opportunity for their companies. They view their role as making sense of changes in the business environment and figuring out what opportunities they create.

George N. Hatsopoulos, the founder and CEO of Thermo Electron Corporation, has built a classic Opportunist. Hatsopoulos started his company in 1956 with no idea where it would lead. His early efforts focused on thermionics, a technology for converting heat into electricity using no moving parts. Hatsopoulos failed to develop any commercial products from these early efforts, but his opportunistic strategy has since taken Thermo Electron into businesses ranging from cogeneration (generating both electrical energy and low-grade heat from the same fuel) and pollution control to heart-assist devices.[4]

Hatsopoulos believes that the most important part of his job is identifying emerging problems, then mobilizing people and technology to solve them. He spends a lot of time trying to figure out new economic trends. Hatsopoulos says that his strategy

> requires a broad understanding of society; and also of what drives our society. The more you understand the overall environment—and re-

ally, it's the whole world—the better able you'll be to find the opportunities. If you find needs that aren't being addressed, you can make a much greater contribution, and you will have a greater chance of success.[5]

To gain a broad understanding of society, Hatsopoulos spends a lot of time talking with people and taking part in public policy discussions. He recommends to other entrepreneurs that they attend professional meetings, develop relationships with people at other companies, involve themselves in the broader problems facing their industries, and talk to investment bankers. He also reads a great deal, and always through the lenses of a problem-solver.[6]

Problem-Solving Organizations

Opportunists are natural problem-solvers. George Hatsopoulos, for example, claims that Thermo Electron is a technologically oriented, not a product-driven company. What does he mean? Hatsopoulos wanted to start with a core technology, look around to identify existing needs, then develop products to meet needs. In other words, Thermo Electron's core technology is a solution seeking a problem.[7]

Occasionally, Opportunists create new industries when their solutions find the right problems. In 1946, Russell Kelly decided to start a service bureau. He moved to Detroit, purchased office equipment, rented an office, and hired two employees. Customers would bring typing, calculating, duplicating, mailing, and other business projects to Kelly's service bureau. One day a customer called to plead for a typist to help him with an emergency project. As a favor, Kelly sent one of his employees to the customer's office to help out. Then requests for temporary services started to come to the service bureau from customers who did not want to release company records from their offices. When Kelly realized that sending his employees out to work in other offices could become a bigger business than his service bureau, the idea that pioneered the temporary services industry took root.

Opportunists also solve problems in the more conventional way—they begin with problems, then find solutions. J. Willard Marriott started his hotel and restaurant empire by opening an A&W Root Beer stand in Washington, D.C. During the spring, summer, and early fall of 1927, business was better than expected. In fact, business was so good that Marriott was able to open a second stand

and hire help. But as the cooler weather approached, Marriott was faced with a dilemma. Selling only root beer during the winter months was out of the question. There would be no demand for his ice-cold drinks as soon as the first winter winds hit Washington. But what to do? Selling food was the obvious answer. But A&W did not allow its franchisees to sell food.[8]

What did Marriott do? He decided on a unique food concept. Instead of the standard fare of hamburgers and hot dogs, Marriott decided to sell Mexican food and barbecued beef. Then he flew west to present his proposal to A&W's founder, Roy Allen. When he returned to Washington he had special authorization to sell food at A&W Root Beer stands in his territory. Following an overnight conversion of the root beer stand into a restaurant, the first Hot Shoppe opened for customers.[9]

Another example of an effective problem solver is the Trammel Crow Company. Trammel has built or helped build roughly 250 million square feet of commercial and residential real estate. The company's credits include path-breaking showplaces such as Peachtree Plaza in Atlanta and the Embarcadero in San Francisco, as well as lowly warehouses and strip shopping centers. There are elegant atrium hotels and medical centers, but also trailer parks, and middle-income housing tracts. Trammel has offices in more than 100 U.S. cities, in five European countries, and in Hong Kong.[10]

Trammel views itself as a manufacturer of space, and more especially of adaptable space. For example, the company pioneered the idea of office and service-center malls: warehouses with 14-foot ceilings that could be adapted for high-tech repair centers, fitness centers, and so on. By manufacturing adaptable space, Trammel can adjust to a variety of customer needs. This increases both the company's problem-solving capability and its opportunities by increasing its pool of potential customers. Because Trammel's space has so many potential uses, partners are comfortable signing up customers on the shortest possible lease. Accordingly, they take advantage of a rising real estate market by charging ever-higher rents.[11]

Opportunists are more adept at finding solutions to problems they have personal experience with. For example, I know an inventor who has trained his mind to identify problems and is able to invent products in response to the problems he identifies. His problem-solving ability, however, can be both an asset and a liability. He is able to invent more products than could be developed by many companies, and enough distractions to keep him from following up on any one of them. So what has he done? His family owns and operates a grocery store. In response to competition from new stores in their area the family was forced to lower prices at its store. The store was then not making enough money to stay in business without cuts in operating costs. Given this problem, the inventor focused his efforts on developing a customer self-checkout system.

Technologically, the customer self-checkout system is not as sophisticated as some of the inventor's other products. Modified IBM PCs driven by 50,000 lines of computer code are the brains of the system. Customers lift grocery items from their shopping carts, scan them, then place them in another shopping cart that is weighed on a highly sensitive scale to ensure security. After customers complete their self-checkout, they receive a receipt which they take to a store clerk (each clerk is assigned to four self-checkout lanes) to pay for their groceries.

With his self-checkout system the inventor has created a technology-based product with a vast potential market that also fits his background. The self-checkout system also provides a way to lower operating costs at the family grocery store, and the store offers an excellent test site for the technology. The inventor's success is in no way guaranteed, but he is addressing a problem he is eminently qualified to solve.

Networking Organizations

David Halberstam's account of Yutaka Katayama's career and Nissan Motor Company's early efforts in the United States shows how much an Opportunist's strategy relies on both weak and strong-tie relationships. Katayama knew he was being banished when in early 1960 he was sent to the United States as Nissan's West Coast representative. Nissan's brand-new American endeavor was considered unimportant at the time. Nevertheless, Katayama was delighted about his new assignment. After all, America was the land of opportunity.[12]

Katayama took some time to study the U.S. market. The most important thing he learned was that in the United States the dealer network was critical, that dealers were Nissan's true customers. Nissan America would only be as strong as its network of dealers.[13]

Katayama judged Nissan's dealers using two criteria: how eager they were and whether they had enough automotive savvy to hold the trust of customers. Then, to build stronger ties with dealers, he gave them between 18 and 20 percent of gross profit, compared to the 12 or 13 percent the Big Three automakers paid to dealers. Katayama figured that the only way Nissan could prosper was if the dealers got rich. He told them they were his partners.[14]

Katayama loved meeting people and making new American friends. He preferred to travel alone because he could learn more that way. He could meet people on planes, in restaurants, and in bars. He took every opportunity available to him to make new acquaintances and learn more about America. Katayama's English was not very good, but the language barrier never seemed to keep him from conveying his enthusiasm.[15]

Years later in his tiny Tokyo office, Katayama liked to point at a map of the western United States, which was covered with little dots. "Each dot is a millionaire I made," he would say. Together the dots represented Nissan's enormous success in the United States—a success built almost entirely on relationships developed by Yutaka Katayama.[16]

The Trammel Crow Company provides an example of how a company uses internal networks to generate business opportunities. Trammel Crow, the founder of the company, began forming partnerships in the early 1960s. His first partnerships, based on mutual trust, were informal contracts sealed by handshakes. His partners knew they would get what was due them because of the founder's legendary reputation for fairness. About the partnerships he formed at his company, Trammel Crow said:

> Partnerships make for a humanly rewarding life. . . . There's also an element of right and wrong in it: a fair distribution of the fruits of common labor. We have here a fraternity, a camaraderie, a brotherhood, which I find very satisfying. At the same time, in a partnership, you leverage yourself. I'd rather be one strong man among other strong men than one strong man among weak ones, or a strong man alone.[17]

Until 1978, the Trammel Crow Company was organized as a delicate and complex network of partnerships. Trammel Crow and senior partners provided the know-how to leasing agents and junior partners, while leasing agents and junior partners devoted their significant energies and ambitions to finding, selecting, and developing new business opportunities. The network of partnerships at the company created an entrepreneurial horde. The organization was self-managing, controlled only by Trammel Crow's intuitive selection of new leasing agents and the intense socializing experience new agents received as they worked alongside senior partners. While the company's corporate structure was loose and chaotic, the traditional relationships that had grown up among subordinate partnerships sustained an incredible record of corporate success.

Opportunities to Compete

Yutaka Katayama's offensive strategy was both opportunistic and simple. He reasoned that Nissan should begin on the coasts, creating their beachheads there, slowly earning the money to spend on advertising, and only then expand into the center of the country. "What we should do," Katayama told his U.S. associates, "is get better and creep up slowly, so that we'll be good—and the customers will think we're good—before Detroit even knows about us."[18] Similar to those of most Japanese companies, Nissan America's strategy was to go toward competition, which was perceived as an opportunity. The success of the strategy depended less on a grand plan than on an ability to improvise.

For example, Katayama had to sell Americans, who wanted power and styling in their cars, on a box-shaped vehicle that was grossly underpowered. Every attempt he made to get Tokyo to upgrade and Americanize the car met with resistance. So Katayama improvised. While continuing to pressure Tokyo to change, he focused promotional efforts on Nissan's little pickup, a vehicle there was significant demand for. In fact, Nissan's small, inexpensive, but durable pickup accounted for nearly half of the company's sales before 1965.

Trammel Crow had a different strategy than most real estate developers have. Most developers build buildings with other people's money, depreciate them, sell them, then deploy the profit to start all over again with other buildings. Crow's formula was to retain ownership. "You get rich selling real estate," he used to say, "but you can only get wealthy owning it."

The real secret to Trammel Crow's success, however, is his relentless competitive spirit. One of Crow's early partners said about him, "He believes that persistence is far more important than genius. Never, never, never, give up—that's his motto." Crow relishes opportunities to compete. His personal credo could have come straight out of an Ayn Rand novel: "I believe that my fate is in my hands and no one else's. Nobody's going to take care of us but ourselves. I don't ask the government to help me; I don't ask you to help me. I just do what I have to do, and if I do right, I hope I remember how I did it, so I can do it the same way next time."[19]

Richard S. Worth, the founder of R. W. Frookies, jumped into the middle of a challenge just to see where the opportunity to compete would lead him. Before Worth founded R.W. Frookies he had already started and sold another company—Sorrell Ridge, a maker of fruit-only wild blueberry, peach, and raspberry conserves. Sorrell Ridge was one of the first makers of "all-natural" foods, a product category that moved quickly from the counterculture to the mainstream. When Worth left Sorrell Ridge he wanted to find another all-natural food product that he could develop and sell, but as he wandered through grocery store aisles he found that the cookie section was the only place without alternatives to products filled with chemicals or preservatives. So he decided to enter the cookie business.[20]

Worth developed a delicious, all-natural cookie that was flavored with fruit juice instead of sugar (hence the name—fruit juice, cookie, Frookie). However, having a quality product did not guarantee R.W. Frookies a spot on the grocery store aisle. Every year roughly 8,000 new food products are invented, and most of those products are created by food giants, like RJR Nabisco, which owns 37 percent of a supermarket's cookie aisle. Obviously, R.W. Frookies could not compete with the food giants in ways that required significant capital investment, but it could be more agile. For example, Worth designed freestanding displays for Frookies that could be placed at the ends of cookie aisles. Instead of spending major advertising dollars, he offered stage promotions to boost store traffic—and Frookie awareness. Worth sold 35 percent of R.W. Frookies' stock to bakers, distributors, and individuals who provided professional services to help launch the company. With their commitment and cooperation he was able to make the playing field more level in his competition against the food giants.[21]

Richard Worth improvised an innovative offensive strategy because he had to compete against food giants. Competition offered him and R.W. Frookies the opportunity to be challenged and grow stronger. Opportunists enjoy and seek competition, and by improvising outward-looking, problem-solving, and networking strategies, they lead the competition.

LIBERATING ORGANIZATIONAL FORMS

Opportunists are economic gadflies. Their role is to stir up the economy, puncture equilibria, and provide a constant source of irritation within static and staid industries. Performing this role to its maximum effect requires a liberating organizational form. Opportunists must be able to provide the appropriate balance between freedom and form to involve all their people in finding opportunities.

The founders of Opportunists are classic entrepreneurs who start their companies with visions of acquiring personal wealth. These founders do not initially seek to control others, but they do aspire to gain sufficient wealth and understanding to look after their own needs. They want to be independent, owing nobody anything. Thus, the values of individualism and personal attainment are the core strengths of Opportunists.

Creating liberating organizational forms for Opportunists means offering to everyone the opportunity of wealth and independence. The driving force behind the offensive strategies of Opportunists is everyone's personal vision of what he or she can accomplish.

What are the common liberating forms Opportunists create, and how do they drive offensive strategies? I have identified three such forms: (1) loosely coupled organizations; (2) dividing organizations; and, (3) build-them-yourself organizations.

Loosely Coupled Organizations

Karl Weick, in his book *The Social Psychology of Organizing*, proposes that loosely coupled organizations are more adaptive because independent, smaller organizational units can respond more quickly to unique environmental changes. Loosely coupled units can be custom-fit to environmental conditions. Moreover, if one part of an organization is maladaptive, the effect is minimized throughout the organization.[22] Loosely coupled organizations are also more adaptive because of the freedom and independence allowed separate business units. Of course, with freedom comes responsibility, and loosely coupled units must identify and pursue their own business opportunities.

Thermo Electron Corporation, according to George Hatsopoulos, has 17 separate business units; 5 of them have minority public ownership. He has set up divisions of Thermo Electron as publicly owned companies so managers feel more responsible for their businesses. In addition to receiving the rewards of partial ownership, managers of each subsidiary know that what they do is scrutinized both by corporate management, because Thermo Electron is the majority shareholder, and by minority shareholders.[23]

Hatsopoulos explains why he chose a loosely coupled organization for Thermo Electron:

> I really believe in small companies. But small companies have a big disadvantage. They don't have the support, the financial and management resources, that big companies have. So, you have to find a new structure for U.S. industry that combines the advantages of small companies and the support of large companies. My own answer is to have a bunch of small companies in a family, which gives them financial and management support and strategic direction. But at the same time they are acting as though they are independent companies with their own constituency or stockholders.[24]

Hatsopoulos hopes that in ten years most of Thermo Electron's business units will have minority public ownership.

Carlton Communications PLC's recent acquisition of a video technology company reveals how companies can assemble loosely coupled, opportunistic organizations through acquisitions. Carlton paid a premium price for the company, making its founders instant multimillionaires. But Michael Green, Carlton's chairman and CEO, realized that for his company to continue to receive significant returns on its investment in the video technology company, its founders had to remain motivated. Somehow he had to keep their personal stake in the company high enough to encourage them to work as hard as they did before the acquisition. So Green added an incentive plan to the deal he signed with the company's founders.

Green knew that because he had already made the founders multimillionaires the incentive plan had to offer a lot of money just to get their attention. He also was more concerned about growth in profits than in sales, so the growth measures he used were weighted 75 percent for profits and 25 percent for sales. Finally, Green realized that he could not hold the company's founders forever, but he assumed that if they remained with the company for five years he could work out an orderly transition. So Green offered the founders a five-year incentive package. Over the first three years each founder would receive a $300,000 bonus if the company grew at least 10 percent and an additional $300,000 if the company grew 30 percent. A formula for prorating the second $300,000 was developed for annual growth between 20 and 30 percent. For the fourth and fifth years, the founders would receive $600,000 if the company grew at a 30 percent rate. Again, the bonus was prorated for growth between 20 and 30 percent. Finally, Green devised five-year bonuses to encourage greater than 30 percent compounded growth. If at the end of five years compounded growth exceeded 40 percent, the company's founders received a lump-sum bonus of $5 million to be divided evenly among them. If five-year compounded growth exceeded 50 percent, an $8 million bonus would be awarded to the founders.

I interviewed the founders of this video technology company during the third year of the incentive plan. Not surprisingly, none of them had left, and all were satisfied with the way they had been treated since the acquisition. The founders met with Carlton's people every three months, but no formal board meetings were held. They sent Carlton monthly financial statements, but as long as performance went well they expected little interference. And performance was going very well: The acquisition had actually increased the company's innovative capacity, and compounded growth since the acquisition was between 50 and 60 percent.

Dividing Organizations

Kuniyasu Sakai heads a Japanese company, Taiyo Kogyo, but is an entrepreneur in the American tradition. Observing the negative consequences of rapid company growth and wishing to create a liberation organizational form, Sakai decided to adopt a strategy of keeping organizational units small, independent, and accountable. His offensive strategy is one of company division. Recently, there were 39 companies in the Taiyo Group, all of which are expected to divide before they reach 500 employees.

Company division is like cell division. Each divided company becomes a new, independent enterprise, and Sakai chooses the founder of each new company from among the employees of the company to be divided. The founder must recruit employees, find new clients, and purchase necessary equipment and materials. Each company in the Taiyo Group holds a financial interest in the new company. Mr. Sakai offers founder's counsel and guidance, but he does not decide the direction they take their company in.

Sakai's method of company division creates the same kind of "atomistic" competition described by Adam Smith in his writings. In fact, many of the companies in the Taiyo Group compete directly against one another. Each new company is helped at the start, but then it must survive on its own. Sakai explains:

Dividing a company is always a risk. I divide my company when it is not yet mature. As a result, not only am I greatly challenged, but I must face the uncertainty of the new company's virgin voyage. In fact, at that point, we are in a position that may be on the verge of shipwreck. However, it is this danger that forces the new leader to kindle his spirit. They say everybody can put forth great strength at the scene of a fire. Occasionally I think of myself as an arsonist who sets fires in the hearts of promising young men, in hopes of calling forward their deeply hidden combative instincts.[25]

Sakai, the "arsonist," understands that when managers are faced with a competitive challenge, most of them rise to the occasion. He offers the founders of newly divided companies the opportunity of a lifetime, but then expects them to go head-to-head against competitors to find their own opportunities.

Build-Them-Yourself Organizations

The key to build-them-yourself companies is recruitment. Individuals recruited to join a company build it and their own organizations within it by recruiting others to join. Build-them-yourself companies become groups of build-them-yourself organizations within organizations. Individuals joining the company receive the same opportunities as the individuals who recruited them, and recruiters' organizations are built by those they directly recruit as well as by successive generations of recruits.

Examples of build-them-yourself organizations include Tupperware, Mary Kay Cosmetics, and Amway. A. L. Williams & Associates (ALW) has shaken-up the previously staid and traditional life insurance industry. ALW's 200,000-person sales force sells more term life insurance than any other company's in the country. Its salespeople raid the cash-value policies other insurers sell. The company argues that people should buy term instead of cash-value insurance and invest the sizable difference in mutual funds.[26]

What is most remarkable about ALW, however, is its liberating, build-them-yourself organizational form. Individuals join the company as training reps. When they complete the company's licensing and training program and observe three field training sales, they become reps. Reps can earn money in only one way: They earn 42 percent commission on personal sales. Once reps complete three field training sales, they become district leaders, who not only earn 51 percent on personal sales but can earn money in three additional ways: from field training sales, overrides at the rep level, and diversification. The promotions continue to division leader, regional manager, senior regional manager, and, finally, regional vice president. These last employees earn 125 percent on personal sales, then can earn money in 13 additional ways from the organizations they build beneath them.

Why has ALW been successful? After looking at the incentives, the answer is obvious. ALW is not just selling insurance, it is selling the dream of financial independence to its associates. By selling insurance and recruiting others, new hires are told they can build their own businesses. Not only do they receive commissions from policies they sell themselves, they also get a piece of the action from policies agents they recruited sell. According to A. L. Williams, ALW's founder and chief motivator, "We've got the best part-time opportunity in America—bar none."[27]

ALW was recently acquired by Primerica Corporation. Commercial Credit Group, Inc., the company that owns Primerica, intends to use ALW's network to sell other financial products, like securities, mortgages, and different kinds of insurance. This will allow opportunity-finding activities to go in a variety of new directions at ALW.

MAINTAINING COMPETITIVE LEADERSHIP

Opportunists maintain their competitive leadership by continuing to be the first to pursue newly identified areas of opportunity. Maintaining competitive leadership does not mean sitting on a lead. Opportunists must continue to go head-to-head against competition. As Kay Whitmore, the president of Kodak, said, "Even with a high market share, you must get out there and say, 'I am trying to gain new customers. I am trying to meet new needs.' You have a more forward-looking, more opportunistic approach. You may end up only protecting your market share, but you will, in fact, protect it."[28]

How do Opportunists maintain their competitive leadership and continue to go head-to-head against competition? First, Opportunists are companies driven by individual initiative. The strongest Opportunists enlist the most individuals in the opportunity-finding process. Therefore, a concern at all organizational levels for individual motivation is fundamental to Opportunists maintaining their competitive leadership, because motivated individuals take their companies toward competition. This concern for individual motivation must then be reinforced by business practices and corporate structures.

Individual Motivation

Because Opportunists are individual entrepreneurs, individual motivation begins and continues with the promise of entrepreneurial gains. The way Michael Green motivated the founders of the video technology company acquired by Carlton Communications PLC is a powerful example of how highly valued outcomes can lead to the attainment of lofty performance goals. A. L. Williams & Associates offers another example of how motivationally compelling the promise of financial independence can be. ALW has the "most powerful sales force in the financial services industry," according to Gerald Tsai, Primerica's CEO, because the financial incentives it promises its agents far surpass what any other company promises.[29]

Alta Products is a company that produces high-tech video equipment, such as time-based correctors, for the home entertainment market. Alta's strategy is to sell products that have been available only to video professionals at a low enough price to attract amateur video enthusiasts. Given this strategy, Alta is always looking for opportunities to lower manufacturing costs.

Wayne Lee, Alta's president and general manager, believes that all of his employees are potential opportunity finders. To transform their potential energy into a dynamic force he promises cash bonuses to individuals who propose successful cost-saving ideas. Then he sets aside a percentage of quarterly profits to distribute to all employees as profit-sharing bonuses. Alta manufactures its products in a spartan, 10,000-square-foot warehouse, but Lee says, "My people love this building." Why? Because they know that a significant share of the money they save by remaining in a low-cost facility will eventually find its way into their own pockets.

American Business Seminars (ABS) began as a vehicle for Gary Cochran to market his real estate investment ideas. The initial concept was to buy lists of potential customers, send out mass mailings offering free tickets to seminars, and then sell products at the seminars. Cochran was so successful that others wanted to join him as seminar presenters. Presently ABS is sponsoring seminars on such topics as financial planning, improving memory, and direct marketing, then selling related products. Cochran has devised a simple, straightforward incentive system that pays presenters according to how successful they are at selling products; encourages presenters to continue to develop new products; and, attracts new faces to ABS's stable of presenters. Specifically, presenters receive 20 percent of the revenues from products they sell, then up to 60 percent of revenues from products they both develop and sell.

Entrepreneurial gains are never just given away. They are contingent upon reaching a required level of performance. But for entrepreneurial gains to be motivating, individuals must believe that the required level of performance is attainable. This is why it is dangerous for Opportunists to spread themselves too thin or expose themselves to too much risk. Individuals working for Opportunists accomplish nothing if they give up because they feel overwhelmed by seemingly impossible challenges.

Individuals are equally unlikely to be motivated when they are underchallenged. They lose interest in their work if all they have to look forward to are the same old mundane assignments. Accordingly, Opportunists more commonly fail because they do not challenge their people enough than because they challenge them too much. Failure more often coincides with decisions to pull on the reins too tightly and pursue more risk-averse strategies. This is why Kuniyasu Sakai has been so successful performing the role of arsonist. Of course, Sakai's people would burn out if he started too many uncontrollable fires, but the more common management mistake is never lighting any fires at all under people.

Although Opportunists do not go out of their way to expose themselves to greater risk, they are willing to take risks for opportunities they believe they are uniquely qualified to pursue. This corporate attitude is the key to creating and maintaining an opportunistic offensive strategy. Individuals are highly motivated because they know that their companies will give serious consideration to the opportunities they find, and more often than not they will receive the green light to pursue them. Individuals take greater initiative because they believe that most of the time it will lead to positive results, and their combined initiative becomes an irresistible force for Opportunists intent on maintaining their competitive leadership.

Business Practices

Individual motivation depends on another factor. While entrepreneurial gains contingent upon challenging but attainable performance expectations will motivate individuals, they will not motivate them for very long if individuals conclude that their companies are not being fair with them. More than employment relationships are at stake. The nature of Opportunists' offensive strategies requires them to be continually building new relationships with suppliers and customers. An Opportunist's reputation can either hasten or impede the building of these relationships, and because speed is always critical to the successful execution of the strategies of Opportunists, they can only perform as well as their reputations are good. Trust greases the skids when building relationships both inside and outside organizations. Accordingly, the business practices of Opportunists must be above reproach if they are to maintain competitive leadership.

The contrasting cases of A. L. Williams & Associates and Trammel Crow Company illustrate why fair and equitable business practices are essential to Opportunists' offensive strategies. Although much of the recent criticism aimed at ALW comes because the company rocked the insurance industry's boat, the company brought some of the controversy on itself through its questionable business practices. For example, ALW promises its new recruits something that is too good to be true and in the process creates what one critic has called a "greed-based pyramid." Where there is greed there is often deception. For example, the easiest and quickest way for agents to build their organizations is to tell potential customers and new recruits half-truths. ALW agents emphasize to customers the low cost of term life insurance compared to cash-value policies, while they attract new recruits by promising commissions that are more than double the industry standard. But according to Jane Bryant Quinn, the *Newsweek* columnist, "A. L. Williams agents don't distinguish between the good and the bad. They can make all cash-value policies look bad by illustrating them without the dividends they pay."[30] Moreover, ALW claims to sell the "cheapest insurance in America," but the reality is that the term insurance its agents sell is expensive. After all, the money to pay agents such large commissions must come from somewhere. Even though ALW's commissions are high, its contracts with agents are among the industry's most restrictive, allowing the company to terminate agents at will and often to keep their renewal commissions. Agents are also required to pay back some of their commissions if the policies they sell lapse within two years.[31]

At Trammel Crow Company, however, new leasing agents and partners know that if they work hard and smart they will become wealthy. They do not question whether they will be treated fairly and equitably because they trust Trammel Crow and the organization he fathered. Between contractors and partners the same level of trust exists. Even though TCC partners are known as tough businesspeople who always negotiate hard, they are also people whose word is their bond.

Although ALW has experienced phenomenal successes, its questionable reputation means that its footings are unsecured. The company stands as a house of cards ready to fall. Conversely, TCC stands on a reputation that makes its foundation firm. As we will soon discover, such a reputation does not ensure continued success, but it does cut a company a lot of slack.

Corporate Structures

Because Opportunists are guided by opportunities, separate business units commonly go in totally different directions. Accordingly, Opportunists can appear out of control as opportunistic growth creates inefficiency and disorder in organizational structures. An obvious response is to impose new structures and controls. But these are like tourniquets to Opportunists. Although they may be necessary in a few cases of excessive bleeding, they create a needless blockage and shut off the lifeblood of individual motivation when they are used prematurely and applied too tightly.

After the 1975–1978 real estate depression, Trammel Crow turned to Don Williams to bring some order and rationality to TCC's bewildering network of partnerships. With Crow's blessing, Williams imposed more stringent financial controls and reporting requirements. The standard partnership agreement evolved into a 25-page document of stipulations, contingencies, guarantees, and escape clauses, and partnerships were radically redesigned to resemble more closely a corporate hierarchy. The hierarchy determined both a partner's status and his or her take from any given project. Incentives increased for national partners at the top of the hierarchy but decreased for project partners at the bottom of the hierarchy.[32]

Don Williams remarked that "the day of the Lone Ranger—Trammel Crow—riding into town and making deals, that's gone! The day calls for teams of highly professional people, *disciplined* entrepreneurs." So TCC has become a chic place to work, especially among MBAs trained at Harvard, Stanford, and Wharton. However, MBAs from elite schools are less committed to TCC. They think of themselves as professionals before going to work for TCC and so generally do not feel as indebted to the company because their education has taught them to believe they deserve the opportunities they get.

The changes at TCC have also led to the defections of several senior partners. As one of these senior partners said, "The kind of people who are good at real estate do not respond well to structure. . . . They thought they had to reshuffle the deck, and in the process they broke the traditional relationships that had grown up among the subordinate partnerships."[33]

TCC does not show the signs of imminent decline. It remains a key player in commercial and residential real estate development. But now TCC is driven more by its reputation and size than aggressive opportunity finding. For example, the recent reorganization of TCC into four separate divisions—Trammel Crow Commercial, Trammel Crow Residential, Trammel Crow Interests, and Trammel Crow Ventures—further rationalizes the organizational structure; but it also restricts the freewheeling style of the past.

TCC's new management is more cautious than daring. It carefully hedges against future downturns in the real estate market and is more concerned about controlled growth and defending the company's established positions than pursuing new concepts and markets. Trammel Crow gives credit to Don Williams for making TCC great. But by turning TCC away from competition, Williams has also tampered with the individual motivation that the company needs to maintain its greatness.

How do Opportunists maintain the kinds of loose structures that motivate opportunity finders? Perhaps Opportunists need to adopt the perspective of venture capitalists, who do not expect every venture they invest in to be successful. Rather, they figure that one-third of their ventures will fail, one-third will do little more than break even, but that the final third will enjoy significant enough returns to make them a lot of money. Because Opportunists go in so many directions to pursue so many kinds of opportunities, failures are an inevitable part of doing business. Attempts at corporate restructuring to limit failures are misguided because failures are as much a sign of health in an Opportunist as are successes. Only when success and failure are mixed do Opportunists find the individual motivation that they need to drive their offensive strategies.

6 Visionaries: A Vision-Guided Offensive Strategy

If venture capitalists were deciding whether to invest in a Visionary, what would they consider first? Visionaries have long-term visions, and it often takes them many years to become profitable. Accordingly, venture capitalists will not invest in Visionaries unless they are completely sold on their founding ideas. Venture capitalists must love a founding idea enough to dig deeply into their pockets to fund something that shows no immediate sign of turning a profit. Venture capitalists that invest in Visionaries must literally share the vision.

The founders of Visionaries view their businesses in strictly instrumental terms. Their companies are a means of realizing their visions. Visions guide Visionaries, and their primary concern when dealing with venture capitalists is keeping their visions alive. Therefore, the founders of Visionaries want to find venture capitalists that appreciate their ideas and are more concerned about long-term development than short-term financial returns.

Visionaries are highly focused companies, driven by radically innovative ideas that will either create or redefine entire industries. Even though Visionaries may initially support exploratory work, they will likely withdraw funding if projects drift away from guiding visions.

Star Electronics[1] is a Visionary, producing advanced work stations for design engineers. The company's founder had a vision of an ultimate technology that was not even remotely possible at the time he founded Star. He believed that supporting technologies would be developed over the years—through technical breakthroughs at both

Star and competing companies—making the realization of his vision possible.

The vision guiding Star Electronics continually expanded the company's horizon of creative endeavor. Engineers were sent back to the drawing board and encouraged to reach for new and higher levels of creativity when their designs did not measure up to the standard set by the founder's vision. Star's engineers concentrated on developing radically new technologies. The prevailing philosophy at Star was, if you can design a better product you ought to, and creating market demand is better than following it. Technical leadership was expected at Star. The company wanted its engineers to be so far ahead of everyone else technically that they would never have to look over their shoulders to see what the competition was doing.

The founder of Star Electronics did not conduct a systematic search for venture capital. Through a network of relationships he was introduced to people from VenFund,[2] an established venture capital firm founded by a member of one of America's wealthiest families. VenFund's founder had decided that because the United States had been good to his family, he should do something to strengthen the nation's business structure. He created VenFund to support technical people in the long-term development of important ideas.

The people at VenFund believed they were funding Star's founding idea and that the idea, more than anything else, needed to be preserved. Because Star's founder was the originator of the idea, it was also important to invest in him.

VenFund's people, however, were as tough-minded in their business decisions as they were committed to ideas. When Star's founder presented his business plan to a small staff group at VenFund, they badgered him with their criticisms. When the founder could not tolerate any more of their criticism they sent him home to rework the plan. When he returned a few days later, the grueling process started anew. In this manner, the people at VenFund invested an enormous amount of effort in teaching Star's founder what a business is.

Given the intensity of the learning process, at times Star's founder thought the people at VenFund were his worst enemies. Throughout the process, he wondered why they kept trying when he obviously knew so little about business. Still, he never felt any threat of being removed.

Five years after he started Star, the founder was approached by a Fortune 500 company interested in an acquisition. Negotiations progressed quickly. VenFund remained neutral throughout the negotiations, leaving Star's founder to make up his mind. The founder did discover that VenFund's people had some reservations about the acquisition, but they never forced their opinions on him. Because of favorable terms and the fact that Star still showed no sign of turning a profit, the founder accepted the company's acquisition offer in principle.

As final arrangements were being made prior to the public announcement, Star's founder asked the acquiring firm for a $150,000 loan. The acquirer was happy to advance him the money and reassured him by saying, "Now look, on the outside chance of the deal falling through, don't worry. We'll give you plenty of time to work things out before we call the note."

The acquirer wanted to treat the purchase of Star as a nonmaterial event and did not want to submit a prospectus. The New York Stock Exchange, however, insisted that a prospectus be filed. The acquirer, for reasons known only to it, refused to file one and promptly backed out of the deal. A few days later Star's founder received a letter in the mail calling the $150,000 note.

Star's founder called VenFund and explained the situation to his main contact there. The contact said, "Forget about it. I'll take care of it." Star's founder did not hear any more about the note until several months later when he was told that the founder of VenFund, who happened to sit on the board of the company that held the note, had gone to its president, bought the note, and then resigned from the board saying, "Don't ever call me again if you can't keep your word."

Several years later, after Star began to turn a profit, one of VenFund's people reminded the founder that they still held the note and told him that when it fit into his plans he might want to repay it. VenFund never charged interest on the note.

Star's founder said later, "We had a number of very good experiences with [VenFund]. We really had a friendship." The relationship between people at VenFund and Star Electronics was built on mutual trust and respect. But VenFund was willing to come to Star's rescue only because it was deeply committed to helping the company realize its vision of a radically new technology. Because VenFund adopted a long-term view and could help handle many of the short-term disturbances, the people at Star Electronics were able to keep their energy focused on realizing the company's vision.

What lessons do we learn about Visionaries from the relationship that developed between Star Electronics and VenFund? First, Visionaries require more from venture capitalists than just money.

The people at VenFund taught Star's founder how to be a chief executive. On many occasions they ran interference for Star, allowing it to keep its attention on its vision. The service VenFund provided was essential because distractions at Star threatened to dissolve the delicate bonds of will and organizational energy necessary to make the vision a reality.

Second, the long-term vision of a Visionary is a two-edged sword. The fact that Visionaries require a long time to realize their visions means that they are highly vulnerable. Without the protection of the "patient" money that VenFund provided Star Electronics, it would never have survived. Although Star has become a viable company, it remains only marginally profitable because of the immense resources that continue to be pumped into research and development. Star is still several years away from realizing its founder's original vision. At the same time, the vision is what holds Star together. As a 20-year-old company that remains radically innovative, it continues to strive because the founder's original vision has not yet been fulfilled. It is unlikely that Star would still be stretching its innovative capacity if the vision had been less ambitious and shorter term. Moreover, the severest challenge to Visionaries is not necessarily realizing their visions but knowing what to do once their visions are realized.

Finally, we learn that business is not necessarily the business of Visionaries. Visionaries contribute to the economy by generating, then developing new ideas. While Opportunists find opportunities, Visionaries create them in the images of their visions. Visionaries become competitive leaders by operating on the cutting edge in developing new ideas.

IMPROVISING OFFENSIVE STRATEGIES FROM VISIONS

How do Visionaries improvise offensive strategies, and what are the ingredients that turn Visionaries into competitive leaders? First, Visionaries play off a core vision. They create short-term opportunities from long-term visions. Second, the visions of Visionaries must have nobility and purpose. Company visions inspire people and create deeper loyalties when they are noble enough to overpower bottom-line considerations. Finally, leaders leverage their visions. Leveraged visions enlist more people in the work of making visions into realities and magnify the influence of visions.

Creating Short-Term Opportunities from Long-Term Visions

If Opportunists are gadflies stirring up the economic pot, Visionaries are revolutionaries promoting fundamental change. While Opportunists try to make the most of what is, Visionaries try to remake the world by focusing on visions of what should be. Radical visions are at the center of everything that Visionaries do. Visions guide Visionaries by providing the basic harmonic sequence for improvising offensive strategies.

Even though long-term visions are central to everything that Visionaries do, they are not the whole story. The many short-term opportunities created by a long-term vision are what make it a reality. Visionaries become competitive leaders because they hold tightly to their visions while creating the opportunities needed to fulfill them. Persistence, not imagination, is the fountainhead of their genius.

The story of Wacoal Corporation, a Japanese company, has something to teach all U.S. companies, large and small, about how to create short-term opportunities from a long-term vision. Wacoal Corporation is a maker of fine women's intimate apparel. The founder, Koichi Tsukamoto, started the company in 1950 when he was 30 years old. The first thing he did was write down the vision of what he wanted to accomplish over the next 50 years. By the turn of the century, Tsukamoto wanted worldwide brand recognition for Wacoal's products, with 25 percent of the company's sales coming from overseas. This was a radical vision in postwar Japan for at least two reasons. First, because Western apparel was not yet popular among Japanese women, there was no domestic market for such undergarments. Second, given the state of Japan's economy in 1950, it was crazy and pretentious to think of a Japanese company selling Western undergarments to the West.

Tsukamoto created opportunities by educating Japanese women in Western ways to create a domestic market for his undergarments. This was no easy task; new obstacles appeared around every turn. At Wacoal's first fashion show in 1952, the company had to hire strippers, because professional models would not appear in its skimpy garments; all men were banned from the show, including Tsukamoto. Moreover, Wacoal's sales dropped every winter, when Japanese women reverted to the traditional kimono with its warm layers of shapeless undergarments.

Wacoal struggled along for several years without any significant growth. But guided by Tsukamoto's vision, the company continued to create new opportunities for itself. Finally, in the late 1950s, the demand for Wacoal's undergarments began to pick up. Tsukamoto's efforts to create a market for Wacoal's intimate apparel were finally supported by major shifts in Japanese society toward Western values and apparel. Because of Wacoal's early efforts at creating new buyer tastes, the company found itself uniquely positioned to assume competitive leadership in Japan.

Tsukamoto used the decades of the 1960s and 1970s to strengthen Wacoal's lead over domestic competitors. As the Japanese market grew for women's intimate apparel, Tsukamoto's offensive strategy focused on retaining his company's enviable market share. He concentrated his efforts on department store sales, creating opportunities for Wacoal by pioneering, then refining, the idea of department store boutiques. Today, Wacoal's boutiques still account for 60 percent of Japan's department store lingerie sales.

In Tsukamoto's original 50-year vision, he saw the 1980s as the decade to establish U.S. markets. Tsukamoto began preparing to compete in the United States in 1977 when he had Wacoal listed on the New York Stock Exchange. Tsukamoto bought and sold a 30 percent stake in Olga Company, a U.S. lingerie producer, and later acquired the leading U.S. maker of underwear for teenagers. Tsukamoto also borrowed a costume show from the Metropolitan Museum of Art in New York to display in his hometown of Kyoto. Then, he helped mount an exhibit of historic intimate apparel in a New York gallery.

Tsukamoto used these cultural and financial activities to develop deeper recognition for Wacoal among heads of U.S. department stores. He set the stage for November 1984, when his company began to ask for prime space for its boutiques in many major U.S. department stores. Wacoal's U.S. sales have been impressive ever since, and to complete his 50-year plan, Tsukamoto is already preparing to establish markets in Europe in the 1990s.

Visions with Nobility and Purpose

Peter Vaill proposes that one of the keys to identifying "high-performing systems" is that such systems "are perceived to fulfill at a high level the ideals for the culture within which they exist—that is, they have 'nobility.' "[3] Noble organizations perform essential services or produce products that benefit mankind. Centrifugal, not centripetal, thinking is dominant in organizations with nobility. They consistently look outward and try to make the world a better place.

So while Opportunists should never fall in love with a deal, the prescription for Visionaries is the opposite. Visionaries need to fall in love with visions that have both nobility and purpose. They become competitive leaders when their people want to identify with and internalize the high ideals and sense of mission embodied in their visions.

William Murphy, the founder and former chairman of Cordis Corporation, created a company around a vision with nobility and purpose. Accordingly, his feelings for his company and the purposes it fulfilled ran deep. Many people told Murphy that he should not love his company because it was an economic entity. But when he made decisions he refused to exclude his emotional attachment to the company.[4]

Cordis is a medical technology company that focuses on developing and manufacturing things "of the heart." How did the nobility and purpose of Murphy's founding vision affect the way Cordis was run? Cordis was guided by what Murphy called "medical wisdom," meaning its products and strategies needed to benefit the patients they were intended to serve.

At Cordis stories were often told about how medical wisdom overrode profit-and-loss considerations. One of the more powerful of these stories dated back to 1979 and involved pacemakers. Cordis engineers developed a hermetic, leak-proof, lithium battery that they believed would reduce the size and improve the efficiency of their pacemakers. Shortly after introducing the new batteries, however, Cordis became aware of a potential complication when one of its engineers attended a seminar on lithium batteries. The engineer learned that the new construction Cordis was using might eventually cause the batteries to corrode. Although no problems had yet surfaced, Cordis immediately changed the battery's specifications and began to monitor and test the 8,500 sealed-battery pacemakers that were already in use.[5]

As Cordis monitored and tested these pacemakers, engineers discovered another potential problem—a bizarre chemical reaction that caused a gradual depletion of battery power. The company responded immediately, sending an advisory to all physicians who had installed the devices. Although the pacemaker warranty did not apply in such circumstances, Cordis offered to reimburse all third-party costs resulting from the battery problem and to pay for replacement when necessary. The company also notified the U.S. Food and Drug Administration (FDA).[6]

Medical wisdom prompted Cordis to halt production of the sealed batteries at the first hint of trouble; medical wisdom also encouraged the company to monitor the suspect pacemakers for two years and respond quickly and effectively when further trouble was detected. But, most importantly, Cordis's education program, designed to keep engineers informed about the latest developments in science and medicine, was based on medical wisdom. The problem was discovered at an early stage because of the education program.[7]

Cordis's pacemaker business peaked in 1984 with sales of $132 million. Then, due to tightened federal controls limiting pacemaker implants, Cordis's sales of the devices dropped to $94.7 million in 1986, when the company's pacemaker division lost $9.5 million. The problems at Cordis, however, ran deeper than slumping industry sales. In 1984 the FDA again questioned the reliability of Cordis pacemakers and ordered two major recalls. Moreover, the FDA also discovered that four Cordis officials had doctored memos about possible technical problems with the company's pacemakers. Even though those Cordis officials were fired immediately, the company lost its technological momentum because the FDA refused to let it test or market new pacemakers for 18 months. Also, numerous product-liability suits were launched against Cordis.[8]

Cordis temporarily got off track because, after William Murphy retired in March 1985, some employees lost sight of his founding vision, and the company was no longer guided by medical wisdom. Accordingly, an obvious way for the company to get back on track would be to create a new vision with nobility and purpose. Cordis sold its pacemaker division to Australia-based Telectronics Holdings Ltd. in 1987, and later agreed to plead guilty to felony and misdemeanor charges related to its pacemakers and pay the government about $5.7 million in fines and other costs. These two actions gave the company the chance to make a new start. Cordis's new vision continues to deal with things "of the heart": The company has become a leader in the development of diagnostic catheters, which are threaded through arteries to produce images of the heart, and balloon catheters, which are used to unblock clogged arteries around the heart. Analysts predict that the revitalized Cordis will return to profitability under the leadership of its new chairman, Dr. Robert Q. Marston, a longtime member of Cordis's board of directors and president emeritus of the University of Florida.

Visions with dignity and purpose strengthen organizations by inducing clarity, consensus, and commitment around their basic purposes. They raise both individual and organizational aspirations. Visions with dignity and purpose also become focal points for the concerted efforts of individuals and groups because they define work that is significant and goals that are compelling to everyone. They promote strong feelings about what organizations do and inspire people to devote extraordinary amounts of time and energy to ensure that their organizations are leaders in their noble and purposeful endeavors.

Leveraging Visions

Jan Carlzon, the president and CEO of Scandinavian Airlines Systems (SAS), tells a story of Ingmar Bergman, the gifted Swedish movie and play director. Carlzon invited Bergman to dinner one week before the premier of a play he was directing. Bergman replied:

> You are crazy. It would be an insult to all your other guests. It would be like inviting me to dinner one week before my divorce. Do you know why? Because I start to build this play eight or nine months ago. First, I write the synopsis; then I select the artists. I involve them in my play, tell them what I expect from them, help them get the idea. We all work for the same objective: to make this play a fantastic play. But it is my play, my works, my scenery, my thoughts, my everything. So they rehearse, and I help them. I form them. And now—one week before the premier—do you know what is happening? They've taken it over. They don't need me any more. I'm a spillover. Can you understand that? So don't invite me for dinner.[9]

Bergman's description of his experience with the play suggests how visions are leveraged. Visions begin as something personal—pictures in the minds of creative visionaries. Then, they unfold as they are shared and more and more people become committed to them. Finally, visions become fully leveraged when people take them over from the visionary and function independently.

The founders of companies that are Visionaries follow the same pattern when leveraging their visions. Originally conceived in the minds of founders, visions are personal constructions of a company or product's future. Leveraging them requires that they be shared, that people identify with them, and that they guide more and more people's actions. They also require the founder to let go. Leveraged visions are navigation instruments in the hands of many people who multiply the number of opportunities created to fulfill them.

Steven Jobs, Steve Wozniak, and their friends in the Homebrew Computer Club formed a vision in the early 1970s. It was based on a simple but powerful premise: They thought of humans as tool builders and the computer as the most remarkable tool ever built. Their vision focused on putting that remarkable tool in the hands of as many individuals as possible. Because people are inherently creative, they reasoned, 1,000 computers with one-thousandth the power of the most powerful computer in the world in the hands of 1,000 people would have a far greater impact than one person using the world's most powerful computer.[10]

The creation of the Apple I was an important event, in that it solidified Jobs' original vision. The Apple I was designed for hobbyists who wanted to play with software but could not build their own hardware. It came with a digital circuit board but without a keyboard, power supply, or monitor.

From his experience with the Apple I, Jobs realized the need for a computer that could be taken out of a box, plugged in, and used. That computer was the Apple II, a machine that software hobbyists, who were not also hardware hobbyists, could use. With the Apple II, Jobs created a new industry because he made computers accessible to everyone who could not build his or her own. He peeled away the hardware barriers to computer usage.[11]

How did Jobs and Wozniak turn their vision into a computer company? First, they recruited people with compatible values. In its early days, Apple Computer was a band of brash, young mavericks, who were so convinced that they knew where the future of computers was going that they didn't bother to ask anyone else. With a rapidly expanding inner circle, Jobs and Wozniak shared the details of their vision by focusing on the details of the product. Jobs was finicky about the Apple II. He wanted every line of solder on the circuit board to be perfectly straight. He cared that both the inside and outside of the machine looked neat and attractive because in his mind all that counted was the product. All the little, minor details that went into making each and every Apple II communicated the company's big attitude. The Apple II was the embodiment of Jobs' original vision of what computers should be, which he shared with the people at Apple by showing them how every computer should be made.[12]

Jobs also became a highly visible spokesperson for the personal computer industry. He shared his vision with external constituencies for several purposes. First, he wanted to attract more customers for the Apple II. He viewed what he was doing as creating a movement, and part of his role was to convert new members. Second, he wanted to put Apple on the map as a company where the best and the brightest would want to work. His vision was a clarion call to like-minded, innovative computer hobbyists. And, finally, Jobs believed in his vision and wanted it to play a significant part in shaping the future of the computer industry. He wanted to change a mainframe computer culture into a personal computer culture.

Jobs further leveraged the vision embodied in the Apple II by leaving to build the MacIntosh in 1980. He left behind, in what later became the Apple II Division, an army of disciples who were forced to carry forward the vision on their own. This, of course, magnified the vision's influence by giving it a life of its own separate from Jobs. In fact, many of the tensions that eventually led to Jobs' dismissal from Apple resulted from people in the Apple II Division reacting to the obvious favoritism he showed for the MacIntosh Division. They remained committed to the original vision, but not to Steve Jobs.

In building the MacIntosh, Jobs repeated the same process. In 1979, after seeing an Alto computer that had been developed at Xerox's Palo Alto Research Center, Jobs created a new vision, grander than anything he previously imagined with the Apple II. The Alto had a mouse and multiple-font text on the screen, and was a computer that anyone could use. Jobs wanted to build a computer that people didn't need to *learn* how to use.

Using Apple as a financial mechanism, Jobs went off and started the MacIntosh project from scratch. He personally led the MacIntosh team, describing his leadership as "having a vision and being able to articulate it so people around you can understand and getting consensus on a common vision." He was there every day challenging assumptions, ideas, and processes; in doing so he shared his vision in hundreds of different ways. One MacIntosh team member described Jobs as "a muckraker, in the classic sense," to explain his penchant for exposing ideas and work that were somehow deficient.

Jobs and the MacIntosh team spent a lot of time selecting new members based on common interests. A key moment in daylong recruiting sessions came when the team liked somebody enough to show him or her the MacIntosh prototype. If a recruit's eyes lit up they knew he or she was one of them.

As MacIntosh team members internalized Jobs' vision, they became increasingly independent of him. The team became mostly self-managing because members saw the higher purpose they were working for. As one MacIntosh team member remarked, "I'm certainly not doing it for Steve Jobs. I'm doing it for something I think is a much greater good than that. And that's to change something really positively for the better."

Jobs' experiences with Debbie Coleman, the woman he hired to run the MacIntosh factory, reveal the process he used to encourage MacIntosh team members to be self-managing. In an interview with *Inc.* magazine, Jobs said:

> When we started the MacIntosh factory, I made a few mistakes before I finally put Debbie Coleman in to run it, and she turned out to be a good choice. I remember that I'd go out to the factory, and I'd put on a white glove to check for dust. I'd find it everywhere—on machines, on the tops of the racks, on the floor. And I'd ask Debbie to get it cleaned. I told her I thought we should be able to eat off the floor of the factory. Well, this drove Debbie up the wall. She didn't understand why you should be able to eat off the floor of the factory. And I couldn't articulate it back then. . . .
>
> We went along for a while, and the factory became clean, but Debbie and I continued to have conflicts over various things. Then one day I came into the factory, and I saw that she had rearranged some of the machines. Before, they had been randomly placed around the floor. Debbie had moved them for some functional reasons and also some nonfunctional reasons. She'd put them in a straight line and cleaned the place up visually. And I hadn't mentioned anything to her. Well, that told me a light bulb had come on for her, and I didn't need to say a thing about it ever again—and I never did. From then on, she just took off like a rocket, because she understood the underlying principle. And the factory worked great.[13]

Strangely, Jobs further leveraged his vision of the MacIntosh when he was fired from Apple. By the time he left Apple, a large contingent of followers had already shared, depersonalized, and internalized his vision. Although Jobs was no longer their leader, the vision he created continued to lead Apple. Guided by that vision, new people stepped forward and assumed the responsibility for creating new opportunities for Apple.

After leaving Apple, Jobs began to look for something else to do. While visiting a Stanford, Nobel Prize–winning molecular biologist, the vision of a new computer and a new computer company came to him. The professor showed Jobs what some of his students were doing to understand how proteins fold. He wondered out loud if their work could be modeled on a computer more powerful than a PC. Jobs thought, "What if you came up with something that was as easy to use as a MacIntosh and had the power of a work station? What if you unleashed that machine in higher education?" The more Jobs thought about the idea, the more excited he became.[14]

Jobs formed NeXT Incorporated to build the computer he envisioned. At NeXT, Jobs rolls up his sleeves and works with different groups, all the time sharing his vision. He argues with people and they argue back, but their goal is always the same—to build only the best. Jobs sees his job as helping individuals and groups set targets and then getting out of their way. Once a group appears to be on track, Jobs moves on to help another group.

A final lesson can be learned from Steve Jobs that invites us to consider another key ingredient in Visionaries' offensive strategies. Jobs allowed his visions to grow. He began with a broad vision about getting computers and people together, then his vision of the Apple II grew into his vision of the MacIntosh, and the MacIntosh vision grew into his vision of the NeXT computer. Within each vision there was also room to grow. For example, Jobs described his original vision of the NeXT computer as being about a third as good as the computer that was developed. Dynamic and expanding visions create competitive leaders because they promote an internal competition. Visionaries can look back and be satisfied with what they have accomplished, but to remain competitive leaders they must always want to accomplish more.

A LIBERATING FORM FOR RADICAL PRODUCT INNOVATION

The two companies Steve Jobs founded—Apple and NeXT—have a liberating organizational form established around a frequently and consistently articulated vision that is self-managing and reinforced by the careful selection of new recruits. At Star Electronics, however, I observed an interesting variation of the liberating form found at Apple and NeXT. Star had a system of selecting personnel based on mundane first assignments; the company's vision was rarely and only partially articulated; and a laissez-faire system of management prevailed. Why did these differences exist? Perhaps there is no definitive answer, but because Star fostered more radical product innovation— it was trying to do something that had never been done before, while Apple and NeXT focused on putting together technologies that had already been developed and bringing them to the masses—this different organizational form appeared to be justified.

Fundamental to the liberating organizational form found at Star

Electronics are academic values, conventions, and even life-styles. Academic values and conventions spawn unique organizational characteristics. Clearly, definitions of technical innovation are quite demanding at Star. Enhancements around existing technologies are not recognized as genuine innovations. To be truly innovative, a product requires a design that is radically different from its predecessors and offers vastly improved performance capability.

Market success is often downplayed as a criterion for success at Star Electronics. Star's engineers believe that there are no unsuccessful products or projects. This is because even market failures lay a foundation of knowledge and skill that contribute to subsequent technical development. Experimentation with radical alternative designs, then, is a valued activity at Star regardless of where it leads.

Initially, I was confused by Star Electronics' organizational form, which appeared to violate numerous traditional management principles. Chaos seemed rampant, Star's founder's management philosophy and style were especially baffling. Then I came to realize that the organizational form he created and nurtured reflected the academic values of the university electrical engineering department he left soon after he launched Star.

Mundane First Assignments

Like many directors of research organizations, Star's founder believes in recruiting the best and the brightest—in Star's case, the top 5 percent of graduates from the nation's premier electrical engineering schools. But unlike other research directors, he often gives these high-powered new hires job assignments that border on the banal. Why? Often, he claims, because he doesn't know where they will best fit in. Rather than define an area of contribution for an employee, he assigns a mundane task, then waits for the engineer to weary of it.

If engineers are any good, the founder maintains, they will soon return with their own proposals for more challenging assignments. If proposals make sense and relate—however tangentially—to Star's overall mission, engineers are allowed to pursue them. If, on the other hand, engineers continue to perform the mundane work, waiting for someone else to give them another assignment, they are considered the wrong type for Star. They will not be terminated; instead, they will continue to receive low-level assignments until, frustrated, they leave the company.

Although it may appear somewhat callous, the founder's job assignment strategy is anything but a careless default of the law of the jungle. The process is a deliberate selection system, designed to ensure that only those engineers with the desired qualities of academic professionalism, initiative, and autonomy are retained. The following anecdote, related by a respected senior engineer, illustrates one instance of the strategy in action:

> A few years ago, [Star's founder] came to me and asked if I needed a new recruit on any of my projects. I told him that we could maybe use someone to sweep the floors, but other than that, we had things covered. He said, "I've got a new engineer I want you to take on anyway. Find something for him to do." So I did. I put the kid to work testing circuit boards. Within a few weeks, he was coming to me with suggestions for redesigning the boards. That kid turned out to be one of the brightest, most creative engineers I've ever known. From then on, whenever [Star's founder] brought me someone new, I didn't ask questions.

The same philosophy is found in the founder's dealings with upper managers. The vice president of one of Star's two main divisions told us that Star's CEO "will never tell a manager what to do. He figures that if he has to tell you what to do, you're not the right person for the job—and that if you are the right person for the job, you wouldn't do what he told you to do anyway."

In many ways, this approach to management reminds me of Louis Armstrong's often quoted response to the question, "What is jazz?" Implying the futility of abstract definition, Armstrong's reply was simply, "If you have to ask, you'll never know." At Star, deliberately ambiguous job assignments have naturally generated increased stress, particularly for professional managers brought in from other companies. For others, however, the system has provided an opportunity to channel their energy in directions they deem most exciting, challenging, and promising.

Unarticulated Organizational Goals

While Star's founder intuitively knows where he wants the company to go in developing new technologies, he does not clearly communicate it. This results partly from the limitations of his intuitive vision—he only knows what he wants when he sees it—but more importantly because he considers any sort of imposed vision inappropriate for his organization.

A prime example of this reluctance occurred at a recent management retreat. The overriding purpose of the three-day conclave was to identify a strategic direction for the company. A middle manager described what happened:

> The main outcomes [of the retreat] were a feeling that top management was listening, and a set of nominal deadlines to produce a strategic plan addressing the question of where we'll be in five years. . . . As I understood it, the deadline for publication of this strategic plan was October. I understood it was supposed to be something that would be distributed to everyone in the company. [Star's founder] was the one who was going to pull the thing together. . . . I know he showed something to the board of directors, but there was no downloading to the rest of the company. It was never published and distributed to employees, not even to middle managers. Any hope of instilling up and down commitment went right out the window. It didn't give everyone a view of "this is where I am, this is how I fit in, etc." . . . Lower-level people need to know what's OK to do in the long run. That's never identified.

This manager was frustrated by a perceived lack of direction at Star. He assumed that the founder did not have a clear vision of where the company should go, that he was simply muddling through. The founder's second-in-command explains that the founder "is a brilliant strategic thinker, but he never puts it down on paper. It's all in his head."

Fragments of Star's strategic focus are articulated to keep the company from veering too far off course. Often this occurs when the founder suddenly rejects a promising project that a group of engineers has nurtured because it does not conform to his vision. On these occasions the founder obviously has a clear idea of the markets he is interested in competing in and the kinds of technologies he wants to develop. Unlike many CEOs, however, he refuses to articulate his vision unless he has to. Even when he does, it is always in small pieces and to select groups.

Laissez-faire Management

The previous two characteristics of the founder's style imply an extremely loose approach to management. Under this academic management pattern, Star's engineers tend to band together in small, highly autonomous work groups. Beyond granting or withholding resources and sponsoring stringent technical design reviews, upper management makes few attempts to control the groups. The reigning assumption is that the engineers should design and run their own projects. As a result, subcultures develop around these work groups, which become the primary socializing units, facilitating learning by apprenticeship. Group members put in long hours and harbor deep feelings about the importance of their work. The environment within these work groups has thus proved an ideal seedbed for the development of new technology.

At the same time, Star's laissez-faire policy is not without severe dysfunctions. In the words of a middle-manager, "The management problems at Star are horrendous: engineers shooting off in wild directions, program managers trying to decide what to pursue and what not to pursue. It's a wild melee." The consequences of this organizational melee include intense competition between groups for resources; wariness surrounding collaboration and the sharing of ideas (one engineer remarked that "ideas usually get kicked around in close proximity to the people that have them—it's not common for an idea to travel rapidly and uniformly through the company"); vicious political infighting (in some cases, sabotage); and the routine loss of innovative people whose pet ideas are not supported. Intergroup tensions damage relationships between research and marketing, research and manufacturing, even manufacturing and marketing. One manager depicted for us the bad blood generated by an interdepartmental development effort:

> It was a terrible mess—an absolute morass—between program management and internal product development. People were not respecting each other's backgrounds and time frames. . . . We'd get together in meetings, sort of agree on compromises, then go back to normal procedures after we left the meeting. The manufacturing people would go back to their rules; the engineers would go back to changing their drawings every three hours; and the product management people would go back to missing design opportunities in order to keep the customer happy. It was a cesspool of noncommunication.

Allowing these conditions to persist would appear the height of management irresponsibility. Although clearly opposed to the intergroup conflict and professional pettiness cataloged above, Star's founder insists that such dysfunctions are an inevitable by-product of the academic values and conventions that ensure radically innovative work. In his view, these negative effects could perhaps be minimized, but only at the cost of disrupting or stifling what has proven to be a remarkably liberating organizational form.

MAINTAINING COMPETITIVE LEADERSHIP

How do Visionaries maintain competitive leadership? Clearly, persistence is a key. Wacoal, Star, Apple, and NeXT are all companies determined to accomplish what they initially set out to do. When Visionaries persist, their visions do not freely float with available opportunities. Visionaries strengthen themselves by actively creating new opportunities while refusing to compromise the integrity of their original visions.

How Visionaries maintain competitive leadership depends on several other factors. First, what are the different kinds of visions held by Visionaries, and how do different visions affect the offensive strategies of Visionaries? Certainly, Tsukamoto's vision for Wacoal was more concrete than the vision of Star's founder. Second, when should visionary founders share their visions? Is there a best time? Does the point at which visionary founders share their visions influence how long their companies are able to maintain competitive leadership? Third, what is the role of visionary founders in maintaining competitive leadership? Are companies stronger with them or without them? Finally, what are the effects of hiring professional managers on a Visionary's ability to maintain competitive leadership? Are there ever ways for sensitive professional managers to fit in and strengthen Visionaries, or are Visionaries always stronger without professional managers?

Different Visions
•

Visions guide Visionaries, but, depending on the vision, they guide in different ways. For example, a vision can be concrete and firm. Accordingly, it guides strategic decisions each step of the way. Companies hold on to the vision to know what they have to do to maintain competitive leadership. In the case of Wacoal Corporation, Koichi Tsukamoto began with a 50-year vision of what he wanted to accomplish. The vision was concrete, and Tsukamoto persistently played off it to improvise an offensive strategy. Even though he was extremely inventive in creating new opportunities for Wacoal, he held firmly to his original vision, which served as a constant source of strength. It took him head-to-head against competitors and consistently reminded him of his goal of gaining worldwide competitive leadership.

Visions are also intuitive. Guidance offered by intuitive visions can be equally exact, but it is delivered through feelings. Companies with more intuitive visions can never see very far ahead, but by always listening to and going with their feelings they are able to fine-tune offensive strategies. Star Electronics was guided by its founder's intuitive vision of an ultimate product capability. Although Star's founder knew what he wanted the technology to do, he was not as certain about what the technology should look like. Therefore, Star's approach was more experimental, while remaining focused on the founder's vision. Critical to Star's offensive strategy was it founder's ability to know what he wanted when he saw it.

For example, Star supported one of its engineers in the development of a radically innovative technology. But it soon became clear to Star's founder that further development of the technology would not be consistent with his vision. Therefore, he decided to discontinue internal funding of the project. After hearing the founder's decision, the engineer asked if he could leave Star and take his technology with him. Star's founder not only sent the engineer off with his blessing, but he provided the initial capital needed to fund the new venture. Thus, Star was able to support the development of an innovative technology but to avoid becoming distracted by it.

Finally, the two companies founded by Steven Jobs—Apple and NeXT—show that visions can be both concrete and intuitive. Guided by an intuitive vision around bringing together computers and people, Jobs formed successive, concrete visions of machines that removed the barriers keeping computers and people apart. After the development of each machine came the concrete vision of what the next machine should be. Thus, Jobs' offensive strategy was based on an intuitive, long-term vision guiding a series of short-term, concrete visions.

The Best Time to Share a Vision

Although some visionary founders are more productive pursuing visions on their own, they cannot leverage their visions unless they share them. Often when visions are not shared early, they become too complex to share later. Moreover, if companies continue to grow, founders eventually become overwhelmed by their direct responsibilities, but they have not found anyone they can share their work with. There is nobody to carry on the work after the founders burn out. The best time to share a vision, therefore, is early.

The experience of a fast-growing software company illustrates this point. The company was reorganized around a radically innovative product for linking and optimizing the power of microcomputers. Initially the company hired the product developers as consultants to develop the software for internal use. But when a new president was recruited to turn the company around, he immediately saw the broader possibilities of the software the consultants developed. The president's first move was to discontinue the company's current product line so it could devote all its efforts to further development of the new software product.

The president struck a unique deal with the software's developers: He offered each of them significant equity positions in the company in exchange for the software they developed; he also allowed them to remain independent. The developers were encouraged to form a separate corporate entity, contracted to develop additional software products for the company. In effect, the developers operated as the R and D arm of the company but also retained their exclusivity.

In the beginning, the structural arrangement between the company and the developers worked extremely well. Even though the developers sat on the company's executive committee, they were freed of any operating responsibilities. Product development proceeded quickly because the developers retained a singular focus. They worked together extremely well, complemented one another, and their history together enabled them to anticipate what others would do. Moreover, their successes created a wonderful esprit de corps.

More recently, however, problems have begun to surface. The company's success has encouraged other companies to develop competitive products. This new competition has had a positive impact across most of the company, but some cracks are beginning to show in the developers' will and innovative capacity. Because the developers have neither shared nor leveraged their technical vision, they continue to provide most of the company's technical support and new product development. Accordingly, the pressures placed on them have become intense—so intense, that the time for sharing the technical vision with new people has all but passed. Moreover, among the developers the desire is growing to remove what has become an albatross around their necks and move on to other things. If any one of the developers were to leave, an irreplaceable piece of the company's technical vision would leave with him or her.

Keeping Visionary Founders Around

Related to this software company's dilemma is the issue of retaining visionary founders. Clearly, the company needs its software developers to stay around. Much of the company's long-term value rests on the developers' unshared technical vision. It is difficult to imagine the company maintaining its competitive leadership without the developers.

But companies also want their visionary founders to stay around. Like William Murphy at Cordis Corporation, such founders symbolize their visions. Once they leave, important reminders of their visions leave with them, and their companies are more likely to get off track. Clearly, visionary founders must redefine their roles once their visions are shared and leveraged. It is critical for them to step back while others step forward. But they can still help guide the offensive strategies of their companies.

John Sculley's experiences with Steve Jobs, however, show that, in spite of the advantages, it sometimes isn't easy keeping visionary founders around. When Sculley came to Apple, he assumed that at some point Steve Jobs would want to run the company he cofounded. At the time, Sculley believed that he would be willing to step aside five or six years down the road when both Job's and Apple's boards believed that Jobs was ready to become CEO. So, in addition to being CEO, Sculley viewed himself as Jobs' coach: He wanted to groom him to become Apple's next CEO.[15]

Problems developed, however, as Sculley gave Jobs increasing operating responsibility. By 1984, Jobs had the title of executive vice president and a significant operating role, with more than 1,000 people reporting to him. He was no longer content to be Apple's technical visionary and public spokesman; he wanted to be a manager. At about the same time, Apple's board began to express its concerns to Sculley. Board members believed that Sculley was sharing too much power with Jobs and not running the company himself. In effect, Sculley had created an impossible situation for himself. He was sandwiched in between a visionary founder above him and an operating executive below him who was overseeing the most critical parts of the company. And they were the same person.[16]

What should Sculley have done differently? He should have

assumed from the beginning that he was Apple's CEO and that by hiring him, Jobs effectively gave up his operating responsibilities. Then he should have encouraged Jobs to continue to grow his technical vision and contribute to the development of offensive strategies. If Sculley had used Jobs in this way, Jobs would still be with Apple. Moreover, the NeXT computer might have been developed within Apple. Even though Apple remains a highly successful company without Jobs, it has lost much of its technical leadership. It needs a new vision. Its offensive strategy cannot be guided by the MacIntosh vision forever.

Professional Managers

The growth of Visionaries inevitably creates the need to hire professional managers. But professional managers can weaken more than strengthen Visionaries when they either do not understand or do not pay attention to the visions that guide them. Because the cultures of Visionaries are often derived from nonmanagerial occupational values, organizational members may view MBA-trained, professional managers as deviant, further neutralizing their effectiveness. Thus, professional managers are hired at important junctions in the history of Visionaries. Although Visionaries need them to strengthen a firm, the tensions the arrival of professional managers create are just as likely to destroy it.

How do professional managers help strengthen Visionaries without destroying their competitive leadership? At Calgene Incorporated, a biogenetics company, professional managers are expected to become totally conversant with the technology. They read technical papers and biology textbooks. When they do not understand what they read, they are expected to approach one of Calgene's scientists and ask for help. Calgene's scientists, on the other hand, are expected to attend management development seminars.

Roger Salquist, Calgene's CEO, believes that the only way to build trust in high-tech companies is for scientists to understand business and executives-managers to understand science. Both executives-managers and scientists need to participate in the formulation of the offensive strategies that guide companies like Calgene.

One of the most successful professional managers at Star Electronics developed an interesting method of compensating for his lack of technical background. Rather than trust his own judgment in technical matters, he would bring in knowledgeable technical consultants for design reviews and base his decisions on their assessment. He also established a close relationship with Star's founder. The engineers in his division began to realize that although he did not have the technical expertise they possessed, he shared their technical vision. He was at least willing to play by their rules and act as their advocate with Star's founder. Thus, he was granted influence, and his contributions help shape Star's offensive strategy.

7 Capitalists: An Opportunity-Guided and Vision-Guided Offensive Strategy

If venture capitalists were deciding whether to invest in a Capitalist, what would they first consider? Arthur Rock, principal of Arthur Rock & Company in San Francisco, tries to invest only in companies called Capitalists, and what he cares most about is their management. According to Rock, "Good ideas and good products are a dime a dozen. Good execution and good management—in a word, good *people*—are rare. . . . I will continue to look for the best people, not the largest untapped market or the highest projected returns or the cleverest business strategy."[1]

Rock describes how he evaluates the hundreds of business plans he receives in a given year:

> The first place I look [in a business plan] is the résumés, usually found at the back. To me, they are the essence of any plan. . . . I see the plan as really an opportunity to evaluate the people. If I like what I see in there, I try to find out more by sitting down and talking with the would-be entrepreneurs. . . . Some of the questions I ask have little to do directly with the particular business under discussion: Whom do they know, and whom do they admire? What's their track record? What mistakes have they made in the past, and what have they learned from them? . . . I also ask specific questions about the kind of company they want to develop. . . .[2]

Rock also wants to know about management's motivation, commitment, and energy. He wants to invest in people with strong feelings about the businesses they are building. He perceives a huge difference between people who have "fire in their stomachs" and those who see their ideas primarily as a way to get rich.[3]

Finally, Rock looks for people who are honest with themselves and tough-minded. According to Rock, founders need to be brutally honest with themselves. They cannot afford to hear only what they want to hear because they don't have the time and resources it takes to recover from mistakes. They need to make hard decisions. They have to be able to say "No, that won't work" to colleagues who come to them with ideas, or to say "That's a good idea but we can't do it because we have other priorities."[4]

Capitalists are empire builders, not speculators. They focus less on maximizing profits—especially short-term profits—and more on maximizing outputs. According to Lester Thurow, they are great institutions where the fates of the founders are inextricably tied to their creations. Because Capitalists are aggressive, risk-taking organizations, they push the United States to global leadership.[5]

Strategy is structure and structure is strategy in the case of Capitalists. They are well-organized and well-managed organizations because that is the focus of their offensive strategies. While Opportunists and Visionaries aspire to financial and technical leadership, respectively, Capitalists aspire to organizational leadership. They become competitive leaders by building the best organizations and developing the best people. Their visions are of distinctive and excellent companies run by satisfied and motivated people. Because they subscribe to a set of distinctive organizational values, their principal issue in negotiating with venture capitalists is maintaining majority ownership. Capitalists may value the advice of venture capitalists, but they want to formulate their own offensive strategies and decide the kinds of companies they build.

Capitalists both create and find business opportunities. They are likely to encourage their technical people to develop unrelated, interrelated, even competing ideas. They appreciate both incremental and radical product and process innovations. Moreover, they encourage their people to be market-oriented and to find new opportunities by interacting with customers. A concern for market acceptance is the only obvious constant in the offensive strategies of Capitalists, because they want to sponsor almost any idea that will make a positive contribution to company performance.

Gateway Technologies[6] is a Capitalist. Gateway produces custom semiconductors using state-of-the-art, gate-array design technology. The founders of Gateway started their basic research with the help of a five-year federal grant funded at $750,000 a year. With the grant in hand they attained faculty appointments at a major research university. The grant supported the work of 25 researchers.

After leaving the university, Gateway's founders were able to operate an entire year without venture capital. They attributed their ability to forego venture capital to their talent for finding creative stop-gap financing for the company.

Initially, Gateway contacted several divisions of Fortune 500 companies with interests related to their technology. They negotiated an arrangement with one company. In exchange for a $1 million loan to be paid back out of sales, Gateway gave them exclusive rights to market its products for three years.

Due to the flexibility of Gateway's technology, the company could approach opportunity finding from both directions—as solutions seeking problems and as solutions to problems. In other words, the company could offer both off-the-shelf and custom semiconductor designs to customers. One of Gateway's founders remarked, "We can do just about anything as long as the price is right."

When Gateway needed a marketing study, its founders convinced a nearby office of a major international consulting firm to conduct the study at greatly reduced rates in exchange for contacts with other local start-ups. The results of the study were so favorable that many of the consultants working on the project eventually went to work for Gateway.

Gateway also negotiated a two-year, rent-free lease on the building it occupied after convincing the owners that one high-tech occupant would attract others.

Ironically, Gateway's approach to paying its employees during its first year was almost communistic. They were paid according to their needs: Employees who had just finished school and had assumed few financial obligations were paid low salaries; employees with house and car payments, spouses and children, received salaries commensurate with their greater financial burdens.

Operating one year without venture capital was consistent with Gateway's goal of maintaining control over the kind of company it was building. By the time the company needed to raise venture capital, it was already profitable. Moreover, Gateway had an exclusive marketing agreement and sales guarantees for two more years with a division of a major corporation. This placed the company in a very strong negotiating position. It allowed Gateway's founders to retain over 50 percent ownership, even after the second round of venture capital financing, and, more importantly, it allowed them to retain control over the company's offensive strategy.

GROWTH AND DEVELOPMENT

It is natural to think of Capitalists as growing organizations. Given this, we might conclude that only the fastest growing Capitalists are competitive leaders. But this is not necessarily the case. Only those whose offensive strategies combine both growth and development become competitive leaders.

In his book *Management in Small Doses,* Russell Ackoff discusses the differences between growth and development. Growth is an increase in size or number, development is an increase in capability and competence. According to Ackoff, a lack of resources can limit growth but not development. The more developed organizations become, the less they depend on resources and the more they can do with whatever they have. Developed companies also have the ability and the desire to create or acquire the resources they need.[7]

Capitalists use growth to go head-to-head against competition, then competition strengthens and develops them. Thus, competition integrates the processes of growth and development. When companies choose to grow to avoid competition, however, growth often interferes with development. This happens because companies force growth to stay ahead of the competition, and they grow so rapidly that development cannot keep up.

Recent events at Jiffy Lube reveal how forced, rapid growth to avoid competition can interfere with development. Jim Hindman, Jiffy Lube's founder and CEO, built a 7-store operation into a 350-store franchise chain. When Jiffy Lube's success attracted attention from would-be competitors, Hindman hired consultants from Booz-Allen & Hamilton to help him assess the new competitive realities of the oil-change-and-lube business and explain his options to him. Booz-Allen spelled out three options. First, Hindman could sell out. Second, he could continue to open 30 to 50 stores a year. Or, third, he could raise as much money as possible and grow so fast that none of his competitors would be able to keep up with him.[8]

Hindman chose the third option, rapid growth to avoid competition. Following Booz-Allen's analysis, he assumed that rapid growth and competitive leadership were synonymous. But Hindman's preoccupation with rapid growth interfered with development. Looking at Jiffy Lube's balance sheet reveals that the company has grown recklessly. For example, it has provided 100 percent financing to some franchisees and guaranteed the loans and leases of others. The company has deferred $1.3 million in franchise fees and given extended credit to some franchisees on the oil and filters they buy from the company. Accounts receivable more than tripled, to $8.9 million, between 1987 and 1988, when Jiffy Lube earned $6.9 million on sales of $78.2 million.[9]

Jiffy Lube's disastrous financials, however, are only part of the story. Hindman talks about patterning his company after McDonald's as a provider of consistent, high-quality service. He argues that the message to customers should be clear: "The quality care you got in Boise will be matched in Bayonne." But with rapid growth and not enough attention to development, Jiffy Lube's service has gotten sloppy. Why? Because the company is no longer as careful about selecting, training, and offering support to franchisees. Jiffy Lube's growth has outstripped its ability to develop a franchising network that provides consistently excellent service to customers.[10]

Central Bank, headquartered in Springville, Utah, provides a useful counterpoint to Jiffy Lube because it is a company that ignored the conventional wisdom of its industry when it decided it didn't need to be the biggest to be the best. The U.S. banking industry is in the throes of dramatic change. Most bankers agree that the only way to deal with deregulation, interstate and regional banking, as well as the recent merger boom is to go with the flow. For example, I have worked with several merging banks that believe they must become large, broad-based suppliers of financial services to survive the new realities of their industry. And I tended to agree with them—that is, until I met Cal Packard, the CEO of Central Bank.

Packard saw what was happening around him, but he thought he had a better idea. While all his competitors were being swallowed up in mergers and acquisitions, Packard was adamant about remaining independent. Obviously, Central Bank could not provide all the fancy services of regional and interstate banks, but then how many people in the several Utah County communities serviced by his bank either wanted or needed those services? Packard believed that by remaining a community and service-oriented bank, Central Bank could compete effectively against larger banks. He reasoned that his customers would prefer walking into a bank and being greeted by people they knew and they had developed personal relationships with over many years. His offensive strategy was to provide customers with an alternative to large, impersonal banks in which computer printouts spoke louder than long-term relationships.

Of course, Packard's offensive strategy depended on making

the most of limited resources and doing the little things better than his competitors. He knew that if Central Bank did not provide the friendliest and most helpful service to its customers that they would go elsewhere. So what does Packard do to ensure that Central Bank's people are as committed as he is to the idea of service? First, he leads by example. Packard gets heavily involved in community affairs. He is a former mayor of Springville and has been active in the Utah Bankers' Association and in church service. He is involved because he believes in serving the community, but at the same time he provides his people with a model of the banker as community leader. Packard also spends a lot of time making personal calls to new customers to thank them for their business. He frequently visits Central Bank's seven branch offices because he believes that is where everything important happens.

Second, Packard shares the responsibility for making Central Bank friendly and helpful to customers. Although the bank has done extremely well in recent years, Packard takes little credit. He is fond of saying that his only talent is gathering good people around him, then getting out of their way. He develops people to build the bank.

Finally, Packard not only shares responsibility with Central Bank's people, he shares ownership. In recent years, representatives from larger banks have approached Packard proposing to acquire Central Bank. Even though Packard has never seriously considered their offers, some of the bank's major stockholders have felt that an acquisition would provide them with a maximum return on their investments. Since Packard's family corporation only owned 30 percent of the bank, he felt vulnerable to the demands of these major stockholders. So what happened? Packard identified large blocks of Central Bank stock that were for sale for the right price. Then, he negotiated an arrangement with Central Bank's employees where they could buy 20 percent of the total shares using money from their savings and investment plan. Now, the Packard family and Central Bank's employees jointly own a controlling interest in Central Bank. They have formed a long-term partnership based on their mutual commitment to keep Central Bank strong and independent. Packard can also tell his new partners that when they make bad loans or turn customers away, 20 cents of every dollar of lost revenue comes out of their pockets.

It is unclear how long Central Bank will remain a competitive leader in the markets it serves. Although Packard is committed to keeping the bank independent, only a few years remain before he retires and turns it over to his sons. Central Bank is already a fourth-generation, family-led bank; Packard's sons will provide the fifth generation of family leadership to the bank. Packard has both shared his vision with his sons and taught them how to be excellent bankers. There is a family tradition at Central Bank that Packard would never impose on his sons, but he hopes they will carry forward. It is a proud and conservative tradition of each generation building on the work of previous generations. It is a tradition of avoiding quick profits, quick growth, and quick fixes, and going head-to-head against competition to sustain long-term growth and development.

A TYPOLOGY OF CAPITALISTS

The character of Capitalists develops because of the balance they achieve between vision-guided and opportunity-guided offensive strategies. Clearly, however, most Capitalists are guided by one strategy more than the other. So when we distinguish between Capitalists the first question we ask is: What is the balance? Is a Capitalist more vision guided or opportunity guided?

A second question is critically important when distinguishing between Capitalists. Capitalists build both organizations and people. But do they build organizations by developing people or do they develop people to build organizations? In other words, what is the first priority of their offensive strategies—organizations or people? The strategies guiding some Capitalists, like the vision of Gene Hendricksen of Tektronix's Forest Grove Plant, are humanistic. They center on what organizations can do for people. Even though an organization must be successful to fulfill these visions, organizational development is an outcome of human development. Other Capitalist strategies, like those at Central Bank of Utah or Gateway Technologies, revolve around the organization. It is still important to develop people, but to develop them for their contributions to building organizations.

The typology presented in Figure 7-1 is based on these two questions. There are four types of Capitalists: Type 1 Capitalists have more vision-guided and people-centered offensive strategies. Type 2 Capitalists have more opportunity-guided and people-centered offensive strategies. Type 3 Capitalists have more vision-guided, organization-centered offensive strategies. Type 4 Capitalists have more opportunity-guided and organization-centered offensive strategies.

Figure 7–1. A Typology of Capitalists.

	VISION– and Opportunity– Guided Offensive Strategies	OPPORTUNITY– and Vision– Guided Offensive Strategies
PEOPLE– Centered	Type 1	Type 2
ORGANIZATION– Centered	Type 3	Type 4

Type 1 Capitalists

A vision of what people can become and do when given opportunities guides the offensive strategies of Type 1 Capitalists. They are hierarchical, functional organizations, but are organized around work teams, which provide people who work for Type 1 Capitalists with a stronger voice in company affairs and also control individual behavior through agreed upon rules and norms. Because work teams control worker behavior, there are real limits to authority. Type 1 Capitalists are not pure democracies, but they are highly participative organizations.

Herman Miller Incorporated, the office furniture manufacturer, is a Type 1 Capitalist. Founded in 1923, the Zeeland, Michigan, company was originally guided by the vision of D. J. DePree, a vision that emphasized a concern for people. For example, he started profit-sharing and employee-incentive programs at the company long before they were fashionable. DePree's sons, Hugh and Max, succeeded him and further refined his people-centered vision while taking the company public and prospering in the expanding office furniture industry. A recent demonstration of Herman Miller's concern and loyalty for its employees was the promise of "silver parachutes" to everyone. If the company were acquired in a hostile takeover, plant workers as well as executives who would lose their jobs would receive generous severance checks."[11]

According to Max DePree, "covenantal relationships" between top management and all employees are at the heart of Herman Miller's management system. He defines the company's central mission as "attempting to share values, ideals, goals, respect for each person, [and] the process of our work together." The atmosphere at Herman Miller is intense and eclectic. People debate passionately, but no one cares where an idea comes from, as long as it works.[12]

People are hired at Herman Miller more for their character and the ability to get along with people than for their previous accomplishments. The senior vice president of research was once a high school football coach. A marketing senior vice president is a former dean of the agriculture school at Michigan State. And the vice president of people was recruited from Michigan's Department of Corrections, where she was training to become a prison warden.[13]

The DePree family has always tried to leverage its people-centered vision at Herman Miller. But they realized that as long as a family member led the company, the range of their vision would be limited. So several years ago the DePrees informed senior executives that, in order to ensure the fullest career development of promising managers, Max would be the last member of the family to head Herman Miller. To ensure that the commitment was not violated, the next generation of DePrees was not even allowed to work at the company.[14]

All employees at Herman Miller are organized into work teams. Team leaders evaluate their workers every six months, and then each worker turns around and evaluates his or her leader. On the plant floor teams elect representatives to caucuses that meet periodically with line supervisors to discuss production shifts and grievances. If workers at these caucuses don't like what they hear, they can bypass the supervisor and go directly to the next executive level.[15]

Another thing that Herman Miller does to reinforce its egalitarian atmosphere is limit executive pay. The chief executive's salary cannot exceed 20 times the average wage of a line worker in the factory. According to Richard Ruch, Herman Miller's new CEO, "One of the real keys to leadership is making sure you don't find yourself defending the wrong things, such as your own inflated salary." Since 1950, Herman Miller has used the Scanlon plan to reward its people. Every employee receives a quarterly bonus based on various benchmarks, including cost-saving suggestions.[16]

Experiences at Herman Miller also illustrate one of the potential problems with the offensive strategies of Type 1 Capitalists. Recently, the company became so intent on refining its internal dynamics that it began to lose some of its feel for the increasingly competitive office furniture market. In other words, Herman Miller became too vision-guided and forgot to look to customers to find opportunities. Moreover, the company became so preoccupied with its programs for people that it needed to be reminded that such programs are only possible as long as the organization remains strong and competitive.

Until the mid-1980s the office furniture market was growing at a 20 percent annual rate and was providing some companies with gross profit margins above 40 percent. Several start-ups were attracted to the industry, but as long as demand remained high, the new entrants had little effect on established companies like Herman Miller. But when restructuring hit corporate America in the mid-1980s, fewer middle managers meant fewer offices and less demand for office furniture. Suddenly, the office furniture industry became highly competitive, and Herman Miller's sales and profits declined.[17]

So what did Herman Miller do? It set about raising what it called the "business literacy" of its employees. The results of satisfaction surveys customers filled out and the company's return on assets were added to the formula for determining bonuses. Thus, Herman Miller met the challenges of competition through the increased involvement and participation of its people.[18]

Type 2 Capitalists

The offensive strategies of Type 2 Capitalists are guided by the opportunities that their people find by staying in tune with customers and markets. They are flat organizations, composed of loosely coupled, cross-functional teams. Type 2 Capitalists grow as these cross-functional teams identify and pursue new opportunities. Teams eventually become independent operations, then give birth to other teams. Similar to the work teams of Type 1 Capitalists, teams control the behavior of individuals, and enforced norms limit outside authority.

W. L. Gore & Associates is a Type 2 Capitalist. The company is especially well-known for its "lattice organization." Traditional organizations are organized pyramidally, with discrete lines of communication and authority moving upward and downward through a system broad at the base and narrow at the top. The lattice organization looks like a lattice—a regular cross-hatching of lines, representing an unrestricted flow of communication with no overlay of lines of authority. As Bill Gore, the company's founder, defines it, a lattice organization means "one-to-one communication" with whomever you need to talk to in order to get a job done; no fixed or assigned authority, but leadership that evolves over time and that fluctuates with the specific problems at hand that most need attention; and tasks and functions that are organized through personally made commitments, not job descriptions or organization charts. According to Gore, a lattice organization is the best organizational form for "making money and having fun."[19]

Where did the lattice organization come from? When Gore worked for Du Pont he was amazed at how motivated people were when they worked on task forces and at how motivation and performance diminished when the task forces were disbanded and people returned to their previous jobs in the corporate hierarchy. He also noticed that even in the corporate hierarchy, the real work got done through informal rather than formal means. So when Gore founded W. L. Gore & Associates, initially to exploit the properties of Teflon as an insulator for electrical wire, he created the lattice organization to free up the informal system as much as possible by doing away with the formal system.[20]

W. L. Gore reinforces its lattice organization in many different ways. First, the company tries to keep its plants small. Ideally, 150 associates (and no more than 250) work in a plant. Second, W. L. Gore has invested in almost every conceivable communications technology, from electronic voice mailboxes to plantwide paging systems, to make it easy for its associates to contact one another. Third, people in the company consistently encourage lateral communications over vertical communications. Even the newest of associates can ask questions of Bob Gore, Bill's son and president of the company, just as Bob can ask them questions. Should an associate mention to his sponsor a concern relevant to another associate, the sponsor is likely to say, "Have you brought it up with him yet?" In other words, the sponsor will encourage the associate to make personal contact, rather than serve as an intermediary between two associates.[21]

So strong is the value of one-to-one communication that many new start-up research teams look forward to growing large enough to move out of established plants into isolated, cramped, and poorly furnished rental headquarters that enhance direct communications. One such research team grew so large that it outgrew its rental headquarters and had to move into a newly built facility with magnificent front offices overlooking a forest of beautiful pines. Team leaders decided to forego the front offices for interior offices so that they could be closer to manufacturing associates.

Mike Pacanowsky spent a sabbatical year working for W. L. Gore & Associates. He described the company as a 4,500-member improvisational jazz group trying to make music in 25 different buildings at the same time. He further explained:

> Each associate seemed busily engaged in making his own music, and hoping that he or she could find someone playing a compatible melody or rhythm. And once you found a fit, and once the music started getting good, you quickly found a whole lot of others joining in. Now this was not to say that, in each room, there wasn't a lot of counterpoint going on. And often it seemed like there may even be occasions of dueling banjos. And there always seemed to be some lost souls wandering around playing out of sync with everyone else, but they were surprisingly tolerated. Occasionally, everything would seem to break down and there wasn't music anymore, just chaos and noise. Then, in time, a line would rise out of the cacophony, and there would be music again."[22]

Pacanowsky's metaphor offers two important insights about W. L. Gore. First, the system doesn't work all the time. Mistakes are made, but people learn from their mistakes, make the appropriate adjustments, and, finally, things work out. Second, the company is a free-wheeling, people-centered organization. It is not an organization built around one humanistic founder's grand vision, but an organization more like a rehearsal room in which 4,500 individuals try to blend their personal visions with someone else's.

W. L. Gore's associates are guided by four principles: *"Fairness*—Each of us will *try* to be fair in all our dealings. . . . *Freedom*—Each of us will allow, help, and encourage [other] Associates to grow in knowledge, skill, and scope of responsibility, and the range of activities. Authority . . . is not a power of command, only of leadership. *Commitment*—Each of us will make [our] own commitments—and keep them. *Waterline*—Each of us will consult with appropriate Associates who will share the responsibility of taking any action that has the potential of serious harm to the reputation, success, or survival of the Enterprise. The analogy is that our Enterprise is like a ship that we are all in together. Boring holes above the waterline is not serious, but below the waterline, holes could sink us."[23]

The underlying message of W. L. Gore's four principles is represented by the words "each of us." Clearly, each individual matters at W. L. Gore, and the company's success depends on the pooled efforts of each of its associates, who are left on their own to identify and pursue opportunities. In effect, associates are free to do anything as long as it doesn't threaten to sink the company.

The other thing for which W. L. Gore & Associates is widely known is Gore-Tex and the many applications the company has found for that single invention. Bob Gore invented Gore-Tex, an expanded form of Teflon, in 1969. Since then, the company has grown by finding new opportunities to use it. Vascular grafts made from Gore-Tex have been used in over a million surgeries. Gore-Tex fabrics, used in everything from ski gloves, running suits, fashion boots, to gym bags, have become popular among people requiring high-performance clothing and equipment.[24]

The lattice organization at W. L. Gore is uniquely suited for finding opportunities. It encourages the sharing of information and the broad participation of Gore's associates. Gore's people constantly identify and pursue new opportunities because they all believe they can make a difference. The company grows as associates find new applications for Gore-Tex, assemble teams, and build teams into separate operations.

Clearly, vision also guides W. L. Gore. This vision is embodied in the company's four principles and the lattice organization. But an empowering vision enables associates to create and pursue their personal visions. In a nutshell, the company's offensive strategy is to encourage people to do their own thing. For example, at the conclusion of a four-day meeting most of W. L. Gore's business leaders attended, someone asked, "Well, what are we all supposed to do as a result of this meeting?" Bob Gore quickly responded, "I don't think we're *all* supposed to do any one thing. I know that I've come away from this meeting with three or four things I know I want to do, and I hope that everyone else has their own personal To-Dos as well."[25]

Type 3 Capitalists

A vision of a distinctive organization guides the offensive strategies of Type 3 Capitalists. They are organized as functional hierarchies, discouraging functional parochialism while promoting an integrated company vision by moving people through nonspecialized career paths. People working for Type 3 Capitalists become experts in their distinctive organizational forms. Commitment and control are based on employee identification with the values embodied in the visions of Type 3 Capitalists.

Type 3 Capitalists expect that everyone, including founders and top executives, conforms to company values. This reinforces the message that the organization and the values it is based on are more important than any one individual.

A story told at Hewlett-Packard, a Type 3 Capitalist, illustrates the power of this concept. Dave Packard, one of the company's founders and, at the time, its president, was doing some photocopying after hours wearing a white lab coat. A new secretary was closing up the laboratory and saw him. She asked accusingly, "Were you the one who left the lights and the copy machine on last night?" "Uh, well, I guess I did," was Packard's reply. "Don't you know," the secretary chastised, "that we have an energy-saving program in the company, and that the president has asked us to be particularly careful about turning off lights and equipment?" A repentant Packard replied, "I'm very sorry. It won't happen again."

When Hewlett-Packard people told this story, they did not dwell on the fact that the president had failed to follow his own energy-saving policy. Instead, they were impressed that he did not pull rank on the secretary. He felt bound by the rules he set for everyone else and, more importantly, lived one of the "big ideas" of the company: "We are family here. We treat people with respect and as equals."

Hewlett-Packard's founders not only lived the big ideas of the company, they shared and leveraged them. Another big idea is that Hewlett-Packard is "a company of individuals who work together, and who, despite differences in assignment, skill, and experience in the company, are not different in worth or as individuals." A story is told about a recently hired person assigned to deliver something to Bill Hewlett. When he arrived at Bill's office, he addressed him as "Mr. Hewlett." Bill responded, "Oh, you must want my father. My name's Bill."

Many Hewlett-Packard employees reported similar experiences with other senior managers, which helped them realize that they were expected to call *everyone* by his or her first name. Bill Hewlett and senior managers who emulated him used to their advantage the sense of discomfort people often feel when associating with people of higher status to dramatize, share in a memorable way, and leverage an important company ideal.

A story told by William Ouchi, the author of *Theory Z: How American Business Can Meet the Japanese Challenge,* about Hewlett-Packard reveals the nature of the interplay between vision and opportunity that is characteristic of the offensive strategies of most Type 3 Capitalists. Digital watches provided one of the most dramatic new business opportunities in the early 1970s. Because old mainline watch companies such as Timex and Bulova were initially suspicious of the new semiconductor technology, the watch industry opened up to new entrants for the first time in many years. Hewlett-Packard manufactured the key component that was the heart of the digital watch, and a young general manager who recognized the opportunity was persistent about wanting to take the company into the watch business. But top executives were less convinced. They asked whether the digital watch business fit their vision of the kinds of businesses the company should be involved in. They wondered whether this was just a one-shot success or whether Hewlett-Packard could continue to be an innovator and a leader in the watch business for years to come. After careful deliberation, executives concluded that even though the digital watch business did not fit their vision, it would be wrong not to allow the young general manager the freedom to pursue this opportunity. Why? Because another major element of the company's corporate vision had to do with preserving the freedom of employees to pursue projects they believed would be fruitful.[26]

The message of this story is subtle. Also, because the young general manager was allowed to pursue a business opportunity he identified, the outcome may appear inconsistent with our description of Type 3 Capitalists. But look at how the decision was made. Although a business opportunity forced the decision to be made, the decision was guided by the company's vision, not the opportunity. The general manager got his way only because Hewlett-Packard's values supported individual initiative. Accordingly, there was no inconsistency between the decision and the company's organizational vision.

A final story told at Hewlett-Packard illustrates that, although the company's values reveal a deep concern for people, the organization clearly comes first. In the early 1970s the entire U.S. electronics industry suffered a drop in orders, and most electronics firms were laying off people in significant numbers. At Hewlett-Packard estimates indicated that 10 percent cutbacks in both output and payroll would be necessary to match the decline in orders.[27]

The obvious solution was for Hewlett-Packard to follow its competitors and lay off 10 percent of its work force. But top management, demonstrating its concern for the needs of the few who would be affected by layoffs, was committed to not being a hire-and-fire company. After considerable discussion, a novel solution surfaced. Management decided to require everyone from the president to the lowest-paid employee to take a 10 percent cut in pay and stay home from work every other Friday. By distributing the cuts throughout the organization, the company was able to avoid the loss of human resources and the human costs associated with layoffs without weakening the company.[28]

Again, Hewlett-Packard's employees saw a consistency between what top management said and did. They realized that company officials really meant it when they said they didn't want Hewlett-Packard to be a hire-and-fire company. Some employees even assumed from the nine-day fortnight experience that the company would never lay off people. However, company executives saw things differently. Although they were committed to avoiding layoffs whenever possible, they did concede that if alternatives could not be found employees would be laid off to preserve the strength and viability of the firm. If a decision had to be made between saving the organization or people's jobs, the organization would win out.

Type 4 Capitalists

The offensive strategies of Type 4 Capitalists are guided by opportunities to build the organization. They are elite, can-do organizations. Individuals are willing to subordinate themselves to the organization because of the pride they feel from membership. They work in teams, but their identification with the team is always secondary to their identification with the organization. Teams are more like task forces because they form around specific projects, then break up once the projects are completed. Although there is some centralized control around the formation of teams, most of the control in Type 4 Capitalists comes through customer demands. Type 4 Capitalists try to provide whatever the customer wants.

When led by H. Ross Perot, Electronic Data Systems was a Type 4 Capitalist. Outsiders tended to notice EDS's military trappings: the fences and guards, the abundance of flags, the clean-shaven men in white shirts, dark suits, shined shoes, and army haircuts. Certainly, part of Perot's original vision was to create both jobs for people leaving military service and a highly disciplined organization. But these military trappings were simply carryovers from Perot's previous experience in the military. Inside the company, the spirit was more capitalistic than militaristic. The company honored employees in the field with its trust. It encouraged them to make their own decisions, regardless of their title or position in the hierarchy. The company's offensive strategy dictated that results were all that mattered, and compensation was based strictly on performance.[29]

Under Perot, Electronic Data Systems was structured as a shifting collection of loose teams assembled to meet challenges and dismantled when challenges were overcome. These teams were flexible enough to restructure in a few days and deep enough to handle the frequent shifting of key team members. The strength of EDS's offensive strategy came from the ability of individuals and teams to focus on specific opportunities, and from their loyalty to a shared organizational cause.[30]

Electronic Data Systems had no personnel department. Like everything else, hiring was driven down the ranks as the company grew. Decisions were made in the field. Potential recruits were invited to a team interview with their potential peers and evaluated in three ways: (1) Would you want to work with him as an equal on a project? (2) What if he were your team leader? (3) What if you were his team leader? Willingness to accept the company's culture and its code of loyalty were more important than technical skills or experience.[31]

When Perot ran Electronic Data Systems, the company would do anything, as long as it was legal and ethical, to get and keep a contract. This, of course, required a lot from employees. Team members would often get calls on weekends, in the middle of the night, or during vacations instructing them to report immediately or the next day to help another team on a troubled project. The focus was always first, do the job for your customer; second, make money at it; and third, teach someone along the way to do it.[32]

Perot, of course, was always providing the example of what was required in terms of personal sacrifice to be an Electronic Data Systems employee. The day major contracts were signed, Perot would walk up to project managers and hand them slips of paper with his phone number on them. "You can reach me here twenty-four hours a day, seven days a week, if you feel we're not living up to our agreement," Perot would say. Then the team assigned to the project made sure the project manager never had to make a call.[33]

Perot loved to see the company's people stand up to him, particularly out of duty to a customer. If they made mistakes while trying to do their duty, they were forgiven. Perot wanted employees to operate like he did—on instinct, by trial and error, figuring it out along the way. When employees did figure things out they were rewarded handsomely with bonuses and stock. In many ways, Electronic Data Systems under Perot was the classic meritocracy: People were paid for results because results were all that mattered.

When General Motors wanted to acquire Electronic Data Systems, Perot was skeptical. He was especially concerned about merging the cultures of the two companies. At General Motors there was a clear division between management and labor, and executives were privileged, with corporate dining rooms, chauffeured limousines, and hefty year-end bonuses even in hard times. Perot argued that GM's executives should set the example for increased labor-management cooperation. He wanted them to give up their perquisites, get back in the trenches, and listen to the troops. He believed that if executives did not separate themselves from and took care of their people, their people would take care of them. Perot highlighted the major difference between GM and Electronic Data Systems when he said, "At EDS there's no labor and management, everyone's labor."[34]

MAINTAINING COMPETITIVE LEADERSHIP

Capitalists intent on maintaining competitive leadership need both specific and general instructions. The specific instructions correspond to the inherent vulnerabilities of each of the four types of Capitalists; the general instructions apply to all Capitalists.

Specific Instructions

The Capitalist's offensive strategy balances being vision-guided and opportunity-guided, on the one hand, and people-centered and organization-centered on the other. Although Capitalists lean one way or the other along these two dimensions, they are likely to lose their balance if they lean too far.

When Type 1 Capitalists become too vision-guided and people-centered, they are likely to lose touch with customers and markets. This is why it is important for them to participate in intense rivalries. Head-to-head competition seems to remedy their natural tendencies to spend too much time looking inward and too little time being concerned about organizational performance. We see this virtue at Tektronix's Forest Grove Plant, where the intense competition in the circuit board industry provides a heavy dose of reality every day. It is an advantage for Herman Miller to have its main competitor, Steelcase Incorporated, headquartered only 21 miles away. *Fortune* reports that Herman Miller's people "glare like tigers" whenever Steelcase is mentioned.[35] Steelcase brings out the competitiveness in every Herman Miller employee, encouraging them to seek new opportunities and to be more concerned about organizational performance.

When Type 2 Capitalists become too opportunity-guided and people-centered they risk providing too much freedom with too little form. Capitalists need organizational visions to guide them; otherwise they grow in too many directions and lose their integrity. A thousand personal visions do not make a Capitalist. This is why the waterline principle is so important at W. L. Gore & Associates. Sufficient form is imposed on Gore's autonomous teams as long as the waterline is kept high enough.

Type 3 Capitalists that become too vision-guided and organization-centered are difficult to change. Although the vision of a product or service can often remain the same, organizational visions need to change with the times. Of course, they only change when they mix with new opportunities, never simply for the sake of change. New opportunities create reasons for change. Type 3 Capitalists must be sensitive to the balance between too much and too little change. These organizations need to honor the visions that have guided them in the past as they build bridges to reach the new opportunities that will take them into the future.

Finally, Type 4 Capitalists increase the risk of doing something unethical when they become too opportunity-guided and organization-centered. People often do anything to succeed, even something illegal or unethical, when intense pressure on individual and team performance is coupled with an intense organizational loyalty. The problem for Type 4 Capitalists is that their competitive leadership is built on their reputations and the pride their people feel from organizational membership. This is why H. Ross Perot enforced a rigid code of honor on all Electronic Data Systems employees. If even one employee had been caught doing something illegal or unethical, the entire organization would have lost stature.

General Instructions

To maintain competitive leadership, all four types of Capitalists must (1) find an effective balance between being opportunity-guided and vision-guided, and (2) have leaders who lead by example.

Balancing Opportunities and Visions.   Capitalists benefit greatly from the tension between being opportunity-guided and vision-guided, which enables them to grow, develop, and maintain competitive leadership. Recent developments at the Geneva Steel Plant illustrate the importance of maintaining this tension.

Two brothers, Joe and Chris Cannon, purchased the Geneva

Steel Plant from USX Corporation in a $40 million leveraged buy-out. Joe, an opportunist, saw the vacant steel plant as an opportunity to buy low, rebuild the business, and sell high. Chris, a visionary, saw the plant as the foundation for new economic development in the surrounding community.

The Cannons, who call their company Basic Manufacturing and Technologies of Utah (BM&T), have transformed the plant into the largest exporter in the state of Utah. In the nine months between August 1988 and April 1989, the Geneva plant exported $70 million in product, 87 percent of which was shipped to Japanese manufacturers. Moreover, BM&T has developed numerous profitable side businesses using facilities that previously serviced only the Geneva plant, such as the metal shop and the steel pipe plant, to produce products for external markets.

The Geneva Steel Plant derives clear advantages from the creative tension between opportunity-guided and vision-guided offensive strategies. The Cannon brothers have not always agreed on a strategy for the plant. In fact, Chris once initiated legal action against his brother when, in the midst of a stormy disagreement, Joe dropped him from BM&T's board of directors. But overall, the company has benefited from their two perspectives. Chris' vision needs the grounding provided by Joe's opportunism, and Joe's opportunism needs the constraint imposed by Chris' vision.

Leading by Example.   Capitalists are strengthened by the examples of their leaders. For Opportunists and Visionaries the dynamics are different. The leaders of Opportunists want their people to create their own examples, while the leaders of Visionaries share their visions with others but leverage those visions by leaving. For Cal Packard at Central Bank, the DePrees at Herman Miller, Bill and Bob Gore at W. L. Gore, Bill Hewlett and Dave Packard at Hewlett-Packard, and Ross Perot at Electronic Data Systems, the importance of leadership by example is unmistakable.

Leaders of Capitalists set examples when they embody the fundamental values of their organizations. Their examples can be powerful and long lasting. I still recall what the example of Maurice Cohen meant to me when, as a teenager, I was a summer employee for Lechmere Sales Corporation. My father had sold his two-year-old car to Cohen, who was his boss and president of Lechmere, a hard-goods department store with its headquarters in Cambridge, Massachusetts. My father, who was vice president of finance and control, hired me to work in the accounts payable department during summers. We would drive to work together and turn into a parking lot that was empty except for one car parked far away from the store. It was always the same car—the one my father sold to Cohen.

Not many things impressed me as a teenager, but seeing Cohen's car every morning did. I knew that Cohen was a millionaire several times over, but because he drove a car he bought from my father he was somehow more approachable. Cohen also didn't park his car in a private parking space next to the store, but as far away from the store as he could. I remember my father telling me many times that Cohen parked his car where he did because he wanted to save all the good parking spaces for customers. Being an optimistic merchant, Cohen always expected the parking lot to be filled with customers' cars. Cohen also set an example by being the first person to work. With his many successes he had not lost the work ethic of the small store proprietor. He was still the person who opened the store doors every morning.

Maurice Cohen had a good teacher—his father, whom everyone called Pop. Pop Cohen founded Lechmere in a small store across the street from the Lechmere Street Station of the Massachusetts Bay Transportation Authority. When I worked for Lechmere, Pop Cohen was an old man and his health was failing, but he still came to the Cambridge store every day.

Lechmere had a unique merchandising idea. Most of the products on the sales floor were samples. Customers who made purchases were given receipts and instructed to go to a conveyor belt located in the middle of the store to pick up their merchandise. Pop Cohen sat on a chair next to the conveyor belt throughout the day. Often he fell asleep in that chair, but he was always there making sure customers were receiving the best service possible from the company he founded.

Why is leadership by example so important to Capitalists? Because actions speak louder than words. When leaders lead by example they tell their people that nobody can let down and that everybody needs to pitch in and work hard because success is never automatic. The only way that Capitalists maintain competitive leadership is by having a stronger desire than their competitors to be the best. The individuals who lead Capitalists show how to be the best by being the first ones to work every morning and obsessively watching out for customers.

8 Overcoming Competitive Disadvantage to Become a Worldwide Competitive Leader

Canon did something that even powerful U.S. companies like Kodak and IBM could not do. The Japanese company overcame Xerox's dominant position to establish a significant presence in the copier industry. It transformed a noncompetitive business environment into a competitive one. How did Canon do it? Xerox built a wide range of copiers, but Canon standardized machines and components to reduce costs. It also chose a different distribution network than Xerox did, choosing to sell its copiers through office-products dealers. Because Canon's copiers were so reliable and serviceable, the company could delegate service responsibility to its dealers. It also produced inexpensive copiers that it could sell rather than lease to customers. Finally, Canon invented the concept of distributive copying: Instead of selling to heads of corporate duplicating departments, it pitched its copiers to secretaries and department managers. At every turn, Canon's offensive strategy helped it sidestep the entry barriers that had been the downfall of both Kodak and IBM.[1]

Canon's offensive strategy paralyzed Xerox. Xerox knew how to operate in a noncompetitive environment and was especially adept at protecting its dominant industry position against potential competitors, as long as they were willing to play by its rules. But Canon played by another set of rules, and Xerox found itself at a severe competitive disadvantage. For example, Xerox's managers realized that the faster they reduced the company's product line, developed

Figure 8–1.   Two Paths to Gaining Competitive Leadership.

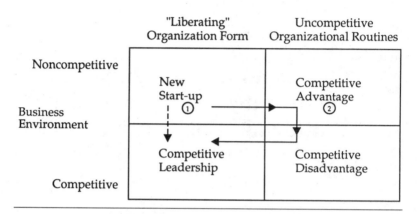

new channels, and improved reliability, the faster they eroded the company's traditional profit base. The entrenched organizational routines established around Xerox's national sales force and service network, its large base of leased machines, and its reliance on service revenues became barriers to retaliation under the new competitive realities brought on by Canon's competitive challenge.[2]

Canon, while it redefined the terms of engagement, went head-to-head against competition. It found a way to challenge a recognized industry leader, then gained a leadership position in the small-copier market. In Figure 8-1, the dotted line represents Canon's direct approach to gaining competitive leadership. If Xerox is to mount a serious attack against Canon for the small-copier market, it must complete the circuitous path represented by the solid line in the figure. Xerox's competitive advantages in the large-copier market actually became competitive disadvantages to the company in its attempts to compete against Canon for a share of the new small-copier market. Xerox's counteroffensive must somehow address these competitive disadvantages before the company can challenge Canon in the small-copier market.

How do companies overcome competitive disadvantages and become competitive leaders? First, executives must create long-term visions of their companies as competitive leaders. New visions promote and sustain needed changes because they help companies see themselves in a new light. Next, companies must find organizational cures for competitive disadvantage. Although visions of themselves as competitive leaders are necessary for companies to promote and sustain change, they begin to change by removing competitive disadvantages. Then, organizational efforts shift to empowering employees to ensure that positive changes become widely distributed throughout companies. Although the wide distribution of changes throughout a company may be necessary, it may be insufficient for gaining competitive leadership unless employees also improvise offensive strategies on their own.

CREATING LONG-TERM VISIONS OF COMPANIES AS COMPETITIVE LEADERS

The first thing that companies must do to overcome competitive disadvantage is change their strategic intent.[3] They need to realize that they can no longer avoid competition with the competitive advantages they have relied on in the past. They must adopt offensive strategies, then confront the new competitive realities. They stay on course by creating a vision of themselves as competitive leaders.

Giving companies visions of being competitive leaders is an executive responsibility. All executive visions are at least two-dimensional. According to Walter Kiechel III, the assistant managing editor of *Fortune,* in order for an executive vision to inspire organizations and people, "it must represent a challenge, an undertaking so big or audacious that it can seem scary, sometimes even to the person who conceives it." In other words, a vision must have *scale.* It must encourage people to lengthen their strides, to stretch themselves, to build new capabilities to make the vision a reality. Kiechel continues: "It [the vision] must reflect some purpose higher than the everyday getting and spending of commerce. The dream of building a computer for Everyman, or saving a great American car company, has the stuff of vision in it. . . . Making another 10 cents a share for the stockholders this quarter certainly does not."[4] Executive visions, according to Kiechel, must have a heroic quality if they are to inspire. They must provide day-to-day, sometimes mundane work with a higher meaning and purpose. They do not move organizations unless they have *substance.*

Scale and substance are common to all effective executive visions, but two additional dimensions are critical to them if companies are to overcome competitive disadvantage. They must also have *scope* and incorporate a *sense of history.* Gary Hamel and C. K.

Prahalad argue that "economies of scope may be as important as economies of scale in entering global markets."[5] What they encourage is global thinking that eases entry into global markets across a whole range of businesses. But global thinking is only one part of executive visions with true scope. For example, executive visions should also account for the strengths of different functional areas, business units, and products. Executive visions with scope capture all of an organization's potential—both present strengths and the new strengths that the company is uniquely positioned to develop and leverage.

Visions to overcome competitive disadvantage require a sense of history to provide a bridge between a company's past and its future. Even when companies are at a competitive disadvantage, there will likely be resistance in them to some of the changes necessary for them to become competitive leaders. According to Stuart Albert, a professor at the University of Minnesota's Carlson School of Management, creating continuity between the past and the future will "motivate change by the promise that at least some valued elements of the past will be preserved and continue in the new arrangement. Almost no situation is so dire that the individual would be willing to give up *everything* about it."[6]

These four dimensions—scale, substance, scope, and a sense of history—are all essential if companies are to use visions of themselves as competitive leaders to overcome competitive disadvantage. The four dimensions are also the building blocks of a process that companies can use to create new visions of themselves as competitive leaders.

Building Block #1: Visions of Scale

During the early years of the space age, success in space was used as a measure of a country's leadership in science, engineering, and technology. The U.S.S.R. beat the United States into space by launching *Sputnik I,* the first artificial satellite to circle the earth, on 4 October 1957. Strong evidence, however, supports the claim that the U.S. Army's Redstone Arsenal, which had developed most of America's Cold War missile arsenal, could have accomplished this feat before the Soviets did if the Eisenhower administration had softened its sponsorship of the Navy's ill-fated Vanguard Project. Vanguard did not succeed; the Soviet attempt did. Only then was the Redstone group, led by Wernher von Braun, allowed to place the first U.S. satellite into orbit.[7]

The National Aeronautics and Space Administration (NASA) was established in 1958 to conduct and coordinate U.S. nonmilitary research into the problems of flight within and beyond the earth's atmosphere. The Redstone group elected to leave the Army and join NASA. They became the core group around which the Marshall Space Flight Center (MSFC) was organized in mid-1960.

Although initial efforts at NASA focused on sending unmanned satellites into orbit, most of the agency's attention and plans were focused on manned spaceflight. It came as a real shock to NASA, therefore, when on 12 April 1961 Yuri Gagarin, a Soviet cosmonaut, became the first man to orbit the earth. With the success of *Vostok I* it became clear to the world scientific community that *Sputnick* was not a fluke. Although the Soviet lead in space was not overwhelming, clearly U.S. scientists' competitive advantage in rocket and space research had evaporated. The space race was up for grabs, and if anything the United States was at a competitive disadvantage to the Soviet Union.

President John F. Kennedy, who had been in office only a few months when Gagarin orbited the earth, made a bold speech in response to that event. He challenged NASA and the entire U.S. scientific community to send a manned spacecraft to the moon by the end of the decade to restore America's leadership in space. NASA, of course, accepted Kennedy's challenge. The Mercury and Gemini programs set the stage for the Apollo program. When the Apollo 11 lunar module, called *Eagle,* touched down on the moon's Sea of Tranquility on 20 July 1969, one of the greatest scientific achievements in all of human history was accomplished. And the United States vaulted ahead of the Soviets in space exploration and research.

Hamel and Prahalad write:

> We seldom found cautious administrators among the top managements of companies that came from behind to challenge incumbents for global leadership. But in studying organizations that had surrendered, we invariably found senior managers who, for whatever reason, lacked the courage to commit their companies to heroic goals—goals that lay beyond the reach of planning and existing resources. The conservative goals they set failed to generate pressure and enthusiasm for competitive innovation or give the organization much useful guidance.[8]

Effective visions, like Kennedy's vision for the U.S. space program, challenge and motivate people. They make something that is presently impossible seem possible and pull organizations into setting heroic goals that are outside the range of any planning process. Effective visions provide the general framework of an organization's mission and engender the individual commitment that specific actions flow from.

Effective visions also restore faith in an organization's ability to deliver on tough goals. They challenge people just enough. Faced with too much challenge, companies panic and are more likely, in their frenzy, to take the wrong actions or to freeze in inaction. Faced with too little challenge, companies are not energized to act. The felt need to change is not strong enough to eliminate uncompetitive organizational routines. But when visions provide just enough challenge, people see clearly what needs to be done, and, feeling confident that they can be successful, they work to make the vision a reality.

One way to create just enough challenge is to make careful adjustments around the rate of change. Something that should take 20 years becomes too much challenge when the goal is to do it in 10 years; it offers too little challenge when companies operate with a 30 year time frame. Generally, overcoming competitive disadvantage takes a long time, and unreasonable pressure can damage faith and distort the process. Visions need to have scale, but companies also need time to accomplish lofty goals.

Building Block #2: Visions of Substance

Robert Waterman, Jr., author of *The Renewal Factor,* tells us that "man is a maker of meanings in a world that sometimes seems without meaning. Few things help us find meaning more than a cause to believe in, or better yet, about which to get excited."[9] Waterman suggests that renewing organizations appear to run on causes. This implies that executives who want their organizations to overcome competitive disadvantages and become competitive leaders must give new meaning to organizational life. For example, the visions a Ford executive creates will have little or no effect unless they help the person tightening the bolts that hold the tires on a Ford Taurus understand that what he does is critical to the quality of an entire automobile. Even though that line worker's part may be small, it is significant because no Ford Taurus is safe to drive unless the job is done right. Ultimately, Ford Motor Company will be judged in the marketplace by the safety and reliability of its cars. Because of the high level of interdependency required in assembling an automobile, each individual at every station along the assembly line must do his or her best if Ford cars are to become the best in the world.

The idea that executive visions need substance to inspire employees is hardly new. Chester Barnard, the former AT&T executive and author of the 1938 classic, *The Functions of the Executive,* described one of the principal functions of the executive as the "inculcation of belief," and Philip Selznick, another classic management theorist and author of the 1957 book, *Leadership in Administration,* discussed how effective leaders provide "definition of institutional mission and role." More recently, Peter Vaill, a professor of human systems at George Washington University, has defined "purposing" as that "continuous stream of actions by an organization's formal leadership that has the effect of inducing clarity, consensus, and commitment regarding the organization's basic purposes."[10] Purposing, according to Vaill, creates feeling and focus in high-performing systems.

Creating a vision with substance is by itself not enough. Leaders of organizations must demonstrate their commitment to visions by acting consistently with them in everything they do. Gene Hendricksen, the manager of Tektronix's Forest Grove Plant, is one of the most participative managers I know. He wants everyone in the plant to have a voice and, either directly or through elected representatives, to participate in all plant decisions. He is incredibly patient with his people as consensus slowly but steadily builds around new structures and processes for making the plant more competitive.

Hendricksen's guiding vision is of the Forest Grove Plant overcoming its competitive disadvantages to become the world's "best cost" producer of circuit boards. It is this vision that drives all changes in the plant. Recently, to make the plant more competitive, the manufacturing engineers were told to move down to the plant floor so that they could work more closely with the Business Element Units (BEUs) they were assigned to. The engineers understood the reasoning behind the decision and reluctantly agreed to move. But week after week they reported excuse after excuse for why they had not moved. Meanwhile, the BEUs were not getting the hands-on engineering service they sorely needed.

Finally, Hendricksen's patience ran out. Without conferring with the engineers, he hired movers to come in on a weekend to move the engineers' desks out of the engineering department into the areas where their respective BEUs operated. Hendricksen never offered an explanation for his action to the engineers, and none of them asked for one. In this case, the plant's needs clearly superseded the manufacturing engineers' professional ties to the engineering department.

Hendricksen's autocratic behavior may have violated his management style, but it had been in the best interest of the plant and was entirely consistent with a vision all of Forest Grove's employees agreed on and held.

Building Block #3: Visions of Scope

If companies are to overcome competitive disadvantages and become worldwide competitive leaders they need to expand the scope of their visions. Scope is expanded when visions are allowed to interact freely with opportunities. Like new air blown into a balloon, opportunities will expand visions in all directions and create new pressures within companies to change. Of course, too much pressure pops visions, but in most cases company visions are not anywhere near their potential scope.

Under Michael Eisner's leadership, Walt Disney Company expanded the scope of its vision on several fronts. Eisner realized that although Disney's image as a moviemaker was getting musty, the company was also sitting on top of some exceedingly valuable assets that were being undermanaged. To tap the video market, Disney now releases at least one of its animated classics on videocassette each year. Disney characters are marketed aggressively, such as by having Snow White visit the floor of the New York Stock Exchange for her 50th birthday and by Disney's producing the halftime show at Super Bowl XXI. The company is also pushing network TV syndication and its Disney Channel. With more than 29 years of *Wonderful World of Disney* television shows, hundreds of cartoons, and nearly 200 feature films, these are natural and remarkably lucrative ways to expand the scope of the company's activities.[11]

Disney is also producing several new films. When Eisner arrived at the company, movies and TV accounted for only about 13 percent of profits. The company wants to triple that output, and its vision is simple: to get as many new movies as possible into the long entertainment pipeline, collecting not only box-office receipts but also added revenues from home-video sales and contracts with pay and broadcast TV. Recently, Disney signed a five-year, $200 million deal giving Showtime/The Movie Channel cable rights to as many as 50 of its Touchstone films. While other studios spend an average of nearly $16 million per movie, Disney spends about $11 million. According to Eisner, "Our movie philosophy is to go for singles and doubles when we make our films. If you go for the home run all the time, you strike out a lot."[12]

Recently, Disney announced it will launch a new record division, tentatively named Hollywood Records. The company believes that by starting its own record operation it can develop new talent rather than engage in bidding wars for established artists. Disney is looking for "cutting-edge music, sold by word of mouth, not mass-produced," which it can bring into the music mainstream.[13]

Disney is also expanding its foreign presence. Mickey Mouse and Donald Duck are now prime-time stars on Chinese television. Tokyo Disneyland is doing a booming business, and although Disney holds no ownership interest in the theme park, it does receive royalties of 10 percent on admissions and 5 percent on sales. Disney does hold a 17 percent interest in the private consortium developing French Disneyland, a 4,500-acre theme park near Paris scheduled to open in 1992.[14]

Another company whose most valuable assets are its cartoon characters is DC Comics. Under the leadership of Jenette Kahn, DC Comics, like Disney, expanded the scope of its vision to overcome a languishing image and sagging sales and regain market leadership. Hired as DC's publisher in 1976, Kahn shared with DC's employees her vision and their shared challenge: to bring Superman into the 1970s. In 1981, as DC's new president, Kahn set about expanding the scope of her vision. She wanted the Man of Steel to be seen everywhere. She strengthened DC's licensing program, aggressively selling the rights to display the likenesses of Superman and other DC characters on products like T-shirts, container labels, and so on. DC published the first *DC Comics Super Healthy Cookbook,* in which Superman and other DC heroes urged children to eat healthy foods. In 1983, Superman peanut butter debuted on supermarket shelves. Then came Superman raisins, Super Hero cookies, and even Super Hero yogurt.[15]

Building Block #4: Visions with a Sense of History

Creating visions of companies as the competitive leaders of the future is a far more complex process when companies are mired in the uncompetitive routines of the present. Any uncompetitive routine is a mixture of positive activities that drive the organization and negative activities that restrain it. Although companies must remove the negative, restraining forces, they must not throw the baby out with the bathwater. Executives, therefore, must walk a fine line as they create visions that honor and retain elements that have made their companies great in the past and at the same time introduce the new elements needed for future greatness.

Michael Eisner has been very careful about retaining the magic that has always made Walt Disney Company unique while he creates some new magic of his own. Clearly, his vision of the future honors Disney's rich heritage. It is a vision that leans heavily on leveraging the company's existing assets, such as theme parks, hotels, movies, TV shows, and, of course, the Disney cast of animated characters. It is a vision of a sleeping giant waking up. Eisner is also leaving his own distinctive mark at Disney. Part of this vision addresses the fact that Disney's audience is growing up. His decision to produce movies with adult themes under the Touchstone label challenged the Disney big-screen tradition of offering only family entertainment. Producing television shows like *Golden Girls* has brought adult audiences to Disney on the small screen as well. Moreover, Eisner is taking Disney magic to places in the world, like China, that Walt himself never dreamed of.[16]

Another company that has created a new vision with a sense of history is Procter & Gamble. According to *Fortune,* Procter & Gamble had become a corporate Kremlin: bureaucratic, risk-averse, and arrogant. In the infamous soft-cookie wars of the early 1980s, the company's Duncan Hines division got burned by Nabisco. Orange Crush soft drinks never came close to competing in the same league as Coke and Pepsi and were finally sold in the spring of 1989. According to several analysts and former employees, most of Procter & Gamble's recent failures were directly attributable to the company's rigid adherence to tradition and the fact that it was out of touch with the rapidly changing business environment. As one former employee noted, "The biggest hang-up is that they don't let a lot of light in the window."[17]

But Procter & Gamble is changing, and in a way that preserves tradition while the company reinvents the packaged goods industry for the year 2000 and beyond. According to John Smale, the company's recently retired CEO, "We're [Procter & Gamble's management] not ancestor worshippers, but we do believe this company's culture is rooted very much in the past." Accordingly, Procter & Gamble blends the best of its past—a willingness to stay with long-term projects (it took Folgers 25 years to become the best-selling coffee in the United States), job security, and a history of promotion from within—with a more dynamic management style that calls for pushing responsibility down in the organization, speeding up decisions, and getting closer to customers.[18]

The most dramatic changes at Procter & Gamble involve the company's relationships with customers. The company used to treat retailers as tough, penny-pinching adversaries. But recently, Procter & Gamble switched from a product to a customer approach. Now teams from finance, distribution, manufacturing, and other areas are assigned to work with the bigger retailers, like Wal-Mart, Kroger, and American Stores. Wal-Mart, for example, worked with Procter & Gamble people in setting up a just-in-time ordering and delivery system. When Pampers or Luvs disposable diapers run low in a store, a computer sends an order by satellite to a company factory, which automatically ships an order of diapers directly to the outlet.[19]

ORGANIZATIONAL CURES FOR COMPETITIVE DISADVANTAGE

Companies with visions of themselves as competitive leaders know where they want to go, but they do not necessarily know how to get there. For companies with competitive disadvantages, however, the first step toward competitive leadership is obvious: They need to overcome their disadvantages. Like injured or sick patients, organizations are unlikely to realize their full potential until a cure is found for what ails them.

In his book *The Social Psychology of Organizing,* Karl Weick suggests that "believing is seeing,"[20] and it does seem obvious that the way executives perceive the competitive disadvantages they want to overcome is influenced by the conceptual frameworks they use to understand organizations. How do executives think about organizations? My experience with them tells me that they think about organizations in three different ways, depending on the level of organizational interdependence they believe exists—whether *pooled, serial,* or *reciprocal* interdependence.

Executives who think in terms of pooled interdependence see organizations as collections of strategic business units (SBUs), each contributing profits or losses to a corporate bottom line. Accordingly, competitive disadvantage is assumed to be based on having too many underperforming SBUs in the corporate strategic mix. The key to becoming a competitive leader, then, is to change the strategic mix by jettisoning some SBUs—the ones for which recovery seems hopeless—and fixing others. To accomplish this task, executives must establish a system of priorities, a process I like to call organizational triage. Then, organizations conduct reconstructive surgery on top-priority SBUs.

Executives who think in terms of serial interdependence see organizations as a series of inputs, throughputs, and outputs, with the final output being a marketable product or service. Given this view, competitive disadvantages are seen as bottlenecks in the process. Therefore, the key to becoming competitive leaders is eliminating the blockage or performing bypass surgery by opening new communication and action channels.

Finally, executives who think in terms of reciprocal interdependence see organizations as complex bureaucracies that are internally focused rather than outwardly directed toward customers. Bureaucracy is perceived as a growing cancer that is eating away the strength and vitality of the entire organization. Competitive disadvantages are seen everywhere in the form of inefficient structures, patterns of interaction, and organizational routines. Executives believe that overcoming these pervasive competitive disadvantages requires systemic treatments—an organizational chemotherapy. A little poison must be injected into the system to kill off the invading cancerous cells of bureaucracy.

Organizational Triage and Reconstructive Surgery

Triage is a hospital emergency room procedure used for the "sorting and allocation of treatment to patients according to a system of priorities designed to maximize the number of survivors." A triage physician will examine patients quickly to determine (1) who cannot be helped, (2) who should receive treatment first, and (3) who can wait for treatment. In organizational triage, the patients are SBUs. Executives conducting organizational triage determine what SBUs would require unreasonable amounts of resources to treat and therefore should be discontinued or divested; what SBUs should be fixed immediately; and what SBUs can be left alone, but may require treatment in the future when higher priority SBUs are healthier and more competitive.

Westinghouse used organizational triage to overcome the competitive disadvantages it had built up over decades of undermanaged acquired growth diversification. In 1975 the company was a misshapen conglomerate that was barely profitable, with only a 2.8 percent return on sales. Like a physician assigned to triage, the new chairman, Robert E. Kirby, assessed the situation and evaluated com-

pany resources. Light bulbs, cable television, and many other businesses were deemed beyond treatment and sold or dropped. Then
capital and resources were channeled into more promising businesses
to accelerate their growth.[21]

Triage continued under the direction of Kirby's successors. In
1988, for example, John Marous, Westinghouse's current CEO, sold
noncontributing businesses with $700 million in sales, including
Westinghouse elevators. Today, the company's remaining 75 business units are arranged in seven groups: industries (24 percent of
company sales); energy and utility systems (22 percent); electronic
systems (21 percent); Wesco (13 percent); commercial (9 percent);
financial services (6 percent); and broadcasting (5 percent).[22]

Selling off losers does not turn companies into competitive
leaders unless they perform reconstructive surgery to turn the remaining companies into winners. The reconstructive surgery Westinghouse performed was some of the world's best. About ten years
ago Westinghouse established its Productivity and Quality Center,
which *Fortune* describes as a SWAT team of some 130 computer gurus,
consultants, and engineers whose job is to help business units "do the
right things right the first time."[23]

A Westinghouse business unit can order a Total Quality Fitness
Review from the Center for all or part of its operation whenever it
wants. Team members from the Center conduct interviews with people at all levels of the organization and even survey customers. They
look for weaknesses in training, processes, and products, finding
ways to improve everything that goes into a product, from engineering to plant maintenance to billing. The results are translated onto a
Total Quality scorecard and presented to the unit manager. Then
Center team members assist managers in organizing teams to discover
and deploy improvements, and remain available to advise and measure results.[24]

Eliminating Blockages, or Bypass Surgery

My colleague, Bill Dyer, was asked by a company for some consulting help. The company was concerned because its productivity
had dropped suddenly and significantly. It had tried everything to
remedy the situation and had called Dyer mostly out of frustration.
Dyer's expertise was in team building, and, not surprisingly, he
diagnosed an organizational problem with a team-building solution.
He spent nearly a month with various work groups processing

problems and improving interactions, but the company showed no noticeable improvements. Then one day Dyer was walking around the shop floor and stopped to speak with a machine operator, who told Dyer that an important machine had been broken for several months and was the cause of the recent downturn in company performance. The operator explained that he had told several different supervisors about the broken machine but that nothing had been done about it.

Dyer determined that the company needed a traditional team-building solution—namely, improvements in communication between machine operators and supervisors. But that was a long-term solution to a long-term problem. Dyer realized that the immediate problem was the broken machine and the immediate solution was to eliminate the blockage it was causing. He reported it to senior management, it was fixed, and productivity returned to previous levels.

When executives think about organizations as a series of inputs, throughputs, and outputs, their principal focus is on getting products and services out the door faster. The point of Bill Dyer's story is that when productivity is slowed by a blockage, the most dramatic improvements in speed come from removing it.

When blockages cannot be identified or are difficult to remove, another alternative available to managers is organizational bypass surgery, which has a two-pronged effect. First, it increases speed, because organizational activity flows through many channels. Second, it increases flexibility. If one channel becomes blocked, there are others for getting the product or service out the door.

John Young, Hewlett-Packard's CEO, believes that speed is at the heart of strategy. The heart offers a useful metaphor: It can only pump blood as fast as it receives it. The logic behind organizational bypass surgery is that output is increased when inputs come from many sources all at the same time. Practically, what this means is that companies that employ flexible, multifunctional teams comprised of individuals from engineering, manufacturing, and marketing are always going to win the race against companies in which engineering, manufacturing, and marketing departments work independently, then throw products over the wall to one another.

Organizational Chemotherapy

Jack Welch, General Electric's controversial chairman, is sometimes called Neutron Jack because he eliminated well over 100,000 jobs through layoffs, attrition, and sales of businesses. After years of upheaval at GE, it is clear that Welch's draconian moves fit into a larger strategy to strengthen the company and make its remaining employees more secure, although not necessarily more comfortable. The target of Welch's moral fervor is the cancer of bureaucracy. He sees bureaucracy in the form of "cramping artifacts that pile up in the dusty attics of century-old companies: reports, meetings, rituals, approvals, and forests of paper that seem necessary until they are removed." Because Welch thinks bureaucracy has created competitive disadvantage everywhere at GE, he has opted for a systemic cure—something like organizational chemotherapy.[25]

Bureaucracy, according to Welch, is evil because it destroys productivity by distracting attention from useful work. Recently, Welch introduced a new program at GE called Work-Out to reduce bureaucratic distractions. The idea behind Work-Out is to get the heads of GE's 14 main business units to join with salaried employees in groups that identify then agree to eliminate unnecessary meetings, reports, approvals, and tasks. For example, through the Work-Out program, GE's medical systems' X-ray unit targeted 55 items for elimination or improvement.[26]

Welch believes that GE needs more leaders and fewer managers to win the battle against bureaucracy:

> Call people managers and they are going to start managing things, getting in the way. The job of a leader is to take the available resources—human and financial—and allocate them rigorously. Not to spread them out evenly, like butter on bread. That's what bureaucrats do. It takes courage and tough-mindedness to pick the bets, put the resources behind them, articulate the vision to the employees, and explain why you said yes to this one and no to that one.[27]

Under Welch's leadership, GE's earnings per share have risen an average of 7.6 percent a year, versus 4.9 percent under his predecessor, the well-respected Reginald H. Jones. Moreover, productivity has grown steadily throughout the 1980s, from 2.5 percent in 1980 to 4.5 percent in 1988. Although it has taken many years of chemotherapy to make a difference in the world's tenth-largest industrial corporation, GE's bureaucratic cancer is definitely showing signs of being in remission. But the challenge continues. Bureaucratic cancer is highly resistant and requires ongoing treatment to prevent reoccurrence. According to *Fortune,* Welch's "ideas and the force he is willing to put behind them—stressing competitive power and changing the bureaucratic character—put him on the leading edge of the art of management."[28]

EMPOWERING PEOPLE

Organizational cures convert visions into concrete action plans. The success of such cures is contingent on the number of managers and workers who can make things happen. A company can only move as fast as it develops people to move it. This is why empowering people is so critical to overcoming competitive disadvantage and gaining competitive leadership.

The ideas behind empowering people all stem from the definition of power Rosabeth Kanter coined in her 1977 book, *Men and Women of the Corporation*. Kanter saw power in strictly utilitarian terms. She defined it as "the ability to get things done, to mobilize resources, to get and use whatever it is that a person needs" to accomplish organizational goals. Kanter also wrote that "when more people are empowered—that is, allowed to have control over the conditions that make their actions possible—then more is accomplished, more gets done."[29] According to Kanter, when people are empowered, the performances of entire organizations are lifted because more people have access to tools for action.

My colleague, Reba Keele, defines empowered individuals as "workers who choose to accept responsibility for their own behavior and its impact on organization success," but mostly focuses on how organizations empower people. According to Keele, an empowering organization "removes the barriers in the organization which make it difficult for individuals to assume responsibility for organizational success." In other words, empowering organizations *enable* power to be exercised through the creation of liberating organizational forms and capital investments in enabling technologies.

In order to empower people, the individual capabilities needed to accomplish organizational goals must be developed. Thus, skill training and feedback about performance are necessary factors in the creation of an empowered work force. Employees must also have reasons for what they do. They need to be motivated to exercise power. Accordingly, trust must exist so people believe they will be treated fairly, and rewards should be structured to encourage people to accept responsibility for organizational success (see Figure 8-2).

Together, these six factors—liberating organizational forms,

Figure 8–2. Factors for Empowering People in Organizations.

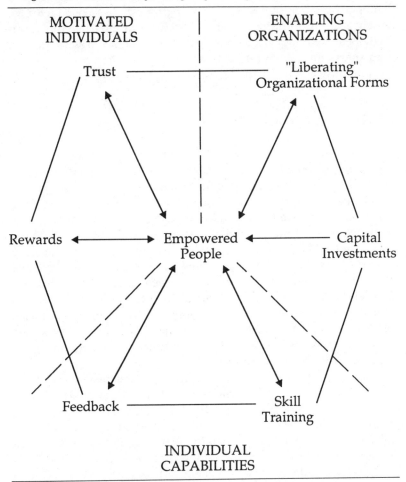

MOTIVATED
INDIVIDUALS

ENABLING
ORGANIZATIONS

Trust ——————————— "Liberating"
Organizational Forms

Rewards ←————→ Empowered ←———— Capital
People Investments

Feedback ——————— Skill
Training

INDIVIDUAL
CAPABILITIES

capital investments, skill learning, feedback, rewards, and trust—
create empowering organizations. They form a seamless garment, in
that no factor is more important than another and all are necessary
to provide the desired effect. For example, clearly a new profit-sharing plan—an empowering reward system—would have little effect
on employee motivation in companies where outdated equipment
imposes insurmountable barriers to profitability. Moreover, these six
factors are a lot like nuts and bolts holding tires on a car. We tighten

up one factor as much as seems appropriate before we move to tighten up another. But once we have tightened the second factor we can always return to the first and tighten it further. Therefore, even though empowering people may be construed as a step-wise process, companies achieve better results when each step is completed many times to ensure that all the factors are tightened together.

Liberating Organizational Forms

Jack Welch remarked that "the idea of liberation and empowerment for our work force is not enlightenment—it's a competitive necessity."[30] Liberating organizational forms empower people by providing them with the appropriate balance of freedom and form. Often, competitive disadvantages develop when companies grow too large for people to see how individual performance affects organizational performance. When this happens, people are psychologically removed from the discipline of competition. Also, the complexity of large organizations limits individual freedom as people concern themselves more with how their behavior affects someone else than with getting something done. Accordingly, restructuring programs at companies like IBM, Procter & Gamble, and Du Pont have focused on making business units smaller to increase autonomy and push responsibility down the ranks.

At Du Pont, one of the side effects of restructuring has been a more innovative, entrepreneurial organization. Empowered individuals have created new businesses that have taken Du Pont into new, lucrative markets. The story of how Jay Daigle, a production worker, and Mal Smith, a research chemist, created a new business with potential annual sales of $200 million illustrates this process.

Daigle decided to raise crayfish part-time to provide some extra income for himself and his family. Raising them took a lot more time than he originally expected because none of the crayfish baits available on the market lasted more than a few hours. He constantly needed to reset his traps. This problem, however, gave Daigle an idea: Why couldn't Du Pont's polymer technology be used as a binder to make crayfish bait last longer? Daigle contacted Mal Smith to help him with his idea.

Smith thought Daigle's idea had merit, but he decided to bootleg the project rather than clear it with his supervisor. New policies at Du Pont encouraging scientists to pursue their own ideas on company time allowed Smith the freedom to experiment with different

concoctions in the lab. And Daigle and Smith continued to get encouraging results as they tested the new crayfish baits.

Once Smith and Daigle had developed a bait that lasted five to
seven days under a variety of conditions, they finally shared the idea
with Smith's supervisor and others at Du Pont. Initially, people were
skeptical. But when Smith and Daigle explained that the popularity
of Cajun cooking had created a tremendous demand for crayfish and
discussed the size of the potential market for the bait, people started
to get interested. Smith and Daigle were given funding and permis-
sion to form a team to pursue the project.

After several months of field-testing the product, Smith and
Daigle approached Du Pont's Agricultural Products Group to propose that they market the bait. But the Agricultural Products Group
concluded that crayfish bait did not fit into its product line. This
forced Smith and Daigle to pursue an alternative path. They made
large quantities of the bait and began giving it away to crayfish
farmers. This created demand, and word that farmers badly wanted
the bait eventually came back through Du Pont's sales representatives to the Agricultural Products Group. Then people from the Agricultural Products Group approached Smith and Daigle and asked to
join the team. The success of Du Pont's long-lasting crayfish bait has
led to the development of new baits using polymer technology for
the crab and lobster industries. Du Pont's liberating organizational
form enabled the idea of one empowered employee to be nourished
and grow into a huge new business opportunity for the company.

Capital Investment

Capital investments empower people for two reasons. First, they
level the playing field. Ownership of Kennecott Utah Copper
changed hands several times because even though the Bingham Canyon mine offered one of the world's richest sources of copper, molyb-
denum, platinum, selenium, gold, and silver, it could not turn a profit.
The company's outdated technology increased mining costs, putting
it at a serious competitive disadvantage against foreign producers.[31]

When BP Minerals acquired Kennecott, however, it committed
to fund a $400 million modernization effort that included the instal-
lation of in-pit ore crushing and the construction of new grinding and
flotation facilities, which transformed the Bingham Canyon mine
into one to the lowest-cost mining operations in the world. Because
the technological barriers to its success have been removed, Ken-

necott's empowered work force can compete effectively in the world copper market.[32]

Second, capital investments are empowering because they build employee commitment. Several factors have contributed to Basic Manufacturing and Technologies of Utah's (BM&T's) dramatic turnaround of the Geneva Steel Plant, such as shifts in world currency rates and lower administrative costs. But the plant's highly committed work force has driven the transformation from outdated steel mill to world-class manufacturer. For example, when the Geneva plant reopened, workers agreed to a 50-cent per hour wage reduction and cancellation of union work rules. Empowered workers also found all kinds of ways to cut costs, increase production, and boost sales.[33]

Geneva's work force, however, would never have risen to the occasion if BM&T had not demonstrated its long-term commitment by investing heavily in plant improvements. BM&T recently hired a consulting firm to develop a strategic plan that includes a wish list of further improvements. According to its strategic plan, BM&T invested around $6 million in a computer system to process steel orders automatically. High on the list of future improvements is the purchase of continuous slab technology that will enable BM&T to produce and market steel to U.S. automobile manufacturers.[34]

Skill Training

Because it increases their perceived probability of being successful, skill training also empowers people. People who possess necessary skills are confident that if they work hard they can accomplish organizational goals. As long as they continue to accomplish those goals, their companies will overcome competitive disadvantages and become competitive leaders.

At Caterpillar, changes in technology have required workers to return to the classroom. Workers are encouraged and expected to learn about product engineering, workplace layout, and quality improvement.[35] Other skills important for empowered workers to learn include the use of statistical tools, problem solving, value engineering, and team building.

Not only does skill training empower people, but only empowered people develop new skills. The empowering process, therefore, is reciprocal. In their book *Dynamic Manufacturing: Creating the Learning Organization,* Hayes, Wheelwright, and Clark propose that manufacturing technology is changing so rapidly that long-term optimal solutions no longer exist. Although there are clearly better ways of doing things, factories are simply too complicated and dynamic to seek a single right way. Therefore, skills training must be an ongoing process, driven by empowered workers, in which learning by doing is a crucial component. According to Hayes, Wheelwright, and Clark, "The key to high productivity is felt to be constant improvement, not the rigorous determination of some optimal 'best practice.' As a consequence, workers are involved directly in redefining the plant layout, how individual tasks and departments are organized, production processes, and their own roles."[36]

Feedback

Going head-to-head against competition has little effect on companies unless the people in the trenches know both what they are up against and how they are doing. Accordingly, communication is an important part of empowering people. Xerox, as part of its formal employee-involvement program, practices what it calls competitive benchmarking. The company studies competitors worldwide in areas such as productivity and marketing prowess, then dares its employees to match them. Then the company provides ongoing information about progress. The resulting improvements in communication at Xerox have made everyone's work more meaningful and have provided the feedback necessary to improve both individual and organizational capability.[37]

At Rockwell International's Missile Systems Division (MSD), tracking and measurement is a critical part of the equation for continuous improvement. MSD's management believes that tracking and measurement removes the arbitrariness from organizational change efforts. It is clear when positive change does and does not occur. People also learn when their performance is tracked and measured. They see how using different approaches to solving a problem lead to different performance outcomes helping them refine the approaches they use; they are psychologically rewarded each time performance improves and punished when it does not. Thus, tracking and measurement subtly shapes employee behavior in positive ways. Finally, MSD's people become empowered because tracking and measurement enables them to assume greater responsibility for their performance and how that performance affects the division's performance.

Feedback, of course, is a two-way street. Empowered people

share information freely up, down, and laterally in organizations. The intellectual roughhousing that Jack Welch encourages at General Electric is part of a conscious strategy to build self-confidence in people at all levels of the organization. Welch expects his subordinates to open up to him just as he expects their subordinates to open up to them. He is constantly bypassing the bureaucracy to communicate directly with employees and encourages employees to communicate directly with him. The goal at GE is to have information flowing in every direction so all employees know how their performance affects others and how the performance of others affects them.

Trust

The challenge of overcoming competitive disadvantages and gaining competitive leadership provides a unique opportunity to renegotiate contracts between management and workers. Most organizational contracts require complete overhauls if they are to provide the level of trust necessary to build and sustain an empowered work force. The kind of contractual arrangement organizations intent on building this requisite trust need appears to be present in relational contracts.

Oliver Williamson, a Yale University institutional economist and the author of the 1975 classic, *Market and Hierarchies,* contrasts classical contracting and relational contracting and discusses the obvious benefits of the latter. Classical contracts emphasize discretion and comprehensiveness. They do not concern themselves with identities of the parties involved, but carefully define the nature of the agreement and possible contingencies and narrowly prescribe remedies. The intent of classical contracting is to leave nothing open-ended. Conversely, relational contracts place less emphasis on an original agreement and more on the identities of the people involved and their relationship. The questions of greatest importance are these: What is the character of the other party? Is the other party trustworthy? Will he or she deal fairly?[38]

How do organizations develop relational contracts between management and workers? They start talking. This is not always easy, because managers and workers invariably form two separate cultures and scarcely ever talk to each other. But as Robert Mahoney, CEO of Diebold, the maker of automatic teller machines and bank vaults, said, "A basic adversary environment doesn't wash if you want to be a competitive global organization." Diebold has set up a committee of managers, supervisors, and hourly workers. According to Mahoney, "They meet once a week, prioritize an agenda, solve problems together. These employees really know what we need to do to improve product quality, reduce scrap, become more efficient."[39]

Recently, there has been a growing realization that offensive strategies can neither deal with the uncertainty nor match the complexity of the business environments most companies operate in. Renewed importance has been given to how people implement offensive strategies throughout organizations. Empowered people are really at the center of all offensive strategies, especially ones to overcome disadvantages and gain competitive leadership. Relational contracts both enlist support and liberate people in organizations. They promote the flexibility and responsiveness among people that companies need to compete successfully in the global economy. Accordingly, many companies are returning to basic values, such as trust, fairness, mutual respect, unity, and caring in order to build relational contracts with their people.

Rewards

In response to new competitive realities, many companies are changing their reward systems. Most of these changes place more of each employee's pay at risk, and they link that pay more closely to performance. Incentive pay makes companies more competitive because while it induces workers to produce more, it also holds down wage and wage-related benefits and allows compensation to rise and fall with a company's fortunes. Incentive pay also encourages worker empowerment because with the better plans workers control their own destinies—how well they perform determines how much they earn.

Empowered employees also influence reward systems. They contribute to their designs, then ensure that only factors critical to company performance continue to be rewarded. They also make demands about the kinds of information about performance they need to raise consciousness about the reward system. At Carrier, a subsidiary of United Technologies, for example, employee initiatives led to the daily posting of plant productivity information.[40]

Many companies intent on overcoming competitive disadvantages and becoming competitive leaders have visited and learned from Lincoln Electric, a manufacturer of industrial electric motors and welding equipment headquartered in Cleveland, Ohio. Since 1934, Lincoln has rewarded workers on a piecework basis: For each acceptable piece they produce, employees receive so many dollars. Workers also receive annual merit ratings, based on their dependability, ideas, quality, and output, that serve as the basis for year-end bonuses. Employee bonuses average 97.6 percent of regular earnings, and the payoff to Lincoln has been 54 years without a losing quarter and a work force that is up to three times more productive than counterparts in similar manufacturing settings.[41]

Although it is difficult to argue against tying pay to performance, it is sometimes hard to do when companies are attempting to recover from competitive disadvantages. Companies often need time to get back on their feet before they implement gainsharing programs. They need their employees to make short-term sacrifices. Alan Wilkins and William Ouchi account for this possibility by proposing a distinction between specific equity and general equity. Specific equity requires that a company's inducements and employee contributions always be in balance; general equity exists when people believe that in the long run their companies will deal with them fairly. In other words, general equity requires trust but also provides for greater flexibility in the distribution of employee rewards than does specific equity.[42]

General equity, however, only works when companies acknowledge their debt to employees and repay the debt as soon as competitive disadvantages are overcome. Lee Iacocca, in spite of his legendary successes, seriously hampered Chrysler's turnaround efforts because he did not understand this important concept. When Chrysler was on the ropes and trying to get massive federal loan guarantees, one of the government's stipulations was that the company gain wage concessions from the United Auto Workers (UAW). UAW representatives were allowed to examine Chrysler's books and, realizing that they had no choice, agreed to accept wage concessions. As a symbol of a new era of cooperation between the UAW and Chrysler, UAW President Douglas Fraser, was appointed to Chrysler's board of directors.

With the help of Chrysler's newly empowered work force, Iacocca paid off the company's federally guaranteed loans early and was able to claim to the public and the government that Chrysler was back on its feet. UAW officials then approached Chrysler's top management and requested a new contract. Now that Chrysler was healthy, the union argued, it was time to pay back the workers for the sacrifices they had made on the company's behalf. But Chrysler's top management balked at the union's request, claiming that the company was not ready to grant such concessions.

By refusing to share rewards from the company's turnaround, Chrysler's top management unempowered its work force and broke the fragile bonds of trust formed between the union and management. Fraser resigned from Chrysler's board, and the union threatened to strike, signaling a return to the old-line policy of union-management confrontation.

IMPROVISING OFFENSIVE STRATEGIES

Jack Welch's favorite management thinker is Helmulth von Moltke, a Prussian general who served as military adviser to the Ottoman court. According to Welch, "Von Moltke believed strategy was not a lengthy action plan, but rather the evolution of a central idea through continually changing circumstances."[43] In other words, von Moltke believed in an improvised offensive strategy. His influence is clearly seen in the way Welch operates at GE. He has a core vision of GE's businesses being number one or number two in their industries and improvises a unique, dynamic offensive strategy to fulfill his vision.

Improvising offensive strategies creates other advantages. My colleague, Gene Dalton, argues that improvisation helps people make something their own. They internalize a strategy when guidelines are general enough that they are forced to improvise specific actions. Accordingly, the strategy is both amplified and integrated into people's existing thought patterns.[44]

Ray Smith, a talented jazz musician, said that "while jazz improvisation puts the musician in direct contact with creating, you can't create something from nothing. Creation is more a process of *organizing* preexisting matter."[45] Applied to offensive strategy, we see that improvisation provides a way for bringing together diverse opportunities in creative combinations. It is an organizing process and a form of art in which intrinsic rewards are tied to the creative spark deep within us.

Improvised offensive strategies are also spontaneous. They are a lot like a statement made by Ross Perot before his well-publicized separation agreement with General Motors. He said, "Revitalizing GM is like teaching an elephant to tap dance. You find the sensitive spots and start poking."[46] As executives poke at their organizations, however, four things are important to remember.

First, it is essential to keep things simple by maintaining a focus. IBM Chairman and CEO John Akers, commenting on his company's lapse from greatness, explained, "We took our eye off the ball." The ball Akers referred to was IBM's customers and their changing tastes. IBM had always been a service-oriented company intent on staying close to customers, but during the mid-1980s it became distracted by the goal of growing into a $100 billion company by 1990. IBM's people started swinging for home runs and took their eyes off the ball. Accordingly, they missed the shift in customers' tastes away from large mainframe computers toward networks of smaller, more powerful machines, and growth in earnings slipped into single digits. What did Akers do to regain focus? He declared that 1987 would be "the year of the customer" and launched a series of programs to bring users in to test their reactions to new IBM products during their design and introduction stages.[47]

Second, companies need to keep competing offensively to stay in touch with their changing business environments. Over the past five years the F. W. Woolworth Company has been literally raised from the dead, transforming itself from a variety store to a specialty merchant that sells in a variety of stores. How did Woolworth do it? According to Harold Sells, Woolworth's CEO, "Shopping malls are our laboratory, where we do our research and development." The company is always encouraging its division managers to dream up new specialty store ideas or to scout out small acquisitions that have big potential. Whenever a division manager comes up with a prospect, the company bankrolls the opening of a few test stores. Says Sells, "We'll open a couple of stores the first year, and if they look good we'll open ten the second year. Then, if we've got a firm feeling we're on solid ground with our concept, we explode it." In 1988, Woolworth improvised its way toward competition by opening 1,100 new stores.[48]

Third, because many offensive strategies are improvised simultaneously, it is important to keep lateral communication channels open. At IBM, for example, a conscious attempt has been made to have business heads resolve disputes among themselves rather than send them up the hierarchy. This has enhanced the flexibility and speed of the decision-making process and has also reduced time wasted in political maneuvering.[49]

The so-called Monday Notes adopted under Werner von Braun's leadership at NASA's Marshall Space Flight Center were originally designed as a tool to improve vertical communications, but they also enhanced lateral communications between improvising groups. Von Braun asked two dozen of his managers to send him a weekly, one-page note summarizing their week's progress and problems. There was no form to be filled out. The only requirements were that the note could be no more than one page and it had to be headed by the date and the name of the contributor. As Von Braun read each note he handwrote a considerable amount of marginalia. Then the annotated notes were reproduced and returned as a package to all of the contributors. The Monday Notes became the most diligently read documents at the space center. By reading the notes, managers knew what their counterparts had been up to and up against. The discipline of writing Monday Notes also prompted several managers to request Friday notes from their subordinates to keep track of progress, share information, and coordinate their improvised work.[50]

Finally, companies that improvise offensive strategies to become competitive leaders assume that there's always a better way. At Du Pont, top executives devised a program called Individual Career Management to institutionalize "there's always a better way" thinking. The program involves a series of discussions that determine how well managers fulfilled specific job requirements during the previous year, what the managers' new goals should be, and whether managers have stretched the boundaries of their jobs. Then, discussions turn to the individual manager's career path. Again, the purpose of the process is to set specific goals and to make the goals as challenging as possible. According to John Hines, Du Pont's vice president of employee relations, "There must be continued improvement. With the kinds of global competition we all face, you have to ask people to continue looking at their jobs in new ways."[51]

At another multinational corporation, new recruits attend an introductory meeting with senior managers. At the end of the meeting the new employees are invited to attend lunch in the company cafeteria. Before entering the cafeteria each employee is handed a small three-by-five-inch card and told to examine the cafeteria operations and, at the conclusion of lunch, to write down at least one suggestion for improving them. This early message to new employees comes through loud and clear: "From the day you begin work in this company we want you to pay attention, to always be on the lookout for ways to make things better."[52]

9 Regaining Competitive Leadership from the Japanese

Ross Perot surrounds himself with symbols that communicate what is great about America. For example, he used to keep Norman Rockwell's *Homecoming Marine* in his office to remind visitors from GM that Americans used to beat the Japanese quite regularly. As Perot realized, the parallels between the Second World War and today's economic war with Japan are striking. Japan surprised the United States in the mid-1970s, not because its economic attack was as sudden as its military attack on Pearl Harbor, but because U.S. companies refused to heed the many warnings. The United States was the same sleeping giant it was at the beginning of the War in the Pacific.

America's self-image was shattered by Japan's initial economic victories. U.S. companies had never expected the Japanese to challenge their global dominance. They did not know exactly how to respond, and, accordingly, they stumbled around at first. But just as U.S. forces did fighting in the Pacific, U.S. companies are gradually learning how to compete against the Japanese. One by one they are going on the attack, and a few companies are actually regaining competitive leadership from the Japanese.

3M is a U.S. company that responded more quickly than most to the Japanese challenge. In the early 1970s, 3M's Scotch brand audio tapes were the recording tape industry's standard. But within five years, Japanese producers, such as Maxell and TDK, had stolen much of 3M's market share. By 1982, 3M, the industry pioneer, had virtually walked away from the audio tape market.[1]

At 3M losing a battle has never meant losing the war. 3M's

management and workers matter-of-factly agreed that enough was enough and made a decision to outcompete the Japanese. In the videotape market, 3M became the aggressor, bent on knocking the Japanese from their dominant position through innovation, efficient manufacturing, and aggressive price cutting. 3M even decided to compete directly against the Japanese in Japan. The company now claims a significant market share in Japan's videotape market and vows to be number one.[2]

What did 3M do to regain competitive leadership from the Japanese? First, the company named as head of its Memory Technologies Group a man who had spent six years in Japan. It also departed from its historic practice of refusing to fund ventures that do not measure up to its standard of returns. Instead, the company tried to position everything with the long term in mind. It spent funds to upgrade and increase capacity at existing facilities, built brand loyalty by providing a whole line of high-quality videotapes, and capitalized on its strengths, particularly its wide distribution system. Finally, the company spared no expense in marketing. For example, it advertised its cassettes during top sporting events and mailed a raft of circulars to people who claimed refunds on its long-standing rebate campaign.[3]

3M's success in the videotape market has given it a new confidence. Many people, both inside and outside the company, believe that the Japanese are becoming demoralized and disillusioned in the market for half-inch videotape. The widely held opinion at 3M is that competing against the Japanese in any market is not a problem.[4]

Other stories, like 3M's, tell of U.S. companies deciding to go head-to-head to regain competitive leadership from Japanese competitors. When companies decide not to retreat but to go on the offensive, they usually find ways to compete against any competitor. Like the Japanese have done so many times in this country, U.S. companies establish a beachhead, then expand out. They approach competition like players of arcade games: They play at one level of competition, and each time they win they move to a higher level. Eventually they lose, but each time they lose they gain new strengths. Finally, they become strong enough to regain competitive leadership.

James Fallows, an editor for *The Atlantic* and author of *More Like Us: Making America Great Again,* understands the American way of doing business, a way based on fairness and possibility. U.S. companies are able to invent new ways to compete, just as people in our society are able to invent new lives for themselves. According to Fallows, the flexibility inherent in our society is our ultimate weapon against Asian economies. The United States may lack a sense of order and discipline, but it compensates for these deficiencies with sheer energy.[5] This is why the United States, the sleeping giant, initially stumbled around but eventually defeated the Japanese in the Second World War. It is also why many U.S. companies will ultimately prevail in the present economic battle with Japan.

Although U.S. companies should be confident about taking on the Japanese, they should not be overconfident. My father likes to tell a story about his first experience with a Japanese company. In the mid-1960s he was the chief financial officer for a large retail buying organization. At the time foreign companies were just beginning to compete in the United States against U.S. manufacturers. My father's company had a large shoe warehouse located on Eleventh Avenue in New York City that was filled with American-made shoes. The company, however, was interested in doing business with both Italian and Japanese shoemakers. A buyer, who was noted for his frugality, was sent to Japan to assess their shoe manufacturing capability. The buyer visited one company and was guided through a warehouse full of athletic shoes. He was impressed by what he saw and decided to place an order for 3,000 pairs of one style of athletic shoe. But the buyer's frugal nature forced him to pick a sample pair of shoes with a slight defect in the heel so as not to waste a good pair. Then, he instructed the Japanese supplier to produce 3,000 pairs of the sample shoe. Months later the order arrived at the warehouse. All 3,000 pairs of shoes were duplicated exactly like the sample pair, including the same flaw in every heel.

Japanese companies have always gone to amazing lengths to be responsive to their customers. When at first they don't succeed, they try, try again. As Andrew Grove, the president of Intel, the semiconductor maker, said, "I never laugh at anything Japanese. They never give up."[6] Just like the Japanese came back from the devastation of the Second World War, they will continue to come back to challenge the leadership of U.S. companies. Therefore, once U.S. companies regain competitive leadership, they cannot afford to fall asleep. Grove also said, "The price of leadership is eternal paranoia."[7]

THREE OFFENSIVE STRATEGIES FOR REGAINING COMPETITIVE LEADERSHIP

All of the many offensive strategies for regaining competitive leadership seem to fall into three categories. Some companies gain competitive leadership by playing the underdog. They go up against competitors that are bigger and stronger, and then, as in judo, they use their competitors' weight against them. Other companies regain competitive leadership by mounting comebacks. They draw on proud traditions, then battle upstart competitors. Finally, companies also manage successful turnarounds. These are usually companies that have developed uncompetitive routines by avoiding competition. Under new management they go on the offensive to develop new strengths from head-to-head competition.

Playing the Underdog

Playing the underdog is an offensive strategy with some unique advantages and disadvantages. One advantage is that there is something inspirational about being an underdog. David is a noble figure charging at Goliath; so is the tortoise racing against the hare or Rocky Balboa fighting Apollo Creed. People will overachieve when their company competes against another that has a clear advantage. It is a situation that provides an unmistakable focus—at least as long as people believe that some chance for success exists.

The inherent danger associated with playing the underdog is that people will realize they are hopelessly overmatched. If and when this happens, the company's best people will jump ship first, further damaging the morale of the people left behind. The company will tend to splinter apart out of a sense of helplessness. Cooperation will evaporate, as everyone waits for the ship to sink.

Micron Technology was at an incredible competitive disadvantage in 1985 when Japanese producers began to dump memory chips on the U.S. market. What is remarkable about Micron's story is that it developed no bunker mentality. Nobody said, "Let's hunker down and try to survive." The company knew that it was facing an immense challenge, but instead of retrenching, it went on the attack.[8]

Joseph Parkinson, Micron's CEO, created a vision of Micron thriving in adversity. He not only refused to give up, he set the company's sights on lofty goals. About Micron's offensive strategy, Parkinson remarked:

> By committing to a survival strategy, you cut everything that doesn't directly contribute to the product going out the door. But you're just postponing the inevitable. It's true that we were intensely focused on cutting costs, which is a survival tactic. But we also continued improving the product, broadening our customer base, innovating new prod-

ucts. That costs money. But that's the only way to play the game—play it to *win*. I'm not interested in survival, not at all.[9]

What did Micron Technology do first? It laid off half its work force. The company went from 1,400 down to 700 people. The cuts were made across the board—supervisors cut operators, managers cut supervisors, and so on. In Parkinson's words, Micron cut down to the "core group"—the people the company needed to come back, the ones most committed to the company, who were needed to make its underdog strategy work. Micron wanted people who would work any shift and do any job, and the core group was it. The company also wanted to get the damage done to morale by putting its layoffs behind it. According to Parkinson, "We told them [Micron's core group], 'This is the crew, this is the boat. We're going to either make it or sink together.' "[10]

Everyone in the core group was asked to take at least a 10 percent cut in pay. Micron eliminated pension plans, life, disability, and dental insurance, and reduced medical and vision coverage. The company further reduced payroll outlays by selling stock to employees from a million-share pool on a payroll-deduction plan that allowed employees to purchase stock with up to 25 percent of their salaries.[11]

Micron Technology, however, refused to cut back in areas that might affect its image. It shut down one of its production lines, but everything else was highly maintained. The company continued to add equipment; it reworked fabrication plants and upgraded its air handling. It even maintained outside service contracts. According to Parkinson, Micron needed to do all the little things to show people that it had a future.

Moreover, Micron kept its R and D people working. While the company was down, the R and D staff developed a new generation of 256K DRAMs (dynamic random-access memory chips). Other people were deployed on the problem of cutting manufacturing costs. According to Parkinson:

> The speed, the performance, the quality of our products—all the decisions for which we're given credit today—are the outcomes of those dark days. It's what comes with being threatened. We learned to squeeze the last ounce of production from the people we kept on board. . . . But remember, we had a great advantage. We had an enemy, and we were sworn to prevail over that enemy, not just to survive the battle. That was our war cry, and we took it everywhere. We had

meetings with all the employees, frequent meetings. Everyone would get all excited. They were like rallies, like revival meetings. . . . The trick is, I think, to manage the situation somehow so that it *does* bring out the best in people. And I think it's a matter of persuading people that they can have an effect on their own destinies.[12]

Besides winning its legal battle against Japanese chipmakers, Micron Technology signed a long-term deal with Intel Corporation in the spring of 1988. The company expects to add 1,000 new employees to its work force by the spring of 1990, and during the fiscal quarter ending February 1988, Micron reported net earnings of $16.9 million on sales of $58 million. In short, the underdog won.

Vanport Manufacturing, a small lumber company located 30 miles outside of Portland, Oregon, played the underdog as it went up against Japanese competitors in Japan. Why was Vanport able to penetrate Japanese markets when bigger, stronger U.S. companies have so often failed? Because it was willing to learn about Japan's customer tastes and to adjust to them. It also received a great deal of help from its Japanese competitors, who believed it was too small to threaten them.

Adolf Hertrich, Vanport's co-owner and CEO, began his conquest of the Japanese finished lumber market with a vision. Federal regulations prohibiting the cutting of whole logs from national forests for shipment to Japan jeopardized the company's future. Hertrich realized that Vanport's future depended on selling finished lumber to Japanese lumbermen and construction firms. But his vision would become a reality only if the company could satisfy Japan's finicky customers by cutting lumber to exacting traditional Japanese specifications. According to Hertrich the decision was simple: "We could go out of business, or we could remodel our sawmill to meet their needs."[13]

Hertrich traveled extensively throughout Japan, meeting with potential customers and inspecting the facilities of their Japanese lumber suppliers. He took pictures and careful notes wherever he went. When he returned to Oregon, he began to redesign his mill from head saw to edger to trim saw. Vanport's log carriage was computerized to accommodate metric measurements. Most important, Japanese specialists instructed company supervisors on the complex lumber-grading systems that are based on such aesthetic factors as color and graining.[14]

It took Hertrich and his people two years before they were finally confident that they could impress potential Japanese customers. To make their point, they built a traditional Japanese guest house from their own lumber and invited overseas guests to spend the night there.[15]

Vanport's strategy has paid handsome dividends. Today, while many local mills lay idle, its 170 nonunion workers labor at double shifts. Sales in 1986 reached $27 million, 90 percent of which are destined to Japan, and the company is consistently profitable.[16]

WordPerfect Corporation of Orem, Utah, uses still another underdog strategy to challenge the Japanese. WordPerfect appointed a development director, then opened an office in Japan in 1987 to study the idiosyncracies and oddities of the Japanese market. The main problem for WordPerfect in Japan, of course, is how to develop word processing software for two- to three-bit characters. The stakes are extremely high, not only because of the huge Japanese market, but because a word processing capability with two- to three-bit characters also opens up China and Korea to WordPerfect. But even without a Japanese translation of its product to sell, WordPerfect has found a way to break even in Japan. An English version of WordPerfect for the IBM PC is selling well in Japan because of the large number of multinational companies with operations there. WordPerfect will soon introduce a new version of its program for NEC, the best-selling computer in Japan. Although WordPerfect's main goal is to develop a bilingual, Japanese-English version, the company is able to continue to operate in Japan and strengthen its ties with both Japanese and multinational customers because it found a problem in the Japanese market it already had a solution for.[17]

Mounting Comebacks

Companies mount comebacks to regain the positions of leadership they held in the past. In other words, former competitive leaders come back by challenging the reigning competitive leaders, who, in many cases, are the Japanese. Many U.S. corporate giants that went to sleep after many years without competition are now waking up to challenge the Japanese. They are formulating offensive strategies to reclaim the leads they lost.

Companies that mount comebacks try to build on the fundamental business practices that worked for them in the past. In many respects, comebacks involve rediscovering the past more than looking into the future. Companies retain the same management teams because an understanding of a company's history and traditions is essential to mounting a successful comeback strategy. Top managers try to return their companies to their glory days by blending the lessons of the past with new competitive realities.

Caterpillar, the heavy equipment manufacturer, used to be able to push, crush, or roll over just about any company that got in its way. Its competitors were too weak to mount a serious challenge to it. Clearly, Caterpillar was king of the mountain, and top management assumed that almost everything was right and very little wrong with internal operations. Then in 1982, Caterpillar suddenly came tumbling down. Oil and other commodity prices plummeted, killing the demand for mining, logging, and pipe-laying equipment. The Japanese began to attack. Caterpillar's blue-collar workers went on strike for seven months, and company losses from 1982 through 1984 totaled $953 million.[18]

But Caterpillar fought its way back. Unlike the Big Three U.S. automakers, Caterpillar never turned out shoddy products. Its machines had set the world standard for decades. Its pride in workmanship gave it something to rebuild on. Its people were still proud of the coat of yellow paint that identified the heavy equipment their company produced.[19]

Caterpillar's products, however, were costly. The company had become vulnerable to attacks by competitors because it had experienced 50 years of nothing but success. It had rarely bothered to cut costs in the past because most of its big-ticket products, like the mammoth D10 tractor with a sticker price of more than half a million dollars, practically sold themselves.[20]

When Komatsu, the Japanese heavy equipment manufacturer, began underselling Caterpillar by as much as 40 percent in the early 1980s, Caterpillar did not retreat. It fought relentlessly to protect its market share. It went on the offensive by cutting prices heavily in its markets around the world. Then the company had to learn how to drive internal costs down. When its situation began to improve, the company did not return to business as usual. I stayed on the offensive by holding down prices, driving costs down, and improving its already vaunted quality.[21]

Caterpillar is also broadening its markets. With its new Century Line, a family of low-end machines ranging from excavators to tractors, Caterpillar is trying to attract a whole new category of consumer—the small-scale owner-operators who build houses, repair roads, and install sewers. The company is also selling a new backhoe loader and the Challenger 65 tractor, an odd-looking contraption with rubber tracks banded around rubber wheels that uses technology Caterpillar tried unsuccessfully to sell to the Pentagon for a mobile missile launcher.[22]

What is Caterpillar's vision of the future? The company's immediate response to the Japanese challenge was to close factories and reduce payrolls. But that was only the beginning. The company phased in a hierarchy-busting reorganization of its entire work force, then invested heavily in modernizing all of its 36 million square feet of factory space to develop Plants with a Future, which involves a total remake of the company's tooling and manufacturing methods.

Caterpillar's strategy was simple. First, its executives studied world-class manufacturers to learn everything they could for mounting a comeback. They traveled the world studying the modernization methods of other companies. Then, with the vision of Plants with a Future in place, Caterpillar shot past its former teachers to regain competitive leadership.[23]

Caterpillar's story is about a company regaining its competitive lead after losing it. To maintain its competitive leadership, both Caterpillar and its people must continue to learn. This is why the company's move to cellular manufacturing is a step in the right direction. Cellular manufacturing is not new, but making it work requires employees and management to alter radically how they view their work. For example, it used to take 11 Caterpillar workers to machine, burr, balance, and wash planet carriers, the main component of transmissions. Now, two workers do the job, running a manufacturing cell consisting of six machines. These two workers must learn how to handle several tasks, work together, and take responsibility for the quality of the parts they produce. Then, their supervisor must learn about different ways to manage them.[24]

Caterpillar is not the only equipment maker that has adopted cellular manufacturing. Deere & Co. is also trying to make a comeback using the cellular approach. This, of course, reveals another virtue of competition: Improvements by one company force its competitors to respond in kind. One company can serve as a catalyst for the comeback of an entire industry.

James Lardner, Deere's vice president for tractors and components, said about cellular manufacturing using computerized machinery that "it takes the least valuable part of man's mind that we've been renting, and lets the computer do that, and frees people to do the things that people's minds do well." A team that takes responsibility for a complete subassembly also creates a new outlook on quality. The buck for shoddy quality cannot be passed because the buck stops with the team. Team members know that their performance needs to improve if their company is going to be successful mounting a comeback.

Although David Halberstam, the author of *The Reckoning,* is not impressed with Ford Motor Company's comeback, many auto industry experts are. What is especially interesting about the comeback at Ford is how the company has rediscovered many of its original values decades after departing from them. The lesson we learn here is that some things are timeless. The values that made Ford a great company in the early 1900s are still relevant in the late 1900s.

Henry Ford founded Ford Motor Company with the vision of making a car he wanted to drive—a car for the common man. Ford built the Model T to fulfill his vision. The Model T had a detachable engine that farmers could also use to saw wood, pump water, and run farm machinery. The car was tough, compact, and light because of Ford's use of vanadium steel, which had been poured for the first time in the United States only a year before the planning of the Model T. The Model T was a brilliantly simple machine. If something went wrong, the average owner knew how to fix it.[25]

Ford's comeback began in 1979 when then president Donald Petersen gave Jack Telnack, the company's top designer, the order to "design the kind of cars *you* would like to drive." Since then Ford has designed cars with its customers in mind. The company is also spending more time dreaming up new concepts. Accordingly, Ford is already moving beyond its highly successful aero designs.[26]

In Ford's early days, employees were skilled artisans who worked together in teams. A job at Ford was desirable because the company was on the cutting edge of technology development and was always trying to do things better.[27] In the 1980s, Team Taurus helped return Ford to its original vision. It brought back the pride of the artisan. Designers, engineers, production specialists, and other groups worked together to shape a totally new car design and to reshape the way cars were developed at Ford.[28]

Ford has also regained some of the manufacturing excellence that was Henry Ford's principal legacy. Moreover, the labor problems that have haunted the company since Henry Ford became obsessed with the ideas of Frederick Taylor, the father of scientific management who alienated workers by championing constant productivity improvements and standardized work procedures, are being moderated by a rediscovered cooperation between management and workers.

Although Ross Perot's new company, Perot Systems Corporation, does not compete directly against the Japanese, it does provide an example of another kind of comeback. Perot Systems was founded by eight former Electronic Data Systems employees who were interested in re-creating the kind of culture that existed at that company before General Motors acquired it. The same management philosophy and management team that made Electronic Data Systems a competitive leader came back under the banner of a new company.

The eight cofounders of Perot Systems started the company with this goal: "Perot Systems will become the premier computer services and communications firm in the world." Then, they pledged that the company will belong to the people who build it; earn after-tax profits in excess of $100 million within ten years; have the strongest balance sheet in the industry and no debt; maintain an atmosphere of mutual trust and respect; and "listen to the people who do the work." Based on their experiences with General Motors, they also stipulated that "Perot Systems will not be sold or merged." Then, in detail, the cofounders spelled out the new company's work ethic, management principles, modus operandi, and personal code of conduct—all identical to those of the old Electronic Data Systems.[29]

Managing Successful Turnarounds

Turnarounds involve new visions, new management, and a commitment to offensive strategy. The rationale governing turnarounds is that new competitive realities require fundamental and sweeping organizational change. In many respects, turnarounds are like the fable of the phoenix. According to Greek writers, only one phoenix existed at any time. At the end of each life cycle, the bird burned itself in a funeral pyre and another arose from the ashes with renewed youth and beauty. Similarly, a complete turnaround requires an old organization to die so a new and more competitive one can come alive. For example, when Lee Iacocca assumed the reins at Chrysler, he renamed the company the New Chrysler Corporation in all its advertising campaigns to signify that the old debt-ridden Chrysler Corporation had been replaced by a new and vital organization.

When Gil Amelio took over as president of Rockwell International's ailing Electronic Devices Division (EDD), he knew he had a real challenge ahead of him. The division had lost money each of the past three years and faced several debilitating financial, strategic, organizational, and human resource problems. Rockwell, which had recruited Amelio from Fairchild Camera & Instrument Company, gave him six months to develop a plan to turn the company around.

Amelio's initial focus was to establish and foster communication at EDD. He tried to identify key players for the turnaround team. During conversations with people, Amelio discovered that basic talent was available in the division, but that it wasn't being used. Division leadership, direction, interdepartmental communications, and teamwork were missing.[30]

One of the first significant actions Amelio took was to rename the division the Semiconductor Products Division (SPD), so division personnel would realize that the old EDD way of thinking—the us-versus-them attitude within the division—was a thing of the past and that everything done from then on would be fundamentally different.[31]

In 1984, SPD lost $19.6 million. Several organizational changes were implemented to address some of the key problems in the division. One core change was the consolidation of both the semiconductor products and telecommunications products businesses into one functional management team reporting directly to the division. The team included the heads of the engineering, production operations, operations support, major programs, and marketing departments. A new division staff was also organized, consisting of heads of the human resources, finance, and planning divisions.[32] Amelio was convinced that SPD should move away from making custom semiconductors and develop and produce standard integrated circuits with larger potential markets. He was certain that SPD's new division structure would support this shift.

Just as the organizational changes were being implemented, Atari, one of the division's principal customers in the electronic games market, canceled all of its orders. The elimination of these orders cut SPD's backlog in half, and the division faced a financial crisis. The entire work force was immediately put on a four-day week, and Amelio ordered massive layoffs.[33]

Major organizational change was initiated at SPD. The central thrust of the change involved offsite workshops with managers representing three organizational levels. The purpose of these workshops was to set strategic priorities for SPD, and a decision was made to move away from the production of standard semiconductors and increase the division's focus on the telecommunications product market. SPD produced two circuit boards that were key components of fax modems.

Soon after the decision to emphasize the production of its fax modem boards, Amelio went to Japan to visit SPD's primary customers for the boards. What he discovered on the trip startled him. Japanese customers were displeased with the 5.1 percent return rate on SPD's fax modem boards. Amelio also discovered that the Japanese had decided to take their business to another supplier who was developing a new 1,200 baud (transmission speed equal to 1,200 bits per second) technology.

Amelio knew that SPD engineers were also designing a similar board to replace their two fax modem boards, but the plan was to introduce the new board in eighteen months. Realizing that his division could not afford to lose the Japanese business, Amelio promised that SPD would develop its new technology in less than four months and provide unrivaled product quality.

Amelio returned to SPD headquarters and dropped his bombshell. Fortunately, he could argue that SPD had no choice. Either they designed, developed, and marketed the new fax modem in four months or they were dead in the water. Amelio did something else that was interesting. He also knew that within a year SPD's customers in Japan expected a fax modem board that could operate four-times faster at 9,600 baud. But Amelio did not challenge his people to develop such a board. He decided that the short-term deadline for a 1,200-baud fax modem board had to be met before SPD addressed customer demand for 9,600-baud technology.

SPD reduced the time to market of its 1,200-baud fax modem board to 3½ months and hit the market window. It also reduced its return rate to 0.2 percent and captured 85 percent of the market in Japan and 63 percent of the worldwide market. SPD also successfully developed a 9,600-baud fax modem board on the heels of the 1,200-baud board.

Although SPD has successfully managed a turnaround, the short-term and long-term competitive challenges facing the division continue. The division will not remain the competitive leader in its industry unless it continues to outperform its competitors, a veritable Who's Who of Japanese companies. Knowing this, Amelio continues to challenge SPD's people, and they continue to adapt their routines and working relationships to maintain their competitive lead.

At Black & Decker the turnaround has been swift and dramatic. A complacent manufacturing mentality has been replaced by what *Fortune* calls an "almost manic, market-driven way of doing things." For 1988 the company reported a 75 percent increase in annual earnings, to almost $100 million, on sales of $2.3 billion. After five straight years of losing market share to Makita of Japan, Bosch of West Germany, and Emerson Electric's Skil, Black & Decker's power tool business is now the fastest growing in the industry—up about 20 percent in the United States compared to overall market growth of around 9 percent a year. Changes in the household products side of Black & Decker are equally profound. In 1988, 40 percent of sales came from products three years old or less. By adding new features and creating award-winning designs, Black & Decker's people are breathing new life into the old business purchased from General Electric.[34]

How has Black & Decker done it? Nolan Archibald, Black & Decker's CEO, started with a vision of the company as a global powerhouse. Archibald's vision required a global strategy, so he abolished the geographical fiefdoms that had grown up at Black & Decker and challenged the company to develop products that could be sold throughout the world. Although the company once made 100 different motors, it now makes 20 and is aiming for 5.[35]

Black & Decker set priorities. Archibald closed five plants, putting over 2,000 workers out of jobs. Then he rolled back wages at other plants. He told workers that their plants had to be competitive or they would be shut down. Then, Black and Decker began to rebuild its manufacturing, engineering, and R and D capability.[36]

Black & Decker expanded market share. Engineers tore apart Makita power tools and analyzed them. Then, the company took on Makita in the fastest growing market segment: midpriced tools for discerning do-it-yourselfers and budget-minded semiprofessionals. The company developed a host of new products—Air Station home compressors and cordless screwdrivers in the power tool business; automatic shut-off irons and cordless blenders in the household products business.[37]

Archibald is fond of saying that "there are no mature markets, only mature managements." He believes in gathering the best possible management talent around him. "You've got to be able to spot it [management talent], you've got to be able to recruit it, you've got to be able to retain it, and you've got to be able to develop it." At Black & Decker, Archibald has done just that, building a classic meritocracy in which the more managers succeed the more responsibility they receive. According to *Fortune,* Black & Decker is run by "a team of smart, proven, driven, aggressive marketers who probably have more rein, at their age, than any group of corporate executives anywhere. They also enjoy what they're doing as much as anyone in business today."[38]

Finally, companies can also be turned around through mergers and acquisitions, but only when both partners possess a clear vision of the turnaround and are deeply committed to it. General Motors' acquisition of Electronic Data Systems, for example, was publicly billed as an acquisition to turn around the giant automaker. Roger Smith, GM's CEO, stated that he wanted the smaller company to infuse GM with the code of the eagle. He wanted to combine GM's huge resources with Electronic Data Systems' entrepreneurial dynamism to create a giant that would finally put the Japanese in their place.[39] What GM appeared to seek was the synergy Marxian sociologists originally conceived—namely, an energy generated from the synthesis of opposites.[40]

Why did GM's acquisition of Electronic Data Systems fail to live up to its billing? There are, of course, many reasons. Obviously, the cultures of the two companies clashed. The problem was also greater than the smaller company's people imagined. GM was literally buried under a mountain of uncompetitive organizational routines. Also, Ross Perot was too impatient about digging GM out. Whatever chance the acquisition had was certainly lost when Perot took his criticism of GM public.

An even more basic problem arose from the fundamentally different views of the acquisition held by the two companies' people. EDS's people believed the public statements GM's top management made. They wanted to turn around GM by remaking the automaker in their own company's image. GM's people, however, were thinking more in terms of mounting a comeback. Accordingly, they were not prepared for the radical changes that EDS's people had in mind. GM's people knew they needed to change, but they were proud of their company and wanted to build on past traditions. They resisted the do-it-our-way attitude of EDS's people, which they interpreted as extreme arrogance. At the root of the problem were the two companies' very different and incompatible views of offensive strategies for regaining competitive leadership from the Japanese.

THE JAPANESE CHALLENGE: THREAT OR OPPORTUNITY?

John Steinbeck wrote a short story, "The Leader of the People," about a grandfather who liked to sit by the fireplace in the evening and reminisce about leading a wagon train across the plains. The grandfather told the stories so the younger generations could feel the pride and spirit of adventure he felt when he was a leader of the movement west. But the story of this old man is sad because his work was done and so was his leadership. He told stories about the past because he had little to look forward to.[41]

U.S. companies do not want to be like the grandfather in Steinbeck's "The Leader of the People," dwelling on the past because the future holds little promise. But to be the best, U.S. companies must be willing to compete against the best. Only by going toward Japanese and other emerging world-class competitors and meeting the test of competition every day will they become competitive leaders.

Of course, another school of thought argues against attacking industry leaders unless they are vulnerable and are unlikely to retaliate.[42] Adherents might also reach the conclusion that the time is right to attack the Japanese industrial machine, but only because they see clear weaknesses to exploit. The Japanese, for example, possess a natural disdain for leadership. Accordingly, Japanese companies find it difficult to adjust to their new roles as world economic leaders. The homogeneous Japanese culture, which preserves the intense worker loyalty that has been key to its economic miracle, also stands in the way of Japan's efforts to internationalize. The ability of Japanese scientists to innovate radically new technologies remains unproven, and there are challenges to Japan's social fabric from a rapidly aging work force, the unraveling system of lifetime employment, and unprecedented prosperity.

But is strength ever created by preying on another's weaknesses? I prefer to see Japan as an ascending economic power that, because of its time-tested capacity to adapt, remains a formidable competitor. At the same time, however, I see the Japanese challenge as an opportunity, as much as a threat, to U.S. industry. Many U.S. companies have learned valuable lessons from competing against the Japanese. Competition has forced them to set new and higher standards of efficiency and effectiveness. They are showing the Japanese that they still have something to learn from Americans, and they are showing Americans that by going on the offensive—pitting their strengths against the strengths of Japanese competitors—they can regain worldwide competitive leadership.

10 The Virtues of Competition

Lester Thurow believes that in the past nations often tacitly ceded industries to one another. The United States, for example, let Japan have transistor radios, while the Japanese gave the United States machine tools. The United States never challenged the French and the Italians for the wine market, and they never challenged the United States in soft drinks. What has changed in recent years, according to Thurow, is that there are no such gentleman's agreements between countries anymore. Everyone wants a machine tool industry, an electronics industry, and a wine industry. Head-to-head competition, therefore, is unavoidable in most parts of the global economy. Everyone is standing in everyone else's corner, and it's unpleasant. Competition makes life turbulent and uncertain. It is eating into a lot of companies' profits. Even worse, companies can lose at competition.[1]

In spite of the unpleasantness competition brings, it has fundamental virtues. First, competitive economies are self-regulating as long as companies do not try to distort the natural processes that drive the free market system. Second, competition promotes organizational learning. When companies go head-to-head against competitors, they discover they must learn and continue learning to be competitive. Third, competition fosters achievement. Whether competing firms win or lose, they achieve more when they compete.

GAIAN THEORY AND THE INVISIBLE HAND

Theories of evolution are one of the first places we should look for an understanding of the virtues of competition. Such theories describe natural systems and the development of the competing fauna and flora within them. They describe competition at its most basic level—as a process of adaptation and natural selection.

In recent years, noted scientists have made several new and startling discoveries, enhancing our understanding of evolutionary processes. One major contributor to the new thinking about evolution is James Lovelock. His Gaian theory offers several startling insights about how environments shape organisms and, more importantly, how organisms shape their environments.

Lovelock maintains that forms of life have changed the land, water, and air in specific, observable ways. He insists that living organisms actually work together to keep the environment comfortable for themselves and that a seemingly willful and intelligent global system arises automatically from the mindless struggle of separate organisms for individual survival. In other words, living organisms, by looking out for their own interests, shape the environment for the benefit of all.[2]

Lovelock's Gaian theory describes robust and complex systems that are likely to survive no matter what. Lovelock maintains that nothing we do is likely to kill the planet. Still, a warning is inherent in Gaian theory that should give cause for concern about the long-term survival of the human race on Earth. Humans have used technology to gain immense power over their environment and, in turn, to separate themselves from nature. But some of the technologies they have developed disrupted the Earth's natural processes. As humans further distance themselves from nature, the potential for disaster increases, because there is no self-regulating exchange between nature and humans. Humans continue to live comfortably while they make their environment more unsuitable for themselves and related species. Although the planet will continue to adapt and survive in spite of human intervention, it may evolve into an unsuitable place for humans to live.

The implications of Gaian theory for organization theory are significant. When I first read about Gaian theory I was struck by one thing—it described processes similar to those orchestrated by Adam Smith's invisible hand, which was competition, or the force by which "the private interests and passions of men" are directed to what "is most agreeable to the interest of the whole society." Smith saw virtue—economic and social benefit—in selfish individual motives as long as they were regulated by the competition arising from the conflicting self-interests of all the members of society. The outcome of multiplying all self-interests was beneficial to collective interests.[3]

How does competition driven by economic self-interest benefit collective interests? Although the economic volatility created when companies aggressively exercise their economic self-interest makes a lot of people—including politicians and economic developers—nervous, David Birch, the director of the Massachusetts Institute of Technology's Program on Neighborhood and Regional Change, contends that volatility is one of the principal signs of a healthy economy. It cleans out bad ideas, old products, and inefficient people, then replaces them with new and more competitive products and services. It provides a way for draining failure out of a system. If an escape route is not provided for failure it accumulates in existing institutions, resulting in disastrous consequences.[4]

Many years ago, Joseph Schumpeter, in his *Theory of Economic Development*, observed another form of volatility. According to Schumpeter, competitive capitalism was driven by the supernormal profits that he called entrepreneurial gains. These gains motivated entrepreneurs to go toward the challenges posed by innovation. They also motivated other businesspeople to change, inducing them to follow the entrepreneur like a herd, and thus extending change throughout the economy and leading to cycles of "creative destruction."[5]

Competition for Schumpeter's entrepreneurial gains creates volatile industries as it sets into motion the forces of creative destruction. This, in turn, exaggerates economic turbulence. But, as Schumpeter observed, the forces of creative destruction are also the forces of progress.

Despite this virtue of competition, companies and the managers who run them try to separate themselves from competitive forces in ways that are profoundly similar to people's attempts to separate themselves from nature. According to economist Milton Friedman, "Every businessman likes to preach about a free market and free enterprise, but he's always in favor of it for other people and not for himself."[6]

How do companies avoid competition, and what happens when they do? First, instead of working within the free market system, companies have tried to change it. Kenneth Boulding, the noted management and systems theorist, observes that a lack of success in "market-justified systems" produces one of two reactions. The first is private discontent, which is directed inward, rather than against the free market system. A company's efforts are focused toward changing its own position within the system rather than toward changing the system. Then there is political discontent with the system itself. Companies attribute their failure to the unfairness of the system and seek to change it. Boulding contends that the future of the free market system depends on which of these two forms discontent takes. If it takes the personal form, the free market system will prosper. If, however, it takes more of a political form, with companies seeking protectionist policies or other trade advantages they have not earned, the free market system is likely to be destroyed.[7]

Second, companies have tried to dominate the free market system to avoid competition. During much of the latter half of the 20th century we lived in a world economy dominated by U.S. corporations that were able to avoid competition because of their immense size and the nature of world markets, which demanded everything produced by U.S. corporations because without global competitors supplies were limited. Corporate strategies based on economies of scale were used to erect entry barriers and/or squeeze out competitors. As U.S. corporations grew larger, their dominance increased and further separated them from the forces of competition.

Change is as inevitable to global economies as it is to planets, and it is always faster. Unfortunately, the further companies separated themselves from the self-regulating forces of competition, the more unaware they became of the economic changes around them. Companies failed to adjust strategies, structures, and operations to new competitive realities, and competitive advantages became competitive disadvantages.

Third, companies have tried to cheat the free market system to avoid competition. Some critics view unregulated competition unfavorably because they assume it encourages winning at all costs. But strategies that involve cheating are noncompetitive. Cheating, in addition to being morally wrong, distorts the natural forces of competition. Organizations that cheat to avoid competition separate themselves from the benefits of competition. They are weakened, not strengthened, when they rely on unethical or illegal business practices.

The most fundamental virtue of competition in nature and the free market system is that it is self-regulating. Of course, the criticisms of both Lovelock's Gaian theory and Smith's invisible hand stem from a lack of faith in this underlying, nearly invisible truth. Critics of Gaian theory, for example, ask how slime molds, plankton, and polar bears even perceive their effect on the planet, let alone coordinate their activities on a global scale, and economists ask similar questions about individual companies and their effects on the global economy. Even if we do not completely understand why, both nature and the economy work extremely well when left to their own self-regulating devices. We should only be concerned about organisms and companies that intentionally distort natural processes to avoid competition.

LEARNING ORGANIZATIONS

When companies enter into direct competition with other companies they learn what they need to do to become more competitive. Moreover, as their competitors learn, they are forced to continue learning to remain competitive. In their book *Dynamic Manufacturing: Creating the Learning Organization,* what Robert Hayes, Steven Wheelwright, and Kim Clark have said about manufacturing organizations applies to all companies desiring to compete in today's global economy: The common denominator of all high-performance organizations is an ability to learn. Learning is the bottom line when assessing the effectiveness of world-class competitors.[8]

One lesson U.S. companies *can* learn from Japanese companies is how to learn. Nissan, for example, decided it wanted to become competitive in Formula One racing. The company sent a racing team to compete at Le Mans in the grueling, 24-hour endurance race. During the course of the race, a television reporter approached Nissan's head engineer and asked him to comment on the poor standing of Nissan's entry. The engineer answered, "We're not here to win. We're here to learn and collect performance data on our technology and on the race." Positioned around the racetrack, Nissan had vans with elaborate monitoring and computer equipment recording and analyzing every facet of the race. The head engineer assured the reporter that within five years a Nissan car would be in the winner's circle, and it would be there to stay.

More and more the people in the Soviet Union are realizing that competition is a great teacher. We are beginning to see dramatic shifts in Soviet economic philosophy, which reflect a greater appreciation for the forces of competition. Competition, however, is not a foreign concept in the Soviet Union. Competition in geopolitics, space exploration, and sports has been nurtured in the U.S.S.R. for decades. For example, the Soviets recently decided that they wanted to become competitive in *beisbol* (baseball) when it becomes a medal sport in the 1992 Olympics. According to *Newsweek:*

> The Soviets know that playing foreigners is the quickest way to get better. A few American college and high school teams have toured the Soviet Union—generally trouncing the comrades of summer—and the

Soviet national team hopes to make an annual habit of its current swing through the States. "One day," says sports official Alexei Nikolov, "maybe the Americans will learn something from us."

For now, the Soviet's goal is modest—to win the European championship by 1993 and keep winning it so they qualify for a spot in the Olympic tournament. But knowing about the Soviet successes in international basketball competition, who can doubt that someday the Soviets will challenge Americans at their national pastime? Soviet baseball enthusiasts will continue to set new goals and accomplish them by going head-to-head against competition and by learning as they go.[9]

Competition teaches companies that they need to do more than react to the moves of competitors. They will not be competitive if they play only defense. Competition teaches them that they need to develop an offensive game plan. A key lesson competitive leaders learn from competition is that they want their competitors to be reacting to them. In the words of Thomas Tyrrell, the CEO of American Steel & Wire Corporation, "If our workers aren't thinking and anticipating, they're never going to be able to make the steps necessary over the next 10 to 15 years."[10]

Raymond Miles and Charles Snow conducted research during the mid-1970s and developed a typology of corporate strategies. Their findings, of course, describe strategies during a time when U.S. companies dominated most domestic markets. They identified three strategic orientations that were effective during that period, one of which was the defender strategy.

The defender strategy discourages learning in two ways. First, defenders protect themselves against competition. They deliberately try to seal off a portion of the total market to create a stable domain. They produce only a limited set of products directed at a narrow segment of the total potential market and aggressively protect their turf against competitors.[11] But when defenders protect themselves from competition they effectively seal off opportunities to learn about themselves and their competitors.

Second, defenders avoid change. Typically, such firms develop single core technologies that are highly cost-efficient, then attempt to protect them from abnormal variations in the business environment.[12] They discourage learning because learning promotes change. Instead of trying to improve continuously, they focus on maintaining the status quo, building performance targets around their uncompetitive organizational routines.

The defender strategy worked until the mid-1970s, because in stable, noncompetitive business environments, companies could defend themselves from competition. But the strategy cannot work against today's more aggressive competitors, because once a defender's defenses are broken down, it can only react to competitors. Defenders are always one step behind competitors because they are passive and routinized, not active and liberated. Instead of shaping events, they are shaped by them because they have forgotten how to learn.

Defenders were once the world's dominant manufacturing organizations. New thinking about manufacturing, however, has replaced the defender's strategy with learning organizations. Hayes, Wheelwright, and Clark argue that it is no longer sufficient for manufacturers to achieve increasingly consistent and precise operations through a combination of reactive, preventive, and progressive controls. They call for a fourth level of control: dynamic control. Achieving dynamic control requires that organizations learn about new equipment, new procedures, new information, different product designs, and higher levels of operator skills and organizational capabilities.[13]

Learning is another virtue of competition. The Massachusetts Institute of Technology Commission on Industrial Productivity reported that "American firms learn fastest not through reading books or gathering intelligence overseas but by being directly confronted with a competitor performing at a much higher level using American employees in America." The new competitive realities have taught America's manufacturing organizations that it is no longer good enough to design elaborate organizational processes and put them on automatic pilot. The lesson is clear: Only thinking and learning organizations are successful competing in today's dynamic global and domestic markets.

THE ACHIEVING ORGANIZATION

Competition vitalizes organizations. It creates excitement and challenge. When companies go head-to-head against competitors they know their survival depends on their ability to rise to the occasion. They do things they would never do unless they had to. Companies are only competitive as long as they meet the test of competition every day. Companies can appear excellent without competition, but it is nothing more than a case of looking good without *being* good.

In his book *The Achieving Society,* published in 1961, David McClelland reported the findings from his long-term study of individuals' need for achievement. As part of the study, McClelland conducted two experiments with people from a variety of cultural backgrounds. The first experiment asked people to throw rings over a peg from any distance they chose. What McClelland discovered was that people with high need for achievement scores (based on results from McClelland's Thematic Apperception Test) nearly always stood at moderate distances from the peg. On the other hand, people with low scores either stood so close to the peg as to make the task ridiculously easy or so far away as to make it impossible. McClelland concluded that people with high need for achievement set moderately difficult, but potentially achievable goals for themselves, where they objectively had only about a one-in-three chance of succeeding. When given the opportunity, they chose just enough challenge for themselves.[14]

McClelland's second experiment offered participants a choice between two ways of winning at a game. They could either roll dice with a one-in-three chance of winning, or they could try to solve a difficult problem that only one person in three before them had solved. McClelland found that although rolling the dice was obviously less work and the odds of winning were the same, people with high need for achievement scores preferred to work on the problem. When given the opportunity, they preferred to compete rather than leave the outcome to chance.[15]

Although McClelland reported many other important findings about the need for achievement, none was more important than his discovery that individuals could be trained to have higher need for achievement scores. McClelland and his colleagues designed a course to increase scores and presented it to executives in a large U.S. firm; to employees of several Mexican companies; to underachieving high school boys; and, to businesspeople from two cities in India. In three of the four cases, data collected two years after the courses were given showed that the people who took the course had done significantly better (made more money, got promoted faster, expanded their businesses faster) than comparable people who did not take the course.[16]

The organizational analogy to an individual with a high need for achievement score is an achieving organization, which seeks just enough challenge and chooses competition over leaving outcomes to chance. How do organizations increase their need for achievement? They continue to go head-to-head against global competitors. The most effective training course is participation in today's global economy. Competition against world-class competitors breeds in companies the desire to become more competitive.

Most of the problems associated with competition between organizations arise because an interest in winning overwhelms an interest in achieving. For example, companies try to avoid competition to escape win/lose pressures, when they might be attracted to the win/win outcomes of achievement-oriented competition. Competition between organizations is the unregulated exercise of industry. It is simple, peaceful, and endless. Of course, competition can be broken up into discrete contests if companies want to keep score, but the thrill of victory is ephemeral because to remain competitive companies must continue to meet competitors head-on. Then, over time competition sharpens the internal workings of organizations.

Organizations achieve only because individuals achieve, and the intensity of individual achievement is heightened when organizations compete. This virtue of competition is like the cry of "There she blows!" in Herman Melville's *Moby-Dick*. Melville described how in the life of a whaler periods of intense work sometimes lasted as long as four days without relief. Then a calm would settle over the ship, and the weary whalers would drop down exhausted and sleep in the mess created in the heat of battle against whales. They would raise themselves when they could, and with swollen wrists and sore bodies clean the deck of the ship. But at any time, the cry of "There she blows!" could disrupt what they were doing and throw them headlong into battle against another whale. Melville appropriately described the lot of a whaler when he said, "Oh! my friends, but this is man-killing!"[17]

In *Moby-Dick*, the competition is against a whale, while companies compete against other companies. But in both cases, competition mobilizes people, then people mobilize organizations. Competition can be a "person-killer," but through it people experience life at its fullest and organizations achieve their full potential.

WINNING ISN'T EVERYTHING

One of my favorite short stories, Ted Walker's "Discobolus," holds a final important lesson about competition. The story is about two English prep school athletes. One was a triple jumper who "added fractions of an inch" to records, and the other threw the discus and "demolished the existing figures by feet and yards." The story focuses on what the triple jumper learned about competition from the discus thrower.

Trav, the discus thrower, saw his event as the purest form of athletics ever devised. He trained seriously to develop strength and perfect his form. He cut an action shot of Adolfo Consolini, the leading discus thrower in the world at the time, out of a sports magazine. He saw flaws in Consolini's technique and in a quiet, matter-of-fact way vowed to be better than the world's best. But what he had in mind was something other than winning.

One day Trav asked his friend, the triple jumper, to watch him throw. Describing what he then saw, the friend said:

> It was beautiful to watch, magnificent, an unforgettable experience. It was like seeing ocean waves for the first time from a childhood beach— the collecting mass, the compression of energy, the gathering of force to a pent stillness, and then the explosive moment breaking, and the dispersal of every shred of power. Five times he crashed out of that calm, lazy coiling down, and every throw was the same. It was as though his arms passed along invisible slots, like the slicked components of a complex machine. Each discus he slung rode the air like some Arctic bird flighting to a place it knew.

The friend saw Trav winning everything in sight, a drawer full of medals, and cups on the sideboard. Then, Trav's response surprised him. Trav said, "I'll win nothing. I've won." Trav had decided to perfect one physical activity that had nothing to do with competing against others. He was competing against himself. He wanted to be as good as his body would allow, and he had reached his goal, so it was time to move on and do something else.

The uniqueness of Walker's story stirs the reader's soul. When Trav had in his grasp the power to compete against others and win, he chose not to use it. He even admitted that choosing not to exercise his power to compete and win was "hellish hard, but it's possible." At least, it was possible for him.

Trav's experience is about transcending head-to-head competition, about reaching for something higher than proving oneself relative to others. It is about proving oneself to oneself. But it would be a mistake for all people to assume that they needed to pursue this higher ideal.

Trav, for example, did not start with this higher ideal. He started with the goal of winning in competition against others. He admitted at one point, "I did enjoy winning last summer, and getting all that glory . . ." Comparing his form to Consolini's was another kind of competition. Only when Trav became the best did he no longer need to compete against others. Certainly, he would have won if he had competed, but it would not have made him better. He could only become better by competing against himself.

Ultimately, a few competitive leaders—whether individuals, companies, or nations—arrive at a point where they can only become better in one of two ways: Either they decide to compete against themselves or they compete at something new. Competing against oneself, of course, is more difficult because people are prone to self-deception. But some U.S. companies, like AMP, the world's leading manufacturer of electrical and electronic connecting devices, dominate their industries to the extent that they compete mostly against themselves, continue to excel, and possess no ambitions for broadening the scope of their present business. AMP, for example, began a program to improve quality by a factor of ten in five years and then in the third year of the program demanded another tenfold improvement in only three years.[18]

When Japanese and American competitive leaders dominate their markets like AMP dominates its market, they more commonly respond by turning to expansionism—companies use competitive leadership in one market as a launching pad for expansion into others. They seek out new competitive challenges by venturing into markets other competitive leaders dominate. The principle of resistance, therefore, is an important part of the strategies of these competitive leaders. They look for new opportunities for head-to-head competition against world-class competitors because they know that the more resistance they push against, the stronger they become.

I like to think of head-to-head competition as being a lot like another field event—the high jump. When I jumped it was usually quite easy to prepare myself for the heights I had already cleared. I had done it before, so I could do it again, I would tell myself. But to improve I needed to go beyond what I knew I could do, and it was often difficult to convince myself that I could. My coach used to tell me when self-doubt entered my mind, "You can do what you think you can do so think you can do it and do it." He never told me I needed to win, but he did expect me to test my limits. If I missed, he expected me to try again.

Many competitive leaders, like Trav, believe that winning isn't everything. Still, they compete because they believe that to be the best they need to compete against other companies that are doing the same thing, and do it better than they do. There is a fundamental virtue to competition when it is approached in this way—as a self-regulating process of learning and achieving. Ideally, head-to-head competition is always testing companies to their limits by providing just enough challenge. Although there are no sustainable competitive advantages, U.S. companies can sustain their competitive leadership by thinking they can successfully compete against world-class competitors and by *doing it*.

Notes

CHAPTER 1

1. Quoted from D. Halberstam, *The Reckoning*, New York: William Morrow, 1986, p. 63.

2. M. E. Porter, *Competitive Strategy: Techniques for Analyzing Industries and Competitors*, New York: Free Press, 1980, p. 4.

3. C. C. Mann, "The Man with All the Answers," *The Atlantic Monthly*, January 1990, p. 58.

4. Adapted from a presentation made by Francis "Butch" Cash to the faculty of Brigham Young University's Marriott School of Management on 14 December 1989 at the Salt Lake Marriott Hotel.

5. T. J. Peters and R. H. Waterman, Jr., *In Search of Excellence: Lessons from America's Best-Run Companies*, New York: Harper & Row, 1982.

6. M. L. Dertouzos, R. K. Lester, and R. M. Solow, *Made in America: Regaining the Productive Edge*, Cambridge, MA: MIT Press, 1989.

7. G. Hamel and C. K. Prahalad, "Strategic Intent," *Harvard Business Review*, May–June 1989, p. 64.

8. B. Emmott, *The Sun Also Sets: The Limits of Japan's Economic Power*, New York: Random House, 1989, p. 272.

9. G. Bylinsky, "The Hottest High-Tech Company in Japan," *Fortune*, 1 January 1990, p. 83.

10. Ibid., p. 86.

11. B. Saporito, "Companies That Compete Best," *Fortune*, 22 May 1989, p. 42.

12. Ibid., p. 44.

13. Dertouzos, Lester, and Solow, pp. 11, 52.

14. M. E. Porter, *Competitive Advantage: Creating and Sustaining Superior Performance*, New York: Free Press, 1985, pp. 212–214.

15. K. Boulding, "Symbols for Capitalism," *Harvard Business Review*, January–February 1959, p. 48.

16. J. Zygmount, "Kenneth H. Olsen: President & CEO, Digital Equipment Corporation," *Sky*, November 1989, p. 62.

CHAPTER 2

1. M. L. Dertouzos, R. K. Lester, and R. M. Solow, *Made in America: Regaining the Productive Edge*, Cambridge, MA: MIT Press, 1989, p. 9.

2. "Missed Opportunities: Americans Hold the Lead in Research but Let Foreigners Develop the Products," *Wall Street Journal*, 14 November 1988, p. R22.

3. M. Goodfellow, "Why Quality Circles Failed at 21 Firms," *Management Review*, September 1982, pp. 56–57.

4. G. P. Shea, "Quality Circles: The Danger of Bottled Change," *Sloan Management Review*, Spring 1986, p. 37.

5. M. E. Porter, *Competitive Strategy: Techniques for Analyzing Industries and Competitors*, New York: Free Press, 1980, pp. 300–323.

6. M. Magnet, "Acquiring Without Smothering," *Fortune*, 12 November 1984, pp. 22–24.

7. P. Drucker, *Innovation and Entrepreneurship: Practice and Principles*, New York: Harper & Row, 1985.

8. J. Dreyfuss, "What Do You Do for an Encore?" *Fortune*, 19 December 1988, pp. 111, 116.

9. R. R. Nelson and S. G. Winter, *Evolutionary Theory of Economic Change*, Cambridge, MA: Belknap Press of Harvard University, 1982, pp. 123–124.

10. R. Henkoff, "This Cat Is Acting Like a Tiger," *Fortune*, 19 December 1988, pp. 72–74.

11. R. H. Hayes, S. C. Wheelwright, and K. B. Clark, *Dynamic Manufacturing: Creating the Learning Organization*, New York: Free Press, 1988, p. 19.

12. Ibid., pp. 271–272.

13. Porter, pp. 47–74.

14. P. C. Reid, "How Harley Beat Back the Japanese," *Fortune*, 25 September 1989, p. 157.

15. Ibid.

16. Ibid., pp. 157–162.

17. L. T. Perry, "Least-Cost Alternatives to Layoffs in Declining Industries," *Organizational Dynamics*, Spring 1986, pp. 48–61.

18. A. Ramirez, "Boeing's Happy, Harrowing Times," *Fortune,* 17 July 1989, pp. 40–43.

19. J. Dreyfuss, "Reinventing IBM," *Fortune,* 14 August 1989, pp. 33–39.

20. T. P. Pare, "How to Cut the Cost of Headquarters," *Fortune,* 11 September 1989, pp. 189–192.

21. Ibid., p. 192.

22. C. Hartman, "Keeper of the Flame," *Inc.,* March 1989, p. 76.

23. Ibid.

24. Ibid.

25. J. Evensen, "Utah Joins in 13-State Fight to Prevent Debit Card's Debut," *Deseret News,* 20 September 1989, p. A9.

26. J. Huey, "The New Power in Black & Decker," *Fortune,* 2 January 1989, p. 91.

27. L. Kraar, "Your Rivals Can Be Your Allies," *Fortune,* 27 March 1989, p. 67.

28. Ibid., p. 76.

29. Ibid., pp. 72–76.

30. T. Peters, "Competition and Compassion," *California Management Review,* Summer 1986, p. 20.

31. L. Kartus, "The Strange Folks Picking on Zenith," *Fortune,* 19 December 1988, pp. 79–84.

32. Reid, pp. 162–164.

33. "Semiconductor Entrepreneur: Joseph Parkinson," *Inc.,* July 1988, pp. 43–44.

34. K. Labich, "The Big Comeback at British Airways," *Fortune,* 5 December 1988, p. 163.

CHAPTER 3

1. Travis Services is not the company's real name. I am not using the company's real name to protect its confidentiality.

2. W. H. Auden (presenter), *The Living Thoughts of Kierkegaard.* Bloomington, IN: Indiana University Press, 1952.

3. G. Hamel and C. K. Prahalad, "Strategic Intent," *Harvard Business Review,* May–June 1989, p. 63.

4. J. Gleick, *Chaos: Making a New Science,* New York: Penguin Books, 1987, pp. 9–33.

5. M. E. Porter, *Competitive Advantage: Creating and Sustaining Superior Performance,* New York: Free Press, 1985, pp. 482, 513–526.

6. Hamel and Prahalad, p. 69.

7. M. E. Porter, *Competitive Strategy: Techniques for Analyzing Industries and Competitors,* New York: Free Press, 1980, p. 4.

8. A. Ramirez, "Boeing's Happy, Harrowing Times," *Fortune,* 17 July 1989, p. 44.

9. Ibid.

10. G. Stalk, Jr., "Time: The Next Source of Competitive Advantage," *Harvard Business Review,* July–August 1988, p. 43.

11. Ibid.

12. H. Wouk, *The Caine Mutiny: A Novel of World War II,* Garden City, NY: Doubleday, 1951, p. 97.

13. Hamel and Prahalad, p. 75.

14. Ibid.

15. R. Smith, "The U.S. Must Do as GM Has Done," *Fortune,* 13 February, 1989, p. 71.

16. J. Wooden, "On Staying Power," *Wall Street Journal,* 23 April, 1986, p. A1.

17. R. R. Nelson and S. G. Winter, *Evolutionary Theory of Economic Change,* Cambridge, MA: Belknap Press of Harvard University, 1982, p. 103.

18. L. Rhodes, "That's Easy for You to Say," *Inc.,* June 1986, pp. 35–41.

19. Ibid.

20. Ibid.

21. Ibid.

22. A. L. Wilkins, *Developing Corporate Character,* San Francisco: Jossey-Bass, 1989, p. 93.

23. Ibid., pp. 94–95.

24. Nelson and Winter, pp. 99–112.

25. Ibid., pp. 99–107.

26. Ibid., p. 112.

27. Ibid., pp. 107–112.

28. D. Halberstam, *The Reckoning,* New York: William Morrow, 1986, p. 328.

29. K. E. Weick, *The Social Psychology of Organizing* (2d ed.), Reading, MA: Addison-Wesley, 1979.

30. P. Sellers, "Why Bigger Is Badder at Sears," *Fortune,* 5 December 1988, p. 79.

31. Ibid., pp. 79, 82.

32. Ibid., p. 80.

33. Ibid., pp. 82–84.

34. Ibid., p. 84.

35. Halberstam, p. 714.

36. Halberstam uses the term *monopoly* or *shared monopoly* to describe what economists usually call an oligopoly. I believe we can assume that Hal-

berstam is making a conscious choice here. His use of terms suggests that the Big Three acted in concert and together had monopolistic control over the U.S. auto market.

37. Halberstam, p. 714.
38. Ibid., p. 327.

CHAPTER 4

1. "Who's Excellent Now?: Some of the Best-Seller's Picks Haven't Been Doing so Well Lately," *Business Week*, 5 November, 1984, pp. 76–86.
2. B. Burlingham and C. Hartman, "Cowboy Capitalist: Inside the Private World of America's Most Public Entrepreneur," *Inc.*, January 1989, p. 60.
3. T. J. Peters and R. H. Waterman, Jr., *In Search of Excellence: Lessons from America's Best-Run Companies*, New York: Harper & Row, 1982, pp. 239–240.
4. Ibid.
5. L. T. Perry and K. W. Sandholtz, "A 'Liberating Form' for Radical Product Innovation." In U. E. Gattiker and L. Larwood (eds.), *Managing Technological Development: Strategic and Human Resource Issues*, Berlin, New York: Walter de Gruyter, 1988, p. 14.
6. Ibid.
7. Ibid.
8. J. Carlzon, "The Art of Loving," *Inc.*, May 1989, p. 41.
9. J. Huey, "Wal-Mart: Will It Take Over the World?" *Fortune*, 30 January 1989, p. 58.
10. M. J. Clark, "Liberating Form," *Brigham Young University Studies*, 15, 1974, p. 39.
11. Ibid.
12. E. deBono, *Lateral Thinking: Creativity Step by Step*, New York: Harper & Row, 1970, pp. 11–13.
13. Ibid.
14. P. Vaill, "Purposing in High-Performing Systems," *Organizational Dynamics*, Autumn 1982, pp. 23–39.
15. R. Keele, "Mentoring or Networking? Strong and Weak Ties in Career Development." In L. L. Moore (ed.), *Not as Far as You Think: The Realities of Working Women*, New York: Lexington Books, 1986, pp. 54–55.
16. K. E. Weick, *The Social Psychology of Organizing*, Reading, MA: Addison-Wesley, 1969, p. 102.
17. J. Steinbeck, *East of Eden*, New York: Bantam, 1970, p. 179.
18. Ibid., p. 180.

19. K. Labich, "The Seven Keys to Business Leadership," *Fortune,* October, 24, 1988, p. 60.
20. Burlingham and Hartman, p. 57.
21. H. A. Simon, *Models of Man,* New York: J. Wiley, 1957.

CHAPTER 5

1. R. Allen and J. Lindahl, "Creed of the Entrepreneur," *Executive Excellence,* January 1989, p. 16.
2. Data-Disk Corporation is not the company's real name. I am not using the company's real name to protect its confidentiality.
3. Beta Partners is not the real name of this venture capital firm. Again, I am not using its real name to protect its confidentiality.
4. G. N. Hatsopoulos, "The Thinking Man's CEO," *Inc.,* November 1988, p. 29.
5. Ibid., p. 30.
6. Ibid., p. 29.
7. Ibid.
8. R. O'Brien, *Marriott: The J. Willard Marriott Story,* Salt Lake City, UT: Deseret Books, 1977, pp. 126–127.
9. Ibid., pp. 127–130.
10. N. W. Aldrich, Jr., "The Real Art of the Deal," *Inc.,* November 1988, pp. 79–80.
11. Ibid., p. 80.
12. D. Halberstam, *The Reckoning,* New York: William Morrow, 1986, p. 419.
13. Ibid., p. 422.
14. Ibid., pp. 422–423.
15. Ibid., pp. 423–434.
16. Ibid., p. 435.
17. Aldrich, p. 86.
18. Halberstam, p. 424.
19. Aldrich, p. 81.
20. P. B. Brown, "Cookie Monsters," *Inc.,* February 1989, pp. 55–56.
21. Ibid., pp. 56–57.
22. K. E. Weick, *The Social Psychology of Organizing* (2d ed.), Reading, MA: Addison-Wesley, 1979.
23. Hatsopoulos, p. 36.
24. Ibid.
25. K. Sakai, *Bunsha,* Tokyo: Taiyo Industry Co., 1985, p. 34.

26. J. B. Quinn, "The Money on Your Life," *Newsweek*, 8 May 1989, p. 46.

27. J. R. Norman and D. Foust, "Meet Art Williams, the P. T. Barnum of Life Insurance," *Business Week*, 15 February 1988, pp. 69–70.

28. B. Saporito, "Companies That Compete Best," *Fortune*, 22 May 1989, p. 44.

29. Norman and Foust, p. 69.

30. Ibid.

31. Ibid., pp. 68–72.

32. Aldrich, pp. 89–92.

33. Ibid., p. 89.

CHAPTER 6

1. Star Electronics is not this company's real name. I am not using the company's real name to protect its confidentiality.

2. VenFund is not the venture capital firm's real name. I have not used the firm's real name to protect its confidentiality.

3. P. Vaill, "The Purposing of High-Performing Systems," *Organizational Dynamics*, Autumn 1982, pp. 23–39.

4. E. Linden, "Murphy's Law," *Inc.*, July 1984, p. 100.

5. Ibid.

6. Ibid.

7. Ibid.

8. P. Engardio, "Why Cordis' Heart Wasn't in Pacemakers," *Business Week*, 16 March 1987, p. 80.

9. J. Carlzon, "The Art of Loving," *Inc.*, May 1989, p. 46.

10. "The Entrepreneur of the Decade: An Interview with Steve Jobs," *Inc.*, April 1989, p. 116.

11. Ibid., p. 118.

12. Ibid., p. 119.

13. Ibid., pp. 120–121.

14. Ibid., p. 116.

15. "Corporate Antihero: John Sculley," *Inc.*, October 1987, pp. 50–52.

16. Ibid.

CHAPTER 7

1. A. Rock, "Strategy vs. Tactics from a Venture Capitalist," *Harvard Business Review*, November–December 1987, pp. 63, 67.

2. Ibid., p. 63.

3. Ibid., p. 64.

4. Ibid., pp. 65–66.

5. C. C. Mann, "The Man with All the Answers," *The Atlantic Monthly*, January 1990, p. 61.

6. Gateway Technologies is not the company's real name. I am not using the company's real name to protect its confidentiality.

7. R. L. Ackoff, *Management in Small Doses*, New York: John Wiley, 1986, pp. 24–26.

8. P. B. Brown, "Looking Out for Number One," *Inc.*, April 1989, pp. 165–166.

9. Ibid.

10. Ibid.

11. K. Labich, "Hot Company, Warm Culture," *Fortune*, 27 February 1989, pp. 74–75.

12. Ibid., p. 75.

13. Ibid., p. 75.

14. Ibid., p. 76.

15. Ibid., pp. 76–77.

16. Ibid., p. 76.

17. Ibid., p. 78.

18. Ibid., p. 78.

19. M. Pacanowsky, "Communication in the Empowering Organization." In J. A. Anderson (ed.), *Communication Yearbook/11*, Beverly Hills, CA: Sage, 1987, p. 357.

20. Ibid., pp. 356–357.

21. Ibid., p. 363.

22. Ibid., pp. 367–368.

23. Ibid., p. 362.

24. Ibid., p. 356.

25. Ibid., p. 365.

26. W. G. Ouchi, *Theory Z: How American Business Can Meet the Japanese Challenge*, Reading, MA: Addison-Wesley, pp. 74-75.

27. Ibid., p.118.

28. Ibid.

29. B. Burlingham and C. Hartman, "Cowboy Capitalist," *Inc.*, January 1989, p. 58.

30. Ibid., p. 57.

31. Ibid., p. 60.

32. Ibid., p. 60.

33. Ibid., p. 62.

34. W. E. Fulmer and J. Kennedy, "Electronic Data Systems (A)," Colgate Darden Graduate Business School, 1986, p. 22.

35. Labich, p. 74.

CHAPTER 8

1. G. Hamel and C. K. Prahalad, "Strategic Intent," *Harvard Business Review,* May–June 1989, pp. 70–71.

2. Ibid., p. 71.

3. Ibid., p. 64.

4. W. Kiechel III, "A Hard Look at Executive Vision," *Fortune,* 23 October 1989, pp. 209–211.

5. Hamel and Prahalad, p. 74.

6. S. Albert, "A Delete Design Model of Successful Transitions." In J. Kimberly and R. E. Quinn (eds.), *Managing Organizational Transitions,* Homewood, IL: Richard D. Irwin, 1984, pp. 169–189.

7. P. K. Tompkins, "Management Qua Communication in Rocket Research and Development," *Communication Monographs,* March 1977, p. 2.

8. Hamel and Prahalad, p. 76.

9. R. H. Waterman, Jr., "The Renewal Factor," *Business Week,* 14 September 1987, p. 120.

10. P. Vaill, "Purposing in High-Performing Systems," *Organizational Dynamics,* Autumn 1982, pp. 23–39.

11. R. Grover, with M. M. Vamos and T. Mason, "Disney's Magic," *Business Week,* 9 March 1987, pp. 65–68.

12. Ibid., p. 69.

13. "Add Records to Disney's World: Eisner Expands Again," *Newsweek,* 11 December 1989, p. 72.

14. Grover, with Vamos and Mason, p. 68.

15. C. Garfield, "Superman to the Rescue," *Executive Excellence,* January 1989, p. 3.

16. Grover, with Vamos and Mason, pp. 62–68.

17. B. Dumaine, "P&G Rewrites the Marketing Rules," *Fortune,* 6 November 1989, pp. 38–40.

18. Ibid.

19. Ibid., pp. 36–42.

20. K. E. Weick, *The Social Psychology of Organizing* (2d ed.), Reading, MA: Addison-Wesley, 1979.

21. T. A. Stewart, "Westinghouse Gets Respect at Last," *Fortune,* 3 July 1989, pp. 92–93.

22. Ibid.

23. Ibid., p. 94.

24. Ibid., p. 96.

25. S. P. Sherman, "Inside the Mind of Jack Welch," *Fortune,* 27 March 1989, pp. 39–40.

26. Ibid., p. 50.

27. Ibid.

28. Ibid., p. 40.

29. R. M. Kanter, *Men and Women of the Corporation,* New York: Basic Books, 1977, p. 166.

30. Sherman, p. 46.

31. C. White, "Geneva and Kennecott: Modernization Gives a Competitive Edge," *Utah Business,* August 1989, p. 32.

32. Ibid., p. 34.

33. Ibid.

34. Ibid.

35. R. Henkoff, "This Cat Is Acting Like a Tiger," *Fortune,* 19 December 1988, pp. 74–76.

36. R. H. Hayes, S. C. Wheelwright, and K. Clark, *Dynamic Manufacturing: Creating the Learning Organization,* New York: Free Press, 1988, p. 248.

37. K. Labich, "Making Over Middle Managers," *Fortune,* 8 May 1989, p. 60.

38. L. T. Perry, "Relational Contracts: Key to Changing Employment Terms During Turbulent Times," *Personnel,* September–October 1984, p. 53.

39. M. Magnet, "The Resurrection of the Rust Belt," *Fortune,* 15 August 1988, pp. 43–44.

40. N. J. Perry, "Here Come the Richer, Riskier Pay Plans," *Fortune,* 19 December 1988, p. 54.

41. Ibid., p. 51.

42. A. L. Wilkins and W. G. Ouchi, "Efficient Cultures: Exploring the Relationship Between Culture and Organizational Performance," *Administrative Sciences Quarterly,* September 1983, pp. 470–472.

43. Sherman, p. 48.

44. G. W. Dalton, "Influence and Organizational Change." In D. A. Kolb, I. M. Rubin, and J. M. McIntyre, *Organizational Psychology: Readings on Human Behavior in Organizations* (4th ed.), 1984, p. 636.

45. K. Sandholtz, "The Jazz Man," *BYU Today,* November 1988, p. 43.

46. T. Mason, R. Mitchell, and W. J. Hampton, "Ross Perot's Crusade," *Business Week,* 6 October 1986, p. 60.

47. J. Dreyfuss, "Reinventing IBM," *Fortune,* 14 August, 1989, pp. 31–33.

48. B. Saporito, "Woolworth to Rule the Malls," *Fortune*, 5 June 1989, pp. 145–148.

49. Dreyfuss, p. 36.

50. P. K. Tompkins, "Management Qua Communication in Rocket Research and Development," *Communication Monographs*, March 1977, pp. 8–10.

51. Labich, pp. 61–64.

52. Hayes, Wheelwright, and Clark, p. 229.

CHAPTER 9

1. P. Houston, "How 3M is Trying to Out-Japanese the Japanese," *Business Week*, 26 August 1985, p. 65.

2. Ibid.

3. Ibid.

4. Ibid.

5. J. Fallows, "Standing Up to Japan," *Los Angeles Times Magazine*, 12 March 1989, pp. 10–14.

6. C. Gottlieb, "Intel's Plan for Staying on Top," *Fortune*, 27 March 1989, p. 100.

7. Ibid., p. 98.

8. "Semiconductor Entrepreneur: Joseph Parkinson," *Inc.*, July 1988, pp. 43–44.

9. Ibid., p. 44.

10. Ibid., pp. 44–46.

11. Ibid., pp. 46, 48.

12. Ibid., pp. 47–48.

13. J. Kotkin, "The New Northwest Passage," *Inc.*, February 1987, p. 94.

14. Ibid.

15. Ibid.

16. Ibid.

17. F. Warner, "WordPerfect: Taking Word Processing Around the Globe," *Utah Business*, August 1989, p. 23.

18. R. Henkoff, "This Cat Is Acting Like a Tiger," *Fortune*, 19 December 1988, pp. 70–71.

19. Ibid., p. 72.

20. Ibid.

21. Ibid., p. 72.

22. Ibid., p. 76.

23. Ibid., pp. 72–74.

24. Ibid., pp. 74–76.
25. D. Halberstam, *The Reckoning,* New York: William Morrow, 1986, pp. 78–79.
26. A. Taylor III, "Why Fords Sell Like Big Macs," *Fortune,* 21 November 1988, pp. 123–124.
27. Halberstam, pp. 90–91.
28. Taylor, p. 124.
29. B. Burlingham and C. Hartman, "Cowboy Capitalist: Inside the Private World of America's Most Public Entrepreneur," *Inc.,* January 1989, p. 66.
30. R. H. Miles and S. Hopkins, "Rockwell International Semiconductor Products Division," Cambridge, MA: Harbridge House, 1988, p. 2.
31. Ibid., p. 3.
32. Ibid., p. 5.
33. Ibid., p. 9.
34. J. Huey, "The New Power in Black & Decker," *Fortune,* 2 January 1989, p. 89.
35. Ibid., pp. 89–91.
36. Ibid., p. 94.
37. Ibid., pp. 90–91.
38. Ibid., p. 94.
39. Burlingham and Hartman, p. 62.
40. L. Ward, *Pure Sociology,* New York: Macmillan, 1907.
41. J. Steinbeck, "The Leader of the People." In *The Long Valley,* New York: Bantam, 1967, pp. 198–214.
42. M. E. Porter, *Competitive Advantage: Creating and Sustaining Superior Performance,* New York: Free Press, pp. 513–536.

CHAPTER 10

1. C. C. Mann, "The Man with All the Answers," *The Atlantic Monthly,* January 1990, p. 58.
2. J. Lovelock, *The Ages of Gaia: A Biography of Our Living Earth,* New York: W.W. Norton, 1988.
3. R. L. Heilbroner, *The Worldly Philosophers* (3d ed.), New York: Clarion, 1967, p. 49.
4. D. L. Birch, "What Goes Up," *Inc.,* July 1988, p. 26.
5. J. A. Schumpeter, *The Theory of Economic Development,* Cambridge, MA: Harvard University Press, 1934.
6. M. Friedman, "Forget Those Phony Problems," *Fortune,* 3 July 1989, p. 69.
7. K. Boulding, "Symbols for Capitalism," *Harvard Business Review,* January–February 1959, p. 44.

8. R. H. Hayes, S. C. Wheelwright, and K. B. Clark, *Dynamic Manufacturing: Creating the Learning Organization,* New York: Free Press, 1988, p. 163.

9. C. Bogert, "First Steppes in Baseball," *Newsweek,* 17 April 1989, p. 41.

10. B. Dumaine, "What the Leaders of Tomorrow See," *Fortune,* 3 July 1989, p. 54.

11. R. E. Miles and C. C. Snow, *Organizational Strategy, Structure, and Process,* New York: McGraw-Hill, 1978.

12. Ibid.

13. Hayes, Wheelwright, and Clark, pp. 220–223.

14. D. C. McClelland, *The Achieving Society,* New York: Free Press, 1967.

15. Ibid.

16. Ibid.

17. H. Melville, *Moby-Dick,* New York: Albert Boni, 1933, p. 382.

18. B. Saporito, "Companies That Compete Best," *Fortune,* 22 May, 1989, p. 40.

Bibliography

R. L. Ackoff, *Management in Small Doses,* New York: John Wiley, 1986.

"Add Records to Disney's World: Eisner Expands Again," *Newsweek,* 11 December 1989.

S. Albert, "A Delete Design Model of Successful Transitions." In J. Kimberly and R. E. Quinn (eds.), *Managing Organizational Transitions,* Homewood, IL: Richard D. Irwin, 1984.

N. W. Aldrich, Jr., "The Real Art of the Deal," *Inc.,* November 1988.

R. Allen and J. Lindahl, "Creed of the Entrepreneur," *Executive Excellence,* January 1989.

W. H. Auden (presenter), *The Living Thoughts of Kierkegaard.* Bloomington, IN: Indiana University Press, 1952.

D. L. Birch, "What Goes Up," *Inc.,* July 1988.

C. Bogert, "First Steppes in Baseball," *Newsweek,* 17 April 1989.

K. Boulding, "Symbols for Capitalism," *Harvard Business Review,* January-February 1959.

P. B. Brown, "Looking Out for Number One," *Inc.,* April 1989.

———, "Cookie Monsters," *Inc.,* February 1989.

B. Burlingham and C. Hartman, "Cowboy Capitalist: Inside the Private World of America's Most Public Entrepreneur," *Inc.,* January 1989.

G. Bylinsky, "The Hottest High-Tech Company in Japan," *Fortune,* 1 January 1990.

J. Carlzon, "The Art of Loving," *Inc.,* May 1989.

M. J. Clark, "Liberating Form," *Brigham Young University Studies, 15,* 1974.

G. W. Dalton, "Influence and Organizational Change." In D. A. Kolb, I. M. Rubin, and J. M. McIntyre, *Organizational Psychology: Readings on Human Behavior in Organizations* (4th ed.), 1984.

E. deBono, *Lateral Thinking: Creativity Step by Step*, New York: Harper & Row, 1970.

M. L. Dertouzos, R. K. Lester, and R. M. Solow, *Made in America: Regaining the Productive Edge*, Cambridge, MA: MIT Press, 1989.

J. H. Dobryzynski, "Fighting Back: It Can Work," *Business Week*, 26 August 1985.

J. Dreyfuss, "What Do You Do for an Encore?" *Fortune*, 19 December 1988.

———, "Reinventing IBM," *Fortune*, 14 August 1989.

P. Drucker, *Innovation and Entrepreneurship: Practice and Principles*, New York: Harper & Row, 1985.

B. Dumaine, "P&G Rewrites the Marketing Rules," *Fortune*, 6 November 1989.

———, "What the Leaders of Tomorrow See," *Fortune*, 3 July 1989.

B. Emmott, *The Sun Also Sets: The Limits of Japan's Economic Power*, New York: Random House, 1989.

P. Engardio, "Why Cordis' Heart Wasn't in Pacemakers," *Business Week*, 16 March 1987.

J. Evensen, "Utah Joins in 13-State Fight to Prevent Debit Card's Debut," *Deseret News*, 20 September 1989.

"The Entrepreneur of the Decade: An Interview with Steve Jobs," *Inc.*, April 1989.

J. Fallows, "Standing Up to Japan," *Los Angeles Times Magazine*, 12 March 1989.

M. Friedman, "Forget Those Phony Problems," *Fortune*, 3 July 1989.

W. E. Fulmer and J. Kennedy, "Electronic Data Systems (A)," Colgate Darden Graduate Business School, 1986.

C. Garfield, "Superman to the Rescue," *Executive Excellence*, January 1989.

J. Gleick, *Chaos: Making a New Science*, New York: Penguin Books, 1987.

M. Goodfellow, "Why Quality Circles Failed at 21 Firms," *Management Review*, September 1982.

C. Gottlieb, "Intel's Plan for Staying on Top," *Fortune*, 27 March 1989.

R. Grover, with M. M. Vamos and T. Mason, "Disney's Magic," *Business Week*, 9 March 1987.

D. Halberstam, *The Reckoning*, New York: William Morrow, 1986.

G. Hamel and C. K. Prahalad, "Strategic Intent," *Harvard Business Review*, May–June 1989.

C. Hartman, "Keeper of the Flame," *Inc.*, March 1989.

G. N. Hatsopoulos, "The Thinking Man's CEO," *Inc.*, November 1988.

R. H. Hayes, S. C. Wheelwright, and K. B. Clark, *Dynamic Manufacturing: Creating the Learning Organization*, New York: Free Press, 1988.

R. L. Heilbroner, *The Worldly Philosophers* (3d ed.), New York: Clarion, 1967.

R. Henkoff, "This Cat Is Acting Like a Tiger," *Fortune,* 19 December 1988.

P. Houston, "How 3M Is Trying to Out-Japanese the Japanese," *Business Week,* 26 August 1985.

J. Huey, "Wal-Mart: Will It Take Over the World?" *Fortune,* 30 January 1989.

————, "The New Power in Black & Decker," *Fortune,* 2 January 1989.

R. M. Kanter, *Men and Women of the Corporation,* New York: Basic Books, 1977.

L. Kartus, "The Strange Folks Picking on Zenith," *Fortune,* 19 December 1988.

R. Keele, "Mentoring or Networking? Strong and Weak Ties in Career Development." In L. L. Moore (ed.), *Not as Far as You Think: The Realities of Working Women,* New York: Lexington Books, 1986.

W. Kiechel III, "A Hard Look at Executive Vision," *Fortune,* 23 October 1989.

J. Kotkin, "The New Northwest Passage," *Inc.,* February 1987.

L. Kraar, "Your Rivals Can Be Your Allies," *Fortune,* 27 March 1989.

K. Labich, "Making Over Middle Managers," *Fortune,* 8 May 1989.

————, "The Seven Keys to Business Leadership," *Fortune,* 24, October 1988.

————, "Hot Company, Warm Culture," *Fortune,* 27 February 1989.

————, "The Big Comeback at British Airways," *Fortune,* 5 December 1988.

E. Linden, "Murphy's Law," *Inc.,* July 1984.

J. Lovelock, *The Ages of Gaia: A Biography of Our Living Earth,* New York: W.W. Norton, 1988.

M. Magnet, "Acquiring Without Smothering," *Fortune,* 12 November 1984.

————, "The Resurrection of the Rust Belt," *Fortune,* 15 August 1988.

C. C. Mann, "The Man with All the Answers," *The Atlantic Monthly,* January 1990.

T. Mason, R. Mitchell, and W. J. Hampton, "Ross Perot's Crusade," *Business Week,* 6 October 1986.

D. C. McClelland, *The Achieving Society,* New York: Free Press, 1967.

H. Melville, *Moby-Dick,* New York: Albert Boni, 1933.

R. E. Miles and C. C. Snow, *Organizational Strategy, Structure, and Process,* New York: McGraw-Hill, 1978.

R. H. Miles and S. Hopkins, "Rockwell International Semiconductor Products Division," Cambridge, MA: Harbridge House, 1988.

"Missed Opportunities: Americans Hold the Lead in Research but Let Foreigners Develop the Products," *Wall Street Journal,* 14 November 1988.

R. R. Nelson and S. G. Winter, *Evolutionary Theory of Economic Change,* Cambridge, MA: Belknap Press of Harvard University, 1982.

J. R. Norman and D. Foust, "Meet Art Williams, the P. T. Barnum of Life Insurance," *Business Week,* 15 February 1988.

R. O'Brien, *Marriott: The J. Willard Marriott Story,* Salt Lake City, UT: Deseret Books, 1977.

W. G. Ouchi, *Theory Z: How American Business Can Meet the Japanese Challenge,* Reading, MA: Addison-Wesley, 1981.

M. Pacanowsky, "Communication in the Empowering Organization." In J. A. Anderson (ed.), *Communication Yearbook/11,* Beverly Hills, CA: Sage, 1987.

T. P. Pare, "How to Cut the Cost of Headquarters," *Fortune,* 11 September 1989.

L. T. Perry, "Least-Cost Alternatives to Layoffs in Declining Industries," *Organizational Dynamics,* Spring 1986.

——, "Relational Contracts: Key to Changing Employment Terms During Turbulent Times," *Personnel,* September–October 1984.

——, and K. W. Sandholtz, "A 'Liberating Form' for Radical Product Innovation." In U. E. Gattiker and L. Larwood (eds.), *Managing Technological Development: Strategic and Human Resource Issues,* New York: Walter de Gruyter, 1988.

N. J. Perry, "Here Come the Richer, Riskier Pay Plans," *Fortune,* 19 December 1988.

T. J. Peters, "Competition and Compassion," *California Management Review,* Summer 1986.

——, and R. H. Waterman, Jr., *In Search of Excellence: Lessons from America's Best-Run Companies,* New York: Harper & Row, 1982.

M. E. Porter, *Competitive Advantage: Creating and Sustaining Superior Performance,* New York: Free Press, 1985.

——, *Competitive Strategy: Techniques for Analyzing Industries and Competitors,* New York: Free Press, 1980.

J. B. Quinn, "The Money on Your Life," *Newsweek,* 8 May 1989.

A. Ramirez, "Boeing's Happy, Harrowing Times," *Fortune,* 17 July 1989.

P. C. Reid, "How Harley Beat Back the Japanese," *Fortune,* 25 September 1989.

L. Rhodes, "That's Easy for You to Say," *Inc.,* June 1986.

A. Rock, "Strategy vs. Tactics from a Venture Capitalist," *Harvard Business Review,* November–December 1987.

K. Sakai, *Bunsha,* Tokyo: Taiyo Industry Co., 1985.

K. Sandholtz, "The Jazz Man," *BYU Today,* November 1988.

B. Saporito, "Woolworth to Rule the Malls," *Fortune,* 5 June 1989.

————, "Companies That Compete Best," *Fortune,* 22 May 1989.

J. A. Schumpeter, *The Theory of Economic Development,* Cambridge, MA: Harvard University Press, 1934.

P. Sellers, "Why Bigger Is Badder at Sears," *Fortune,* 5 December 1988.

G. P. Shea, "Quality Circles: The Danger of Bottled Change," *Sloan Management Review,* Spring 1986.

S. P. Sherman, "Inside the Mind of Jack Welch," *Fortune,* 27 March 1989.

"Semiconductor Entrepreneur: Joseph Parkinson," *Inc.,* July 1988.

H. A. Simon, *Models of Man,* New York: J. Wiley, 1957.

R. Smith, "The U.S. Must Do as GM Has Done," *Fortune,* 13 February, 1989.

G. Stalk, Jr., "Time: The Next Source of Competitive Advantage," *Harvard Business Review,* July–August 1988.

J. Steinbeck, "The Leader of the People." In *The Long Valley,* New York: Bantam, 1967.

————, *East of Eden,* New York: Bantam, 1970.

T. A. Stewart, "Westinghouse Gets Respect at Last," *Fortune,* 3 July 1989.

A. Taylor III, "Why Fords Sell Like Big Macs," *Fortune,* 21 November 1988.

P. K. Tompkins, "Management Qua Communication in Rocket Research and Development," *Communication Monographs,* March 1977.

P. Vaill, "The Purposing of High-Performing Systems," *Organizational Dynamics,* Autumn 1982.

L. Ward, *Pure Sociology,* New York: Macmillan, 1907.

F. Warner, "WordPerfect: Taking Word Processing Around the Globe," *Utah Business,* August 1989.

R. H. Waterman, Jr., "The Renewal Factor," *Business Week,* 14 September 1987.

K. E. Weick, *The Social Psychology of Organizing,* Reading, MA: Addison-Wesley, 1969.

————, *The Social Psychology of Organizing* (2d ed.), Reading, MA: Addison-Wesley, 1979.

C. White, "Geneva and Kennecott: Modernization Gives a Competitive Edge," *Utah Business,* August 1989.

"Who's Excellent Now?: Some of the Best-Seller's Picks Haven't Been Doing So Well Lately," *Business Week,* November 5, 1984.

A. L. Wilkins, *Developing Corporate Character,* San Francisco: Jossey-Bass, 1989.

————, and W. G. Ouchi, "Efficient Cultures: Exploring the Relationship Between Culture and Organizational Performance," *Administrative Sciences Quarterly,* September 1983.

J. Wooden, "On Staying Power," *Wall Street Journal,* April 23, 1986.

H. Wouk, *The Caine Mutiny: A Novel of World War II,* Garden City, NY: Doubleday, 1951.

J. Zygmount, "Kenneth H. Olsen: President & CEO, Digital Equipment Corporation," *Sky,* November 1989.

Index

224   INDEX